Lawful Abuse:

How the Century of the Child became the Century of the Corporation

Other Works by Robert Flynn

North to Yesterday

In the House of the Lord

The Sounds of Rescue, the Signs of Hope

Seasonal Rain

A Personal War in Vietnam

When I was Just Your Age
(with Susan Russell)

Wanderer Springs

Living With the Hyenas

The Devil's Tiger
(with Dan Klepper)

Growing Up a Sullen Baptist

Tie-Fast Country

Slouching Toward Zion

Paul Baker and the Integration of Abilities
(with Eugene McKinney)

Echoes of Glory

Burying the Farm

Jade: Outlaw

Jade: The Law

Lawful Abuse:

How the Century of the Child became the Century of the Corporation

Robert Flynn

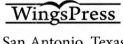

San Antonio, Texas
2012

First Wings Press ebook editions:
October 2012
Epub ISBN: 978-1-60940-278-5
Kindle ISBN: 978-1-60940-279-2
Library PDF ISBN: 978-1-60940-280-8

First Wings Press paperback edition:
February 2013
Printed Edition ISBN: 978-1-60940-277-8

Wings Press
627 E. Guenther
San Antonio, Texas 78210
Phone/fax: (210) 271-7805
On-line catalogue and ordering:www.wingspress.com
All Wings Press titles are distributed to the trade by
Independent Publishers Group
www.ipgbook.com

Library of Congress Cataloging-in-Publication Data

Flynn, Robert, 1932-
  Lawful abuse : how the century of the child became the century of the corporation
/ Robert Flynn.
     p. cm.
  ISBN 978-1-60940-277-8 (pbk. : alk. paper) -- ISBN 978-1-60940-278-5 (epub
ebook) -- ISBN 978-1-60940-279-2 (kindle ebook) -- ISBN 978-1-60940-280-8
(library pdf ebook)
  1.   Children--United States--Social conditions--20th century. 2.   Children--
Government policy--United States--20th century. 3. Corporations--United States-
-History--21st century. 4. Corporations--Government policy--United States--21st
century. I. Title.
  HQ792.U5F59 2012
  305.2309730904--dc23
                              2012037074

CONTENTS

Preface

America has never known what to do with needy children, especially unwanted ones. "Unwanted" included children of unmarried parents, orphans, runaways who abandoned their families, those whose parents had abandoned them because they were unable to feed them, those who were physically or mentally damaged by filth and other brutal living conditions, and those who were of an unwanted color, culture, or origin.

In the 1790s, while President Washington and Congress were in Philadelphia trying to establish a new form of government, they and other citizens were appalled by a "multitude of half-naked, dirty and leering children" roaming city streets, sleeping in alleys, picking pockets and robbing stores. Girls who had seen only "eight or twelve summers" were "addicted to immoralities of the most loathsome descriptions." (*Huck's Raft*, Steven Mintz)

Some boys were sternly warned to get off the street. Some were roughed up by police or other adults as a warning. Some were arrested and sent to jail where they learned survival lessons from hardened criminals. Some of the girls were abused by police and other adults. Such children needed little education; fathers or other bosses taught boys their duties and mothers or other controllers taught girls what they needed to know to survive in a world dominated by men. Boys left the farm or the home in search of a better life and girls married early to escape the drudgery. Few were successful at either.

The cornerstone for the family was a livable wage. Without it a man could not conscientiously begin a family. With no means of family planning toddlers had to work under the supervision of the mother. Children had to work under the supervision of the father until mature enough to work under a boss. Livable wages came at the price of long hours on the job, twelve, fourteen, as many as sixteen hours a day, even for children.

Sometimes the work hours were determined by quotas that could mean even longer hours and seven-day work weeks with little time to spend with wife or children. Jobs such as lumbering, building railroads required fathers and boys to be away from their families for extended periods of time. Deck hands might spend months, even years at sea before returning home, possibly with enough money to begin a family or to support a family until he returned from the next voyage. Those were the dreams families were built on.

On the frontier, a hard-working man could get by with a hardworking wife and children who worked as long as there was light. Farmers welcomed children because of the need for free or subsistence labor.

In the cities even good fathers had difficulty finding work that would provide the necessities for a family. Many jobs did not pay enough to enable young men to provide for families, resulting in unwanted children and unwed mothers. There was no effective family planning and even good fathers could not watch their wives or children go hungry or naked or die for lack of nutrition and health care. Fathers abandoned the family hoping someone would take care of them until he could return with a job that would allow them to live together. To prevent the father from leaving, boys left the family or were driven out to support themselves. All too often, daughters also were forced onto the street.

Immigrants from Christian Europe and England knew that the Bible required care for widows and orphans, that the Hebrew prophets condemned those who grind the poor, and that the Gospel of Matthew quoted Jesus as saying that those who fed the hungry, clothed the naked, cared for the sick, even "the least" of them, were his followers and would dwell with him forever; those who did not feed the hungry, clothe the naked, care for the sick, welcome strangers were doomed for the alternate eternity.

However, Jesus contradicted the American Dream that with free and fertile land, clear and abundant water, anyone willing to work hard could find success, and for those who dared even wealth. Unspoken was the big IF: if they were able to kill or drive off the Indians and steal their lands and escaped injury and illness to themselves and their family and avoided too many children.

There was ample evidence that not everyone could work hard or work at all, that families burdened with a member who was physically or mentally disabled were doomed to a cycle of poverty, that many arrived in this new land already in debt and servitude, and that generally those who did the hardest and most dangerous work received the least reward.

There was no child welfare and no regard for them. They were burdens or at best, nuisances. If they were hungry they got food wherever and however they could or they starved. If they were sick they got well or died. Thousands of children were living and dying on the streets. In New York City the number was 30,000.

Nevertheless, for the many the American Dream trumped the Gospel, enthroning Mammon as America's god. But it left others with a troubled conscience. Those who acted on their conscience were called reformers, progressives, and child-savers.

Lawful Abuse:

How the Century of the Child became the Century of the Corporation

The Battle for the Family

Families were expected, and sometimes required by law, to care for relatives, but some poor, especially recent immigrants, had no families, no support system. Most of them had no way to return to their native lands, no source of help with language to know where jobs were, how much the jobs paid, or what the jobs required. Some had no way to support a family and no place for a family to live. Wives or daughters could usually work as servants but that sometimes required that they live on the premises, separating them from their family. Those families that did remain together lived in squalor with no schools, churches or social life. Their plight was similar to the southern slaves they replaced. And they kept wages low for workers across the country.

Christians and moralists agreed that poverty was a blot on the American Dream of unlimited economic opportunity and upward mobility. It weighed heavily on their consciences. They resolved the conflict by calibrating between the "worthy" poor and the "unworthy" that Jesus had called "the least of these." The worthy poor, sick, elderly, disabled, widows and children were provided, sometimes temporarily, "outdoor relief:" food, firewood, medicine. The "unworthy poor" taxed a diminishing faith in the biblical requirement of charity. The poor were blamed for their poverty. They were lazy and their drunken licentiousness gave them more children than they could feed. Nevertheless, Christian morality required that assistance be given the degenerates.

Assistance came in the form of the vendue system, the privatizing of public poverty for private profit. The unworthy poor, sometimes the worthy poor were lumped with them, were auctioned to the lowest bidder who would provide a poorhouse and care for a fee and whatever work he could get from them. Usually that meant "picking oakum," loosening hemp or jute fibers in rope. The fibers were soaked in tar and used to calk seams in boats. It was work that even children and the physically and mentally disabled could do as long as there was light. Providence, Rhode Island reported that picking oakum was the only labor required of the poor.

Understandably, some counties and states pushed the poor into an adjoining one resulting in "warning out" paupers, telling them they were unwelcome. Before aid was given, the poor had to prove settlement, that they had been a resident of state or county for a specified period of time. An 1823 Massachusetts law stated that "Overseers of the Poor... shall certify that no part of such account is for the support of any male person, over the age of twelve, and under the age of sixty years, while of competent health to labor.

With little regulation the welfare of the paupers depended almost entirely upon the kindness and fairness of the bidder. If motivated by Mammon a bidder could increase his profit by cutting expenses, denying wholesome or adequate food or necessary medical care. And there was little protection from abuse.

In 1859 Thomas Hazard reported a visit to a poorhouse "in the most deplorable condition imaginable. The house in which they were huddled, was old and dilapidated...the furniture was absolutely unfit for the use...of savages. The mattresses and bed clothing were filthy and ragged. Not a sheet nor a pillow case was to be seen...An insane woman...was ordered from her filthy lair (where she was confined by the corner of a bedstead being pushed against the door)...a caricature of despair clothed in filth and rags...a dish of unripe, watery potatoes, was all the food to be seen, or that was visible in the house...When stripped of all disguise, selling the poor to the lowest bidder, is simply offering a reward for the most cruel and avaricious man that can be found to abuse them."

By the middle of the 19th century as many as 150 infants' bodies were found in New York City each month as parents tried to avoid the poorhouse. There were an estimated 30,000 "orphans, foundlings, waifs, half-orphans, street arabs, street urchins" living on the streets of the city. Their only options were confinement in jails, almshouses and orphanages. Twenty-six-year-old Congressional minister Charles Loving Brace believed that institutional care harmed children. Work, education and family life could turn them from drains on society to useful adults. Brace formed The Children's Aid Society that in 1854 sent street children west to live with families that could raise them as their own and educate in them moral and spiritual values. That was the beginning of foster homes.

Rural areas in the west were free of vice and rich in farmers who could use extra field hands. Housewives could train and use homemakers. From 1854 to 1929 "orphan trains" took more than 200,000 newborn babies, infants, children and teenagers who were orphans or whose families could not feed them from the streets of the city to rural homes in the west, Mexico and Canada.

The children got off the train in Midwestern towns and were placed on a platform or a church altar to be examined for health, strength, intelligence in a manner similar to slave auctions in the South. Children not selected returned to the train for a trip to the next town. Few families could take more than one child so siblings were separated and the children were told to never speak of their other parents. Two orphan train boys grew up to be state governors. One grew up to be Billy the Kid.

Some children were adopted by loving families, some were abused, some were indentured servants until they were old enough to escape. But it was the best thing that Americans had done for unwanted children.

The trains were controversial from the beginning. Abolitionists believed it to be a form of slavery and defenders of slavery saw it as a plot to make slaves unnecessary. The trains transported 250,000 unwanted children until the Great Depression and the Dust Bowl left few families able to feed and care for any child. The last orphan train carried unwanted children from New York City to Sulphur Springs, Texas in 1929.

The New York Foundling Society, operated by the Sisters of St. Vincent de Paul, kept a cradle in the foyer of their building where mothers could secretly leave babies. As knowledge of the cradle spread there were too many babies for the Sisters to care for. They began "baby trains" so that devout Catholic families could request the child of their dreams.

In 1856 a New York report stated... "The poor houses throughout the State may be generally described as badly constructed, ill-arranged, ill-warmed, and ill-ventilated. The rooms are crowded with inmates; and the air, particularly in the sleeping apartments, is very noxious... with low ceilings, and sleeping boxes arranged in three tiers one above another...inmates sicken and die without any medical attendance whatever. In one county almshouse, averaging 137 inmates, there were 36 deaths during the past year, and yet none of them from epidemic or contagious disease.

"Many of the births occurring during the year are doubtless the offspring of illicit connections. During the last year, the whole number of births was 292. The indiscriminate association of the sexes generally allowed strongly favors this assumption...the only pretence (sic) of a separation of the sexes consisted in the circumstance of separate stairs being provided at each end of a common dormitory; and a police regulation, requiring one sex to reach it by one flight, and the other sex by another, appeared to be deemed a sufficient preventive of all subsequent intercourse."

In two counties, "the food supplied was not only insufficient in quantity, but consisted partly of tainted meat and fish. The inmates were consequently almost starved. They were also deprived of a sufficiency of fuel and bedding, and suffered severely from cold."

> *Personal Note:* A modern reader of these accounts, not knowing the origin, could be excused for believing they referred to Nazi concentration camps.

Other laws provided that "any child...hereafter be found begging for alms, in any of the cities in this state, and whose Parent or Parents, is or are not a charge to such City, as a pauper or paupers, it shall and may be lawful for any magistrate of such city to take up and send such child or children to the almshouse...there to be detained and supported until such child...shall become of sufficient age to be bound out..." Bound out was indentured servitude and the age of the child varied by state. Mothers saw their families split up as minors were bound out, boys bound to farmers usually until the age of 21; girls bound as household servants until 18. After which they were at the further mercy of an ofttimes blind society that could not see them as "worthy."

In 1835 "Simeon Bingham aged seven years who is now a pauper" was bound until he was twenty-one "to learn the craft, mystery and occupation of a farmer, and at the end of the said term shall and will allow and deliver unto the said apprentice one good new suit of holyday (sic) clothes, of the value of at least twenty five Dollars suitable for winter and also two good suits of common or every day clothes, of the value of at least twenty Dollars and also one new bible (sic) and shall pay him fifty Dollars if the said Apprentice shall faithfully serve his said master during the said term." The master would decide whether or not an apprentice deserved such a reward.

The Records of the Court of Wardens, 1846-1848, Orange County, reveals the melancholy story of an infant orphan. "September 7, 1846: Ordered that the Treasurer pay to Mrs. Kendall W. Wait thirty Dollars for taking care of Elizabeth Truelove for six months. Ordered that the Treasurer pay to Mrs. Wait Four dollars per month for taking care of Elizabeth Truelove, an infant, for two months and twenty Dollars for the next six months. Ordered that the Treasurer pay to Howel Gilliam five dollars for taking care of Lucy Truelove (mother of Elizabeth).

"Ordered that the Treasurer pay to John W. Carr four dollars for finding coffin & burying clothes of Lucy Truelove. September 6, 1847: Ordered that the Superintendant (sic) pay to Mrs. Price twenty dollars semiannual allowance the support of Elizabeth Truelove from 1st April last & fifteen dollars for the next six months up to 1st April 1848. April 5, 1848: Ordered that the Superintendant (sic) pay to Mrs. Price fifteen dollars semi-annual allowance for the support of Elizabeth Truelove to 1st Oct. next. September 4, 1848: Ordered that the Superintendant (sic) receive Elizabeth Truelove, an infant, as a pauper at the Poor House."

War brought more separation of families. 1847 Orange County, North Carolina ordered the Superintendent to "bring the children of Young Barbee to the poor House," that $12.50 be paid to C. W. Johnston "for the support of the children of Young Barbee who is at present a volunteer in the N.C. Regiment in Mexico. Ordered that the Superintendant (sic) pay to Murrell Chisenhall twenty dollars for taking care of the children of Young Barbee before they were brought to the poor House. . .Ordered that Superintendant (sic) be directed to bring the children of Calvin Bacon (who is now a Soldier in Mexico) to the poor House."

Husbands and wives, or adult children and parents who were dependent on each other, were also separated and sometimes moved every year depending on the bids. Marjory Boyes and her children were separated. "Marjory Boyes was struck off (auctioned) to Israel Merrill at 16 cents per week. Mary Boyes was struck off to Nathaniel Baker at 37 cents per week Elenor Boyes (sic) was struck off to Reuben Sawyer at 48 (sic) per week Jonathan Boyes was struck off to Peter Young at 42 cents per week."

A reformer reported, "I really don't know what meaning the county superintendents of the poor attach to the word Education... But if they mean anything which elevates the mind-anything which ministers to the moral feelings or the intellectual powers-anything which will help to get a living, or to discharge intelligently the duties incident to citizenship-there is no such thing given to the youth in our county houses.... In many cases the teacher is a pauper, generally an old drunkard, whose temper is soured and whose intellect is debased, and who spends the school hours in tormenting, rather than in teaching his pupils.

"I have found many children bound out by the superintendents who never received one hour's education during their apprenticeship, and who, at the age of twenty one, were cast loose on the world no better than the heathen. How can children brought up in this way be expected to become anything else than criminals or paupers? They have no ambition to acquire property, and if they had, they have no means to acquire it. They cannot enter into trade, because in order to do this with any success they must be able to read, write, and cypher, and this they cannot do. Each of these is a seed of pauperism, which will bear plants that will again bear seed, and in time will overrun the State with a burden of pauperism and crime, which it will be unable to bear."

Reformer Dorothea Dix wrote, "There was no school for the children; they were at one time sent to the district school in the immediate vicinity, but parents objected to having their children associate 'with the children of the paupers,' and these were sent home. The county provided no teacher, and the house afforded no person supposed competent to teach. The children took their education therefore into their own hands, and were acquiring a sort of knowledge which years of careful instruction will fail to eradicate."

Despite such conditions many were convinced that "the greatest evil of all (sending needy children to almshouses), creates and perpetuates paupers, by accustoming all the children in them to an easy, happy life in an almshouse, where they are well fed, clothed and instructed, so that the inducement for them to labor for their own support–and that of their parents–is completely lost sight of."

Others believed that the vendue system was corrupt and degraded both those in and outside the system. By 1875 some states took over regulation of poorhouses, and placed the poor in county-owned farms or workhouses managed by a superintendent where they could grow their own food or work to pay for their own care. It would also allow them to live in permanent homes rather than being threatened with moving every time they were auctioned. Then, as now, an overriding concern was to provide adequate assistance at the lowest possible cost.

The efforts to make paupers self-supporting failed and reformers pointed out that poorhouses and poor farms were poor places to raise children. Some states prohibited children in poorhouses and removed mentally ill patients and others with special needs to separate facilities. Nevertheless, a few persisted until the middle of the 20th Century.

In the East, state boards dealt with the poor, but in Texas, as in most other western states, the poor were another job for the county commissioners. A federal government report regarding Texas poor laws in 1904 stated, "The County Commissioners have the duty to provide for the support of paupers, resident of their counties, who are unable to take care of themselves, to send indigent sick to county hospitals where such are established, and to bury the pauper dead. The commissioners may, by contract, bind a county in any reasonable sum for pauper support, and are authorized to employ physicians to the poor, etc. The almshouses are under the management of the county commissioners. Except for these general provisions, there are no special statutes governing in detail poor relief and the management of almshouses."

Popular opinion decided who was worthy and who was not. In Texas there was a general opinion that poverty was a crime and poorhouses were sometimes a combination jail and poorhouse. Although not debtors prisons, the poor were punished for being poor, regardless of the reason.

The Poor House Story includes records by states and in some cases counties. In the 1887-88 Texas census 35 counties reported poor farms. Bexar County (San Antonio) had 167 indigents, 10 colored, 114 foreign born, $7.50 cost per month. Bandera County reported 7 indigents, no colored, 1 foreign born, cost $10.80. Baylor County, 1 indigent at $15. Bosque County: 15 indigent, 1 colored, $17.50. Somerville County paid the most: 2 indigents, no colored, no foreign born, $20.

> *Personal Note:* My father was born in 1887. I have not been able to find a poor farm in Hardeman County where he was born, or in Wilbarger County where he spent most of his life after 1888, and where I was born in 1932. I remember as a child hearing my parents speak of the "poorhouse." They pretended it was a joke but even as a child I was aware of the fear and horror that they might live there some day.

There were private orphan asylums some founded for the benefit of children whose parents perished in epidemics. In 1846 an epidemic in the German settlement of New Braunfels in the newly minted state of Texas left a number of orphaned children. Private citizens, incorporated as the Western Texas Orphan Asylum, reared and educated those who had no relatives. In addition to regular school courses the girls were taught housekeeping and the boys agriculture. The name of the asylum was changed to West Texas University, and in 1853 advertised elementary, Latin, and high school departments.

Others shelters were established by philanthropists, benevolent societies and religious organizations limiting their charity to particular religious, racial, or ethnic groups. Most were selective in admission and able to dismiss children when they wished. Some of them received public as well as private funds, regardless of the First Amendment, but they served a small number of the children who needed charity.

Texas was rural but in the cities churches attempted to address the need. In 1867 the Catholic Diocese of Galveston, with fifty-five churches, built an orphanage on the grounds of St. Mary's Infirmary. The hospital had originally cared for orphans, but yellow fever required a separation of orphans and patients and in 1874 St. Mary's Orphan Asylum opened. Girls were kept until they were eighteen years old. At the age of ten, boys were sent to St. Mary's College to continue their education.

1892, Dr. Arthur Carroll Scott was appointed chief surgeon for the Santa Fe Railroad's hospital in Temple. In 1898 Scott and Dr. Raleigh White established the Kings' Daughters' Hospital for the care of the indigent which became the Temple Sanitarium in 1905, a general hospital and nurses training school. In 1922 the name was changed to Scott and White Memorial Hospital.

The Island City Protestant Orphans Asylum was founded in 1878 in Galveston, Texas. In 1879 it became the Island City Protestant-Israelite Orphans Home. The building was damaged in the 1900 hurricane and the children, unharmed, had to be moved for a time to the Buckner Orphans Home, established by Baptists in a rented house in Dallas. William Randolph Hearst held a benefit at the Waldorf-Astoria Hotel to benefit the orphans of the Galveston hurricane and in 1901, the institution became the Galveston Orphans' Home.

In 1894 eight Galveston women founded the Society for the Help of Homeless Children, establishing a day nursery and "temporary home for homeless white children" who needed shelter from sick, negligent, or abusive parents. The "Home for the Homeless" as the Lasker Home was first called was open to children who paid, partially paid, or did not pay. The third class referred to children the Galveston Orphan's Home refused. The Hebrew Ladies Benevolent Society subsidized indigent Jewish children, Baptist women sent sandwiches, Methodist women clothed several children, and Episcopal women sent treats to the children. The 1900 hurricane swept away the home and many of the children.

Conditions were better for children in the East than in the West where the American Dream was kept alive by get-rich-quick opportunities for the strong, bold and ruthless. If one worked hard, maintained good health and were armed and lucky, unbranded cattle could be found in the brush, gold and silver discovered in the hills, and oil and fertile soil in the plains. All free for the taking after the federal government disposed of the Indians. The weak, the lame, the unlucky need not come but desperate and greedy men left families in search of instant riches.

A few struck it rich, most struck out, dooming their families to a future reminiscent of that of Joseph's family in Egypt after Joseph died and his survivors were enslaved. The work was hard, rural and often dangerous. At least 8000 Irish immigrants died hand-digging New Orleans' New Basin Canal (1832-1838). Slaves were considered too valuable to risk. This was neither the first nor the last time that economic considerations determined policy as profits trumped morality. Rural churches followed the gun and plow but circuit riding preachers had little to offer except patience and prayer.

By 1900, 49% of farmers were tenants. In 1910, 52% were tenants. Sharecroppers were the poorest of the 200,000 tenants in Texas. Some wives and children lived in squalor and upward mobility seemed unlikely. "There is something rotten in Texas when over 50% of our farm families are homeless renters, the *Houston Chronicle* editorialized in 1912.

> *Personal Note:* As a depression era child on my father's farm I learned early what work was, but my father owned the farm. I did not realize at the time what a huge difference that made. Bringing in the cows from the pasture to be milked and fed in a few years became bringing, feeding and milking the cows. Feeding the chickens and gathering their eggs became cleaning the hen house and the chicken pen and wringing their necks, sometimes two at a time, so that they could be dressed and placed in the frozen food locker in Vernon. Those chores continued after I began school plus weeding the orchard and garden, pruning the grape vines,

mowing the yard and worst of all, walking home from school, putting the strap of a cotton sack over my shoulder and picking cotton or pulling bolls until dark.

Like most farm boys I learned to drive a tractor to get out of the cotton field, but in the summer my older brother, Jim, and I chopped cotton for our father until our farm was free of weeds and then we hired out to others at 50¢ an hour for 10 hours, $5 a day. Once laboring in the hot cotton patch I figured out that I could make more than $1,700 a year chopping cotton. Then I remembered there were school days, and Sundays and holidays, but I was still banking money for my college education.

As hard as I thought my life was it was easy compared to that of my future wife whose father was a sharecropper. Alfred used someone else's land, seed, and farm equipment, and his own children to produce crops for a share of the produce, one-fourth of the cotton and one-third of the wheat. My wife and I now own my father's farm and the percentage is still the same. Alfred's children, including my future wife that I had not yet met, worked whenever they could and when the school bus went by they lay down in the field hoping the other school children wouldn't see them. They also prayed that it wouldn't rain because then they would have to go to school and tell the teacher, the principal and their classmates where they had been. When it rained they prayed the rain would never stop because then they would have to go back to the field and back to hiding when the school bus went by.

Because Alfred was not a good farmer they frequently moved to a different farm and farmhouse. The houses were almost identical, bare walls, bare floors, paint on the outside an ancient memory and on the inside a distant dream.

Most of the children I went to school with, in a two-room rural school out of sight of any town, were children of sharecroppers. One year they would be in my school and the next year they wouldn't. If their father was a good farmer and they were good workers they moved to a better farm. If their father wasn't a good farm only their hard work might get them a second year in the same house on the same land.

I visited their homes and the homes of my parents' friends. I remember some clapboard houses that had dirt floors, but the floors were clean and frequently swept. My brother and sister and I were instructed to say no if we were offered food because farm etiquette required that they offer something and it might be the only food they had in the house. If they insisted, we looked at our mother and she nodded okay if she were certain we were not depriving them. But against all odds, most of the children were upwardly mobile. Most of them went to college. Some, especially the women taught school. My wife was the first in her family to graduate from college and she earned two degrees, taught high school English, became a school librarian and published eleven biographies.

In 1874, a 13-year-old boy was beaten to death by his father for refusing to bring beer when there was no money in the house. Such things were "family matters" that states had best leave to fathers. A few months later a bruised 8-year-old girl with whip marks and burns was found in a foster home. There was nothing the law could do but attorneys for the American Society for the Prevention of Cruelty to Animals (ASPCA) argued that if she had no rights as a child she should be considered an animal that was protected by law. That led to the Association for the Protection of Children.

Maryland was the first state to make "wife-beating" a crime, punishable by a one year prison sentence (or 40 lashes, it was 1882). Four years later, a North Carolina court took a step backwards, when they ruled that a man cannot be criminally charged on a domestic violence complaint unless there is permanent damage or the instance was "malicious beyond all reasonable bounds." If a husband beat his wife daily without disabling her or causing life-threatening injury she had nowhere to turn for help.

Personal Note: In the 50s, Jean and I lived next to a house separated from our neighbors by about a foot. The young couple living in the house had a fight almost every Friday night that was difficult not to hear. There was a lot of cursing and screaming and sometimes slaps and blows were exchanged. The wife called her father who came to their house, explained her duty to her husband, reminded her that her parents advised her not to marry him, and told her she had made her bed and now she had to lie in it. That was a cruel cliche that I heard parents say about others, sometimes their own children, but not my parents and not about me, my older brother and sister.

On another occasion the wife next door called the police. Two officers came to the house, tried to calm the situation, and explained to her that they could take her husband downtown and question him until he got over his anger, but that when he came home he was likely to be angrier than he was at the moment. The only choice they saw for her was to be gone when he came home or to move out of the house.

In 1911, a New York court ruled that domestic violence was best left to psychiatrists or mediators who could use conversation to resolve the issues. Sometimes only one spouse had to be present. The Association for the Protection of Animal Welfare and the Association for the Protection of Children were established before domestic violence was considered a legal issue.

In America, the 19th Century women's movement challenged husbands' rights to forced sex with their wives. Marital equality required a woman's right to her body and to control fertility they proclaimed. Family planning was available only to the rich and usually required abortion. English philosopher John Stuart Mill saw spousal rape as a means to the subordination of women. Moses Harmon, a Kansas school teacher, publisher and supporter of women's rights was prosecuted and sent to jail under the Comstock Act that prohibited sending obscene material through the US mail. Discussion of spousal rape and women's bodies was obscene.

Rape is an offense under state rather than federal jurisdiction so the laws against spousal rape are murky. English Common Law exempted a husband from charges of rape as long as the couple were married because marriage gave conjugal rights to a spouse, and marriage could not be revoked except by private Act of Parliament; therefore, a spouse could not legally revoke consent to sexual intercourse, and if there was consent there was no rape. The United States adopted the same law but it has slowly evolved. From the beginning the progress that has been made has been done by activists for women's rights.

South Dakota was the first state to remove the marriage exemption in 1975. North Carolina became the last state to do so in 1993. In eight states, wives can also be prosecuted for spousal rape. Some states exempt husbands if their wife is living with them. Some states exempt husbands even if they are separated, even if the wife has filed for divorce if the divorce has not been finalized. In 1999, in 33 of 50 states spousal rape was a lesser crime that might be reduced to assault, battery or spousal abuse. In all states there is a marriage exemption to the charge of statutory rape if one spouse is under the age of consent in the jurisdiction where the act took place.

Churches and private organizations attempted to protect children from the evil of society and to protect society from evil children but it took decades for Christian citizens, government officials and do-gooders to confess that delinquency and neglect were the consequences of poverty, and that no child should be punished for hunger.

Reformers, "child savers," Sermon-on-the-Mount Christians vowed to make the 20th century the Century of the Child. Where a country's heart is there its funding will be also, and it wasn't in its children. To improve the lot of the child they had to improve the lot of the family. That meant a livable wage for workers so they could support families, family planning, getting children out of mines, factories and fields and into schools that trained citizens to maintain a democracy. It also required better health care for healthier children, and institutional help for those born with physical and mental disabilities and those whose damage was caused by work accidents and epidemics.

The simple concept of childhood innocence was changed to a more complex understanding of children's sexuality making crimes such as statutory rape and carnal abuse possible. In 1900, 20% to 30% of all children had lost a parent by age 15. As late as 1911, a survey of Polish immigrants revealed that the children of unskilled laborers contributed 46% of their families income and children of skilled laborers contributed 35%. (Huck's Raft)

Some education was required in every state by 1918, and the 40-hour work week with overtime became law in 1937. A federal law regulating child labor was adopted in 1938. "Separate but Equal" education was declared unconstitutional in 1954 leading to a more common educational experience. By 1972 every state had laws requiring doctors and teachers to report suspected child abuse. Child abuse also included neglect that placed a child at risk. At least 10 states have abuse laws that exempt religion and corporal punishment from the child abuse law. A few states exempt religion and poverty. In some states, abuse of children by neglect is state policy.

There was the opposition they expected from the robber barons and corporations. What they had not expected was opposition by the government and often by the church.

Despite the opposition there was progress but well-wishers came to understand that to accomplish their goal they had to have fair representation in government.

The Battle for Representation

A citizen's voice is in the ballot and most of the time that's the only voice in government a citizen has. Although, "We the people" speak through the ballot, from the beginning our "representatives" have been distrustful of giving voice to all the people. The founding fathers wanted to hear the voice of the landed gentry, white men of property. White men were slow to share power. Early Americans regarded democracy as a synonym for disorder and mob rule. They restricted the vote to those who had "a stake in society," property owners and taxpayers, code for white males. White Protestant males. Five colonies prohibited Catholics from voting; four colonies barred Jews. In nine of thirteen colonies mothers, and many fathers, had no say in how the government regarded their children.

The Declaration of Independence stated that government received its legitimacy from the consent of the governed. After the Revolution, by 1790, all states had eliminated religious requirements for voting. Six states allowed free black men to vote, as the Constitution left voting rights to the states. In 1800 only three states allowed all white men to vote. Many men lost their property and their right to vote in the Panic of 1819, and by 1830 ten states permitted all white men to vote, eight restricted voting to taxpayers and six still required property ownership. In 1860, five states still required voters to be tax payers and two required property.

In those hallowed days, white males lined up on two sides in the village square so you could survey your opponents, perhaps give the evil eye, scorn, mouth or yell threats at a timid citizen and frightened him from his side before the heads were counted. Later the ballot was introduced but none were furnished. Each man had to prepare his own ballot and take it to the polls through jostling crowds of other men who believed he was voting for an unapproved candidate. There were fist fights, knife fights and shootings. Eighty-nine voters were killed during election day riots. Slowly states moved toward secret ballots. In 1888, Massachusetts was the first state to hold a secret ballot, and in 1892, Grover Cleveland became the first president to be elected by secret ballot.

Every state that joined the Union after 1819 denied black men the right to vote. In 1855, only five states allowed black men to vote without restrictions. Abraham Lincoln had talked of giving black soldiers the right to vote but between 1863 and 1870 fifteen Northern states refused to do so. After the Civil War many Republicans believed free black men required the vote to gain and protect their rights. And, of course, to protect their families, their children. In 1868 the Republican Party called for a Fifteenth Amendment that would prohibit states from denying the vote based on race or previous condition of servitude. Theoretically.

> *Personal Note:* In 1989 I accompanied some other Americans to visit an arts college outside Vientiane, Laos. In a meeting with the arts faculty, I noticed that people in the paintings of faculty or students were block figures like Soviet sculpture. Laos are svelte, and the paintings looked nothing like the Lao people. I asked if they used nude models. "Yes," the rector said. There was chatter among the faculty and when it quieted, he said, "Theoretically, yes. Practically, no." Since that time my definition of "theoretically" has been more acute.

Black men had as much right to vote as white men would give them. Still, black men had a voice, at least in some states, when women did not. Women's representation came from their husband or father. Theoretically. Some blacks shared the opinion of some suffragettes that some white men were more concerned about the treatment of horses than about the treatment of women and children.

The amendment giving black men the right to vote resulted in the rise of the Ku Klux Klan, the suppression of Southern black voters through intimidation, lynching, property ownership laws, poll taxes, lengthy residence requirements, complex and burdensome literacy tests, gerrymandering and fraud. In 1891, the Federal Elections Bill to oversee elections and enforce black voting rights in the South failed in Congress. Some states in the North and West adopted the Southern plan to keep black men from voting. In 1924, Oregon was the last state to adopt a literacy test for voting. ("Winning the Vote," Steven Mintz)

> *Personal Note:* Texas restricted voting with a poll tax. The tax didn't seem onerous to white people, not even dry land farmers like my father. But it was more than the money for blacks. There was the condescending humiliation and

disapproval of the white officials and white bosses, "Why do YOU want to vote?" Many blacks lived in the country, few had cars during the Depression years, there was no public transportation for blacks and a trip to the county seat meant a long walk when all that they needed: groceries, medications, notions, church were available at a closer town. Texas, part of the Solid South, had only one party and membership was restricted to whites. Every political office was determined by the primary, except for the White House, and blacks could not vote in the Democratic primary.

For the general election, large employers, including farmers since November voting came during fall harvest season, paid the poll tax for employees and told them how to vote. Farmers gathered truckloads of field workers, paid their poll tax and sometimes offered them a dollar or a beer for their vote. We never had enough workers to tempt my father to do that, and in 1944, the Supreme Court ruled that the Texas Democratic Party could not bar blacks from voting in the primary. In 1957, the Civil Rights Act allowed the Justice Department to seek injunctions and file suits in voting rights cases, but it scarcely increased black voting.

Personal Note: As a white evangelical Christian it gives me no pleasure to state that in the South, most Protestant churches stood on the same side as the "segregation forever" politicians. I still recall the horror I saw in the face of a favorite relative when I said that Martin Luther King, Jr. was the greatest Christian in American, and probably the greatest American of the century. Still I was M.I.A. in the freedom marches, the freedom riders, the sit-ins. From 1957 to 1959 I taught at a white Baptist college in North Carolina. The only time race became an issue on the campus was when a young Cherokee woman wanted to enroll in the school. Immigrants were still telling native Americans where they could live? Where they could go to school? As far as I could tell all the faculty and most of the students had no problem with a Cherokee in the classroom, but there was rumbling off-campus and the KKK announced a rally near the Cherokee reservation. The Indians fired a few shots in the air and the KKK scampered holding their skirts up to facilitate speed. Still, nothing happened on or off-campus, but we did hear Will D. Campbell whose clear voice rose above all the voices of hatred to declare that segregation was not only wrong, it was a sin.

In 1965, Martin Luther King, Jr. began a voter registration drive in Selma, Alabama, and led hundreds of black residents to the courthouse to register to vote. Nearly 2,000 of them were arrested, including King. A federal court ordered law officers not to interfere with registration. Black applicants stood in line for as long as five hours before being allowed to take a "literacy" test. Not a single black voter was added to the registration rolls. Also in 1965, the states ratified the Twenty-Fourth Amendment barring a poll tax in federal elections. Lyndon Johnson signed the Voting Rights Act, and sent federal examiners to seven Southern states to register black voters. At last blacks had representation in their government. It wasn't an equal voice but it came closer to fair representation.

The Constitution says "We the people," and "persons," rarely "he." The Constitution did not declare that women could not serve in Congress, the presidency, on juries or in voting. The Fourteenth Amendment that modifies Article I, section 2, of the Constitution was ratified in 1868. Included in Section 1, are clauses that read, "No State shall make or enforce any law which shall abridge the privileges or immunities of citizens of the United States; nor shall any State deprive any person of life, liberty, or property, without due process of law; nor deny to any person within its jurisdiction the equal protection of the laws."

Those clauses seem clear enough. Even if women weren't "citizens," they were "persons" as stated in the last clause, but enforcement of the clauses has been spasmodic. Nevertheless, they became important in the fight of women, gay, lesbian and transgendered citizens for equal representation, and to fight for family. Wyoming Territory was the first state to give women the vote in 1869, and Utah, Idaho and Colorado soon followed. In 1872, women argued that nothing in the Constitution stated that women citizens had no right to vote. Despite the 14th Amendment, in 1875 the Supreme Court ruled that women's right to vote would require legislation or a constitutional amendment. In 1878, the 19th Amendment was first introduced in Congress. By 1912, women could vote in nine western states. Challenging male-only voting in the courts gained women little favor but they paraded, held silent vigils and bravely faced heckling, derision, and jail. Some of them suffered physical abuse.

Suffragettes campaigned on the value of their moderating influence on behavior and as a counterbalance to the voice of recent immigrants. Opponents argued that dirty politics would corrupt women, increase discord in the home, and be the first step on the slicky slide of the masculinization of the gentler sex. Suffragettes supported the war effort of World War I by selling War Bonds, wrapping bandages and making clothing for the doughboys. They also battled for better education and moral support of children whose fathers were overseas. In posters they were strong, clean, echoes to the propaganda of "Huns killing children and raping women." In 1920, Tennessee became the last state necessary for ratifying the amendment. Women, too, had representation in government.

> *Personal Note:* Ironically, and shamefully for Texans, in 1963 when Lyndon Johnson was sworn in to replace the martyred John Kennedy, Sarah T. Hughes, the woman judge who gave him the oath of office, could not serve on a jury in Texas. When Lyndon Johnson signed the Civil Rights act, the political South took a sharp turn to the right. As always, the religious South followed.

In 1962 the Supreme Court ruled that because of the First Amendment public school students could not be required to hear or recite prayers written by the government. Government imposition of religious prayers on students should have been offensive to everyone. Instead, it caused a brainless reaction. How could young people be required to pray if the government, backed by public school officials, didn't require it? In 1963, in a separate decision, the Supreme Court ruled that any sponsored practice in public schools must have a secular purpose, must neither advance nor inhibit religion; and must not result in excessive entanglement between government and religions. Religious and other private schools used that as a key to opening closed minds. In their schools students would be allowed (p.c. for required) to pray and read the (a chosen) Bible.

Children born after World War II have no idea what America was like before they were born. The 50s were the golden years of "Leave it to Beaver." Soldiers came home to wives they didn't know and children they had never seen or with dreams of starting a dream family that would have the dream childhood they never had. They moved to suburbs where children could build tree houses or club houses and explore undeveloped land.

The 60s were years of progress and privilege. Integration, the Civil Rights and Voting Acts had given black Americans the prize they had fought and many had died for, representation in government and in the media. Integration gave black children access to good school libraries, well-equipped science labs, new rather than hand-me-down books, desks, lockers, and athletic equipment. They had the opportunity to make friends with different visions of a world in which they had a place.

The 60s were also a time of strife. In the South integration, voting, sitting in a restaurant, seeking justice in court came at a price, and often the price was insults, threats, blood and too often, death. Martin Luther King,Jr., who had saved America from a civil war as Lincoln had saved America in a Civil War, was gunned down, to the satisfaction of more than the killer, for being a black who acted like an American and a Christian.

Across the country there was strife over Vietnam. Usually Lyndon Johnson is blamed for Vietnam, but I think historians will be less inclined to do so. Eisenhower refused to sign the peace accord between Vietnam and France, supported South Vietnam's refusal to hold elections that the peace accord required, and signed the SEATO (South East Asia Treaty Organization) treaty that committed the US to the defense of South Vietnam. According to the Constitution, that treaty, ratified by Congress, carried the same weight and validity as the Constitution.

Kennedy was the last person who could have refused to honor the treaty. He represented another political party. It would have been costly, but he could have said he was not going to honor the treaty. He did not. To this day, some people do not know that every nation that signed the treaty joined in the defense of South Vietnam. There were more foreign troops, other than US, defending South Vietnam than there were UN troops, other than US, defending South Korea, or in Bush's coalition that made war on Iraq. Contrary to what many believe, according to Kennedy's last statements regarding Vietnam, and declassified documents in the National Security Archive (nsarchive.org), Kennedy had no intention of abandoning South Vietnam.

It would be difficult to choose a time when LBJ could have withdrawn from Vietnam. Not shortly after Kennedy was shot. Or after the assassination of Diem, the only politician most Vietnamese knew or when Indonesia, the fourth most populous nation in the world, withdrew from the UN and aligned itself with China or when China exploded a nuclear weapon. Largely forgotten is the fact that LBJ tried to reach a peace agreement with North Vietnam but South Vietnam walked away from the table before a treaty was agreed upon and refused to return. That act by South Vietnam infuriated Americans, especially young men eligible for the draft, as much as any event during that war but few know why the South Vietnamese delegation walked away from the table. LBJ knew.

> *Personal Note:* In 1989, I returned to some of the hamlets, that the Marines called "villes," I had been in during the war. In Vietnam, a village is not a geographical location but a political one. Hence, My Lai 1, My Lai 4, etc. Accompanied by a "handler" from Hanoi I interviewed citizens in those hamlets. None of them could name a South Vietnamese leader other than Diem. He was hated by most of them, but he was known.

In 1980, Anna Chennault, the widow of Flying Tiger hero Gen. Claire Chennault, revealed in her autobiography, *The Education of Anna*, that John Mitchell, Nixon's campaign manager and later Attorney General, and Senator John Tower (R-Texas) asked her to prevent a peace agreement with North Vietnam fearing that such an agreement would put Hubert Humphrey in the White House. She was to tell South Korea, Thailand and other SEATO nations not to trust LBJ and to tell Hanoi that Nixon would give them a better deal because he wouldn't have to demand as much as Johnson would. The attempt at peace collapsed. In 1972, Nixon had Kissinger send a letter telling China that the US would accept a Communist Vietnam. (nsarchive. org) On the basis of that Nixon reached an agreement with China and the Soviet Union to work toward normalization of relations.

US intelligence told Johnson why his attempt at a peaceful settlement collapsed, but Johnson thought the country was in such turmoil that news of the treachery of one political party would split the nation and destroy the Republican party. LBJ refused to go public with the information but did tell Democratic candidate Humphrey who agreed not to go public with the information putting his country before his party. What would happen to the country, they both wondered, if the treason became known and Nixon was elected anyway?

Johnson also told Senator Dirksen and said, "That's treason." "Yes it is," Dirksen agreed. That story also appears in Seymour Hersch's biography of Kissinger, *The Price of Power*, 1983, and in at least three other books. Somehow it is unknown to most people despite a free press. However, the misinformation most people have about Vietnam has disillusioned them about their government.

> *Personal Note:* I voted for Humphrey in 1968 and Nixon in 1972 because I thought Nixon could achieve peace in Vietnam. I defended Nixon during Watergate as long as I could but until recently I did not know of Nixon's treachery. The war would go on for three more years after Nixon's letter to China, signaling surrender. Most veterans of that war blame Congress for failing to support South Vietnam.

After the Watergate burglary, the publisher of the *Washington Post* made an agonizing decision to give press freedom to Woodward and Bernstein or Nixon's thuggary might not have been known until he was out of office. The Supreme Court has consistently ruled that only the publisher has freedom of the press. Editors, writers, columnists have only the freedom the publisher gives them. Giving press freedom to two young reporters almost destroyed the Post. Most newspapers receive about 70% of their income from advertising, 30% from subscriptions, but the price of advertising is based on the number of subscriptions. For magazines it's about 50% each, and for network TV, it's 100% advertising. Angry subscribers to the Post cancelled subscriptions because they had been forced to face the truth. That hurt, of course, but the big hurt was the corporations that stopped their ads. Their message was clear: You don't have the freedom to do that without taking us into account. The news media took the lesson to heart. Don't threaten corporate income or corporate image.

Later Dan Rather reported that when he was a White House correspondent he didn't know the pressure that the Nixon White House put on his bosses who "took the heat, so I didn't have to, who said 'the buck stops here.' The more likely motto now is: 'The news stops... with making bucks.'"

Republicans also learned a lesson—think tanks to produce the product, public relations experts to develop the message, well-rehearsed "experts" to echo the talking points and reinforce the message on radio and TV talk shows, ad campaigns to spin facts in corporate favor, and friends in the media to place it where you want it—the lead story on the front page or opening shot on TV, or buried in the middle pages in the middle of a MEGO (my eyes glaze over) report. Control the media or buy them.

Conservative foundations and corporations joined right-wing religious media in pouring tens of millions of dollars into buying media outlets and influencing the perception of the nation. Dozens of religious, right-wing and neo-conservative media outlets promoted the vision of an America in decay—moral decay by the "religious" media, economic stagnation by neo-conservative media—with selected targets. "Liberal," that usually means tolerant, enlightened and libertarian, when added to schools, government, the economy, the public welfare, became condemnatory.

For children and their families, the Vietnam treason, the Watergate deceit was not as harmful in the long run as Nixon's "Southern Strategy" to dismantle the Civil Rights Acts by turning the Solid South—solidly Democratic since "Reconstruction"— to solidly Republican. Many southern politicians were Republicans anyway, running in the Democratic primary. Some called themselves "Dixiecrats," dedicated to preserving segregation, Jim Crow laws, white supremacy under the guise of "the southern way of life." By code words and phrases Nixon, and later Reagan and the Bushes, would intimate that they would support segregation, racial discrimination and aid to fundamentalist churches.

In 1970, the Internal Revenue Service stripped Bob Jones University of its tax-exempt status. BJU was a fundamentalist Christian college that proudly announced its segregated policies. BJU sued and in 1972 the Supreme Court ruled that any institution that practiced segregation was not a charitable institution and therefore not qualified for tax-exemption. Although the abortion decision and the integration decision occurred before the Carter administration, the "Religious" Right blamed Jimmy Carter, a Southern Baptist, from the South who had turned against the sacred Southern Way of Life.

The Bob Jones decision turned the Solid South Solidly Republican. Many Protestant churches in the South had started schools to avoid integration. With the Bob Jones decision, the schools lost their reason for being, segregation, or white Christians would have to pay taxes on their private schools. Both the Jewish Bible (Old Testament) and the Christian Bible (New Testament) say that believers should pay their taxes. Both Jesus and the Apostle Paul told Christians to pay their taxes. The "Religious" Right opposed taxes, except for national defense.

Black Americans had paid extra taxes to make up for the tax exemption given to church and private schools that their children were not allowed to attend. For them, and many others, it was taxation without representation. But for the "Religious" Right and much of the South, taxation without representation was their right. Jerry Falwell, pastor of a megachurch and president of a Christian college, complained, "In some states it's easier to open a massage parlor than to open a Christian school."

> *Personal Note:* I attended Baylor University and taught at Gardner-Webb and Baylor, both Baptist schools, and Trinity, a Presbyterian university. Trinity had integrated the school before 1954 and it was the first Christian school that I was associated with to have black students. That was in 1963. When I retired in 2001, there were still no black professors in the English Department.

The Reagan Regression

Ronald Reagan made his first campaign speech as the Republican nominee at the Neosha County Fair. The seat of Neosha County was Philadelphia, Mississippi, known for one thing, the brutal lynching of three young men trying to register black voters. On the 25th anniversary of their murders, 1989, Congress passed a non-binding resolution honoring the three men. Senator Trent Lott and the rest of the Mississippi members of Congress refused to vote for it.

If two of the three men trying to register black voters had not been white men from the east, Neosha County would still be unknown. When the bodies of the three civil rights volunteers were found, fourteen black bodies were found with them, fourteen black men whose "disappearance" was unnoticed outside the county. Some thought Reagan opening his campaign in such a small place was dumb; southerners knew it was eloquent.

"I believe in states rights," Reagan declared. He promised to "restore to states and local governments the power that properly belongs to them." In the South that promise was heard in several ways. To many black people it meant the South had at last won the Civil War. Many whites believed Reagan had announced the end of federal pressure and that he would leave it to states to enforce integration and voting rights. In the struggle to maintain white supremacy, Reagan was on their side.

Blacks heard clearly that for them the government was going to be the problem. Lee Atwater, Republican strategist explained the "Southern Strategy" in an interview at Case Western Reserve University. "You start out in 1954 by saying," (he repeated the N word three times.) "By 1968, you can't say (N word)—that hurts you. Backfires. So you say stuff like forced busing, states' rights, and all that stuff. You're getting so abstract now you're talking about cutting taxes, and all these things you're talking about are totally economic things, and a byproduct of them is blacks get hurt worse than whites."

Tom Turnipseed, manager of George Wallace's campaign for the presidency, and also running in opposition to "big government," said later, "Let's face it: 'big government' was a code term aimed directly at voters who objected to civil rights. Despite the rhetoric, it was all about race." (David Podvin 8/10/04)

NeoRebels and Yankee union busters thought they heard a hint of the Southern economic philosophy: there was no such thing as a classless society and there must be a mudsill race of inferior people under the foundation of those meant to lead civilization to prosperity and refinement (http://www.pbs.org/wgbh/aia/part4/4h3439t.html). That had worked fine until the Yankees interfered. After the Civil War the Yankees imported the Irish, Chinese, Italians to replace the slaves as the mudsill people who did the dirty, difficult and dangerous jobs at subsistence wages as indentured servants, wage slaves and debt-slaves of the meanest, greediest corporations to whom they were numbers with dollar signs. With them, America became the most productive nation on earth. But like slaves, the mudsills had to be kept out of the political process by any means possible or they would threaten the wealth, the political power and social status of the ranks above them.

Some who heard Reagan's speech as a state's right to its own economic plan applauded; others thought 50 economic plans would lead to economic chaos. The idea has been resurrected by a Georgia Republican who has introduced a bill, with 60 cosponsors, that would eliminate Internal Revenue and give states exclusive rights to collect a 23% federal sales tax. (*The Washington Spectator* 8/1/12) For the poor, that would mean a 23% tax since every dollar they earned was required for subsistence. For the rich who owned villas in Italy and Spain, apartments in Paris and Rome, who bought their clothes in Europe and cars in Germany, Italy and Japan the tax would be negligible.

The "Religious" Right believed Reagan supported tax exemption for religious and private schools, and perhaps subsidy by nonbelievers. Reagan was a nominal Christian at best but some heard a whisper of Christian supremacy and fervently hoped that Reagan would stop the social destruction of the Southern Way of Life and the scientific destruction of the fundamentalist literal interpretation of the Bible.

Ironically, the backbone of literal fundamentalism, "You must be born again," is not literally true. It must be understood as metaphorical. As Nicodemus knew, you cannot literally be born again.

> *Personal Note:* I am an evangelical Christian. I consider myself to be a "born-again" Christian in the sense that I need a rebirth of my spiritual self and I need it every day. Jesus told only one man, Nicodemus, that he must be born again, because Nicodemus was a literalist. You literally can't be a literalist and be a "born-again" Christian. Jesus told another man that he must sell everything he had and give it to the poor and to follow him, because the man was a "materialist." You can't serve God and Mammon. I use Mammon, the Biblical word for riches, because those who love riches most don't consider riches an idol or their prayers, praise and rituals to Mammon a sin.
>
> All Christians who believe that salvation is by God's grace through faith and not in works or sacraments are evangelicals. To broaden their base, fundamentalists began calling themselves evangelicals. Because of the history and rigidity of fundamentalism, and because members of the media are not able to distinguish between fundamentalist and evangelical, some evangelical churches gave up their legitimate claim to "evangelical." I refuse to do so but I am not a fundamentalist. I don't believe in an "inerrant" Bible. I've read the Bible. Anyone who has read the Bible knows that there are mistakes in it, some, perhaps many, the mistakes of scribes laboriously hand-copying the Bible

before the invention of the printing press. There are no original copies of the Bible, and the manuscripts selected to be in the Christian Bible (NT) were not chosen until a few centuries after they were written. Christians don't even agree on which manuscripts should be included in "their" Bible. Some Christians regard some books, the Gospel of John, for example, to be more valuable than Leviticus or Numbers.

Fundamentalist Christians have always allegorized America as the New Israel, the City Built on a Hill. During the Civil War it was the Confederacy that was the New Jerusalem and that belief buoyed Confederates through trying times. From the pulpit they heard that God was testing them, trying their faith and steadfastness. As times turned dark the sermon became God punishing them for their sins. They must repent of their sins or God would deliver them to the godless Yankees. None of those sins was slavery, racism or pride.

Many Americans have done the same allegorizing. The "whore of Babylon" was Rome and the Caesars to early Christians. During the Reformation it was Rome and the pope. During the Civil War, for the South, it was Washington, D.C. and Lincoln. I remember as a child hearing in church and sometimes at home that it was Rome and the pope, Stalin and Communism, Hitler and Fascism, Roosevelt and the New Deal. Later it was the Soviet Union, Communist China, Lyndon Johnson and the War on Hunger, Saddam Hussein. The wonderful thing about allegory is that you can change the principal characters. Today Babylon is Washington, D.C. to the many politicians who demand that voters send there.

Noah's curse on Ham for the sin of his father, Canaan, was an everlasting curse on people of color condemning them to menial work as mudsill people. That was the biblical basis for slavery. The Tower of Babel has been the United Nations, the New World Order, Congress, and I believe at the moment, an election year, it's Congress again.

The allegory of the New Israel is the root of American exceptionalism. Unlike other nations (sometimes Israel is included)

America was created by God. Therefore, we are excepted from the things we condemn in others such as genocide, slavery, torture, war for political or economic profit on defenseless or near defenseless nations. For fundamentalists, the Bible can be used to justify genocide (Hitler, an avowed Christian, did that), slavery (Southern slave owners did that), mistreatment of women to keep them in their lower status (almost all churches do that, especially the Catholic Church), homosexuality (many preachers and politicians do that). The Bible is seldom used to preach "in Christ there is neither male nor female," rarely used to preach fasting as a remedy for gluttony although fasting is mentioned far more times in the Bible than homosexuality and gluttony is a choice, to damn divorce and remarriage as an adulterous lifestyle, or revile envy and covetousness because consumerism is 70% of the American economy, the Goose that lays the Golden Eggs.

Integration divided the evangelicals and fundamentalists in the South. It was a division that would grow in size and noise. Four years after the Brown decision outlawing segregation, Jerry Falwell, pastor of a megachurch, preached, "If Chief Justice Warren and his associates had known God's word and had desired to do the Lord's will, I am quite confident that the 1954 decision would never have been made... When God has drawn a line of distinction, we should not attempt to cross that line." The "Religious" Right was unable to stop the slow but relentless march against segregation. Falwell's church, like many white churches in the South, established a private school, Lynchburg Christian Academy for white children to spare their children the indignities of integration. Between 1961 and 1970 there was a 242% increase in the number of non-sectarian private schools in the Southeast; most were racially segregated. Five years later Falwell founded Liberty University.

As Paul Krugman pointed out (*New York Times* 11/19/07), in his 1976 campaign Reagan talked about how upset workers must be to see an able-bodied man using food stamps at the grocery store. In the South, the food-stamp abuser was a "strapping young buck" buying T-bone steaks. Reagan didn't use explicit racial terms. Neither did Richard Nixon. "Reagan paralleled Nixon's success in constructing a politics and a strategy of governing that attacked policies targeted toward blacks and other minorities without reference to race—a conservative politics that had the effect of polarizing the electorate along racial lines." (*Chain Reaction: The impact of race, rights and taxes on American politics*, Thomas and Mary Edsall)

Falwell believed Reagan to be the answer to his prayers. Falwell abandoned the traditional Baptist belief in strict separation of church and state, and the Southern Baptist Convention followed him in a flip-flop of turncoat proportion. Falwell saw the federal government as essential to restoring the primacy of white Protestant Christianity and Falwell's southern values. In 1976, Falwell held a number of "I Love America" religious rallies across the nation to restore "traditional" morality, catching the attention of a Christian advocacy group called Christian Voice. Robert Grant who had headed Christian Voice declared that the "Religious" Right was a "sham controlled by three Catholics and a Jew." The Catholics, Paul Weyrich, Terry Dolan and Richard Viguerie, would become important Republican right workers.

The Jew was Howard Phillips, a three-time candidate for the presidency, who became a Christian convert to Christian Reconstruction that wants to restore the laws of the Old Testament and New Testament to family and church but with separation of church and state at the national level, dog-eat-dog capitalism and minimal state power over economics. The state, under God, enforces God's Law, provides national security and stays out of the way. Reconstructionists (aka Dominionists) are Postmillennialists, believing that Christianity will progressively and eventually rule the earth. They have little tolerance for religious plurality in the public square.

Phillips left Christian Voice and the three Catholics encouraged Falwell to establish the Moral Majority (MM) as a southern-extension of the "Religious" Right. Falwell brought with him his "Old Time Gospel Hour" radio program and its mailing list and publication that was sent to sponsors. Falwell insisted that the MM include Catholics and Jews for a broader appeal. MM political action committees campaigned on moral issues they believed were the opinions of most Americans such as censorship of publications and entertainment that were "anti-traditional family," prayer in schools despite Jesus command not to pray in public to be seen, opposition to the Equal Rights Amendment that would have given equality to women, despite what the Apostle Paul wrote (Galatians: 3: 28), opposition to sex education in school, the villainization of homosexuals and rejection of "the homosexual agenda," outlawing abortion, targeting non-Christians, especially Jews, for conversion to Christianity.

The Moral Majority and other fundamentalists saw Reagan as their messiah.

Reagan came with problems for fundamentalist Christians, Catholics and social conservatives. Increasing divorce among conservative Christians was the threat to the family. In the 1970s, "Christianity Today" ran eight articles or editorials regarding it. Jesus said that anyone who divorced and remarried lived an adulterous lifestyle. (Matt. 19: 8,9) Reagan was divorced and had married a pregnant mistress. Nevertheless, fundamentalist leaders did not call for laws outlawing divorce and abortion was not an issue. That was a problem for Catholics not Protestants. Divorced women lost stature and divorced women who remarried risked being shunned, especially if they married an older and richer man. Love was rarely believed to be a motive in that circumstance. For men, both were generally accepted, unless they were ministers or in some cases deacons. There was tacit agreement that homosexuality would become the threat to the family.

Personal Note: I had never heard of homosexuality at home or in church until I enlisted in the Marines. I had heard jokes about "queers," and assumed that meant odd and effeminate. Some of my fellow Marines had been arrested for picking up and mugging gay men. A judge had given them a choice between jail or the Marines. Some said they wished they had chosen jail but I believed they were joking. I would have bet my life there were no gay Marines. Now I know there must have been. I just didn't recognize them.

When I returned to Baylor as a student I had a gay roommate but I didn't know it. When others said he was gay I defended him. Some years later I did know he was gay and I didn't know how to deal with the change in our relationship. He had betrayed me by letting me defend him because I didn't believe he was gay. If he had revealed he was gay I probably would have moved out and shunned him. Some years later I wrote him a letter of apology because I did not understand. He did not reply.

When I returned to Baylor as a faculty member, the Dean of Men asked me to come see him. When I did he asked me to identify gay men who were among the student body. I was puzzled because I had no idea why he had asked me. Did he ask other faculty members who had been in the military to spot gays? I knew by then that I could no more determine who was gay by their appearance than any one else could. Out of loyalty to my duty, I did pick out one gay man. When I asked other faculty and students they assured me he was not gay. They were right and he has been married for many years. That was the end of my duty at spotting gays.

There remained a problem for Catholics. Reagan, as governor of California, had signed the most liberal abortion law in the nation before Roe v. Wade. For most Protestants, the Roe decision was overdue. Women were regarded as having a lower status than men but even when pregnant the lives of women were considered sacred. At the 1971 national Southern Baptist Convention, Southern Baptists were called upon "to work for legislation that will allow the possibility of abortion under such conditions as rape, incest, clear evidence of severe fetal deformity, and carefully ascertained evidence of the likelihood of damage to the emotional, mental, and physical health of the mother."

Prominent Southern Baptist fundamentalist, W. A. Criswell, pastor of First Baptist Church, Dallas, declared his satisfaction with Roe v Wade. "I have always felt that it was only after a child was born and had life separate from the mother that it became an individual person, and it always has, therefore, seemed to me that what is best for the mother and for the future should be allowed." W. Barry Garrett of Baptist Press wrote, "Religious liberty, human equality and justice are advanced by the Supreme Court abortion decision."

Personal Note: When Jean and I married in 1953, our Southern Baptist pastor warned us that should she get pregnant we should avoid Catholic doctors and Catholic hospitals because they would sacrifice a mother's life to save a fetus. Baptists thought that was both unwise and deplorable prejudice. Some considered it barbaric.

During her child-bearing years we heard the same from other Southern Baptist pastors, preachers and friends. Among ourselves we said, "You can always have another baby." We presumed Catholic husbands said, 'You can always get another wife."

In male dominated cultures there has always been birth on demand. A woman's primary duty was to provide a male heir for her husband. If she did not, her husband was free to use another woman for the purpose. The chosen woman had no will of her own. (Genesis 16) It wasn't rape because the woman had no rights.

In wars, the victors often killed everyone and Moses ordered Hebrew warriors to do so. Neither pregnant women nor their fetuses were spared. However, warriors could take virgin girls for personal use. (Numbers 31) A woman's only alternative to birth on demand was abortion or suicide, often the same thing.

Even for men, birth on demand was not always desirable. Christian theologian Tertullian (160-430 A.D.) described surgical implements for such use. Augustine (354-430 A.D.) argued that "there cannot be a living soul in a body that lacks sensation due to its not yet being fully formed." Thomas Aquinas (1225-1274 A.D.) believed that in the first stage of pregnancy the fetus was "vegetative," in the second "animal," and that it became a soul only in the third stage. Whether induced or not, fetuses were not given Christian burial. The Catholic Church did not permit the baptism of fetuses that did not show a human form. However, that changed when the immaculate conception of the mother of Jesus became dogma (1854). Most Protestants think the immaculate conception refers to the birth of Jesus. It does not. Mary was conceived the usual way but was freed from "original" sin because of her future obedience.

Until 1821, in America there were no state or federal laws against abortion. Growing Catholic population and political power moved states toward control of human reproduction with laws criminalizing contraception and abortion. The Supreme Court overturned the last state law against contraception in 1965. By the time Roe v. Wade was decided in 1973, nineteen states explicitly permitted abortions in some circumstances, although only four allowed a woman choice for non-medical reasons. Then, as now, women with choice were those with money.

Outlawing abortion was a problem for fundamentalists because of a literal interpretation of Gen. 2:7, that Adam did not become a living soul until God gave him the breath of life. Other Christians had problems with stripping women of the right to their most private property after centuries in which women were not permitted to own any property. Read Jane Austen.

Baptists had no earthly authority other than the Scriptures to decide doctrine or declare dogma. Neither the Jewish nor the Christian Bibles mentioned abortion. Jesus said that nonexistence was not the worst fate. "The Son of man indeed goeth, as it is written of him: but woe to that man by whom the Son of man is betrayed! Good were it for that man if he had never been born." (Mark 14:21)

Jeremiah wrote, "Cursed be the day wherein I was born: let not the day wherein my mother bare me be blessed. Cursed be the man who brought tidings to my father, saying A man child is born unto thee; making him very glad…because he slew me not from the womb; or that my mother might have been my grave, and her womb to be always great with me." (Jeremiah 20:14-17) Job also wished that his mother had aborted him. (Job 3:1-17) Ecclesiastes 6:3 declared that unless a man has a good life and proper burial, abortion is better. The prophet Hosea prayed for God to punish wayward Israelites with abortion. "Give them, O Lord: what wilt thou give? Give them a miscarrying womb and dry breasts." (Hosea 9:14)

A better indication of the status of a fetus might be Exodus 21:22-25. If a man accidentally caused a woman to abort a fetus, then he had to pay the father for the loss of his property, the fetus. However, if there were injury to the mother then it was eye for eye, hand for hand. Some try to force the interpretation that it refers to injury of the fetus but how many incubators did the Hebrews have? How nearby were they? As Dr. James Morse points out, "Why even bother to fine the man at all if the child lived and suffered no injuries?"

"Christianity Today" published an article from a Dallas Theological Seminary professor criticizing the Catholic position on abortion as unbiblical, using the text above as an example. In his book, *Broken Words: The Abuse of Science and Faith in American Politics*, Jonathan Dudley quotes the article and points out that today the magazine would not publish the article and Dallas Theological Seminary would not hire the writer. "At some point between 1968 and 2012 the Bible began to say something different," Dudley wrote.

The Code of Hammurabi was similar and the understanding has not changed. "If a man strikes a woman causing her fruit to depart, he shall pay ten shekalim for her loss of child. If the woman should die, he who struck her shall be put to death."

In Leviticus God commanded Moses to say that if a man lies with his uncle's wife or his brother's wife, "they shall die childless" or "be childless." (Leviticus 20: 20, 21) Previous verses regarding sexual immorality required death by stoning or fire. How was the punishment of childlessness carried out? Wouldn't abortion or infanticide be required?

Before reading the Bible too literally, read Hebrews 7: 9-10. Levi existed in the loins of his great-grandfather. Is that where fundamentalists or Catholics believe life begins?

Baptists, and some other Christians, fell back on Ephesians 5:22-25. Wives were to submit to their husbands. Husbands were to love their wives. When fundamentalists gained control of the Southern Baptist Convention, women lost their power, even those who had been pastors, university or seminary professors, or officers in the Convention. A woman was to have no authority over a man. If women controlled reproduction they would not be submissive but have power over men. Baptists, and some other Christians, chose to ignore the previous verse in Ephesians. "Submit yourselves one to another in the fear of the Lord." For men, love is a verb that requires no action other than declaration. For women, declaration of love means submission. Was submission to mean birth on demand?

The government was the answer to the purpose of women, who owned a woman's most private property, decided how it was to be used, and what it was for. According to the Guttmacher Institute 73% of US abortions are economically motivated. Abortion would drop significantly if medical, financial and emotional support were provided during pregnancy along with day care post-partum services. It would drop further if we re-thought our adoption policies and dealt with the values taught to our kids about the worth of others and of intimate relationships, and—especially for boys about using others for one's own pleasure. If that were the purpose of pro-life proponents. (*USA Today*)

The "Religious" Right wanted the government on their side, claiming that government neutrality was war on Christianity because it refused to accede to their demands for money, power and supremacy, regardless of what their fellow Christians believed or Jesus commanded. The voice of Mammon spoke louder. They had the voice of thousands of radio and TV stations, of right wing politicians and corporate citizens to whom they are willing to bow.

In order to preserve tax exemption for their schools, to gain a better grip on their slipping control over women, to regain government prayers in the school, to prevent science from teaching reproduction and destroying a literal Bible, maintain Christian supremacy in public places, deny gays equal rights and family and only God knows what other reasons, many Protestants and Catholics agreed to work for some of the same causes. After wars that devastated Europe, after persecutions and midnight assassinations, years of arguments and dissension, Catholics and Protestants were able to unite to create a common demon—the threat to marriage by homosexuals and abortion. (For a broad view of abortion see "Is Abortion Always Murder," by Dr. James O. Morse, US Army, Retired.) For the most thorough discussion of the conversion of Fundamentalist and Evangelical Christians to the political right read *Thy Kingdom Come* by Randall Balmer, professor and Episcopal priest.

The strangest bedfellow was Rev. Sun Myung Moon, a South Korean theocrat and pastor of the Unification Church, who claimed to be the second coming of Jesus. The first Jesus had failed because he died before producing children to carry on his mission. Rev. Moon was going to rectify that by producing many children through more than one woman. He, his children and his followers, would sweep away democracy and individualism to built a one-world God-ruled state. Moon, a billionaire, had propped up the *Washington Times*, owned by Unification Church, with more than $3 billion and spent millions on "conservative" speakers and conferences including Jerry Falwell.

Falwell endorsed the *Washington Times* and spoke in behalf of Moon at a Coalition for Religious Freedom conference. Moon was in prison for tax evasion. In 2004 Moon, who had called America "Satan's Harvest" and American women "prostitutes" was given a room in the Senate Dirksen Office Building where he was crowned "King of Peace." Moon's followers claimed that as evidence that the US was bowing to the new Messiah. (Institute for Policy Studies; *Bad Moon Rising*, John Gorenfeld)

Reagan needed fundamentalists as much as they needed him. After Nixon signed agreements with China and the Soviet Union, June 1, 1972, Nixon announced to the nation, "Last Friday, in Moscow, we witnessed the beginning of the end of that era which began in 1945. With this step, we have enhanced the security of both nations. We have begun to reduce the level of fear, by reducing the causes of fear for our two peoples, and for all peoples in the world."

Some people thought the Cold War was over and began to talk of a "peace dividend," that the trillions of dollars that had been wasted on the Cold War could now be spent on schools, highways, health, and the welfare of the people. The CIA had been saying for years that the Soviet Union was collapsing of its own dead weight. Even some conservatives believed that capitalism was superior to communism and that communism would destroy itself.

That wasn't what the military/industrial complex that had become the military/industrial/media (MIM)complex wanted to hear. Talk of a peace dividend caused Gerald Ford to dismiss the reports of the CIA and the faith of conservatives. Ford's Secretary of Defense, Donald Rumsfeld and Chief of Staff Dick Cheney began to rebuild the state of fear claiming that the Soviets had secret weapons that nobody, including the CIA, knew about but them and that billions of dollars must be diverted to defense contractors.

"The Soviet Union has been busy," Rumsfeld announced in 1976. "They've been busy in terms of their level of effort; they've been busy in terms of the actual weapons they've been producing; they've been busy in terms of expanding production rates; they've been busy in terms of expanding their institutional capability to produce additional weapons at additional rates; they've been busy in terms of expanding their capability to increasingly improve the sophistication of those weapons. Year after year after year, they've been demonstrating that they have steadiness of purpose. They're purposeful about what they're doing."

The CIA called Rumsfeld's position a "complete fiction," stated that the Soviet Union was disintegrating from within, could barely afford to feed their own people, and would collapse within a decade or two if left alone.

Dick Cheney who could spot secret Soviet weapons as far away as he could someone else's oil encouraged Ford to appoint a committee including Paul Wolfowitz to prove the increasing Soviet threat.

According to Adam Curtis' BBC documentary, "The Power of Nightmares," Wolfowitz's group, "Team B," concluded that the Soviets had developed terrifying new weapons including a nuclear-armed submarine fleet that used a sonar system that didn't depend on sound and was undetectable by US technology. The BBC asked Dr. Anne Cahn of the US Arms Control and Disarmament Agency during that time, her thoughts on the secret Soviet WMDs. "They couldn't say that the Soviets had acoustic means of picking up American submarines, because they couldn't find it. So they said, well maybe they have a non-acoustic means of making our submarine fleet vulnerable," Dr. Cahn said. "Even though there was no evidence... The CIA accused Team B of moving into a fantasy world."

The neocons said it was true, and organized a group—The Committee on the Present Danger—to promote their worldview. The

Committee produced documentaries, publications, and provided guests for national talk shows and news reports. They worked hard to whip up fear and increase defense spending, specially for weapons systems offered by the defense contractors for whom the neocons would later become lobbyists. (CommonDreams.org)

Declassified reports of the Pentagon contractor BDM Corporation available at the National Security Archive (nsarchive.org) reveal that US intelligence was guilty of "overestimating Soviet aggressiveness" and underestimating "the extent to which the Soviet leadership was deterred from using nuclear weapons." The Soviet military high command "understood the devastating consequences of nuclear war" and believed that the use of nuclear weapons had to be avoided at "all costs."

Nevertheless, Reagan saw an opportunity to reverse Roosevelt's New Deal by taking money from the middle and lower class and throwing billions of dollars at the MIM complex. All he had to do was fan the fires of fear and the media, top brass and think tanks would spread the smoke. Reagan campaigned on the claim that the Soviet military was stronger than the US military and that the USSR outspent the United States by 50% on defense. (David Podvin 8/10/04) That wasn't true and Reagan gave no basis for his statement but it was believed and once started, Eisenhower's fear became a nightmare and seemed unstoppable.

> *Personal Note:* When news came that one of San Antonio's military bases was going to be closed, I opposed the closure. So did the schools, the local media, the Chamber of Commerce and other businesses, our congressional representatives. It's possible that nothing had united San Antonians since Pearl Harbor.

The Department of Defense (p.c. for War) receives more than 50% of all federal discretionary spending. It is the biggest employer in America with 1.4 million men and women in uniform, 850,000 paid members of the National Guard and Reserve, and 650,000 civilian employees. There are hundreds of companies providing goods and services for the military requiring about 5.2 million domestic jobs. Plus 25 million veterans, Washington think tanks, pundits and politicians eager to question the patriotism of any American, including those in uniform, who don't bend over to war-profiteers. (Stephen Walt, *Foreign Policy*, 1/6/09)

That's the "Defense" Department that has needed to defend the country only one time since it changed its name, and that was against 19 hijackers armed with box-cutters. The "Defense" Department failed miserably, leaving the nation defenseless for an hour and a half. If it had been China or Russia that had attacked us, this nation would have ceased to exist.

Although they wanted God's name on everything, the trust of the "Religious" Right was in nuclear weapons and a strong national defense at the cost of children, education, health care and the homeless, including homeless veterans.

They, like Reagan, were anticommunist and, in the right wing tradition, anyone who opposed them was a Communist. They pledged "to defend the free enterprise system" that—like "family values" and "Bible morality"—was never defined, but put them on the side of corporations.

Local MM chapters focused on local issues and candidates, endorsed certain candidates, called on ministers to give their congregations political direction, suggest correct candidates, warn that the government had expelled God from schools and other public places, and vote for candidates who would permit the Ten Commandments in public places and prayers in public schools.

> *Personal Note:* There's a dirty secret about the government throwing God out of the schools and forbidding students to pray in school. God is wherever the Almighty's people are, and that includes all people. The government may chunk your idol out of public places but no government can remove God from any place. Christians can pray anywhere. They don't require kneeling, clasping their hands, closing their eyes, speaking aloud, facing any direction, a prayer shawl or prayer rug. I have prayed in Protestant churches, Catholic churches, Islamic mosques, Hindu and Buddhist temples, public buildings such as courthouses, and every public school I have been in. Any Christian can. A minute of silence is a mute attempt to express Christian supremacy. The "Religious" Right can pray anywhere. What they want is to be seen and heard. They see the government as the solution.

The "Religious" Right also want the Ten Commandments posted in schools, courthouses and other public buildings. Drive around your local churches, temples, and synagogues and see how many of them have monuments of the Ten Commandments on their grounds. If Jews and Christians don't want to display the Ten Commandments on their property why does the "Religious" Right want them in your face on public property, even though it's a violation of two of the Ten Commandments? For the same reason we stamp God's name on graven images called money, and use God's name in a national pledge, as an amulet, a charm, a rabbit's foot against government-and-media induced fear of the Soviet Union. The Supreme Court declared that using God's name on coins and pledges was constitutional because it was using God's name for a secular purpose. That's the definition of blasphemy.

More than MM organizations Reagan needed the media outlets of the "Religious" Right. Many religious organizations have recorded sermons and lectures that have been broadcast as public or community service on radio and TV. There are also nonprofit religious radio and TV outlets, and non-commercial TV networks such as Daystar Television Network (Marcus and Joni Lamb), Trinity Broadcasting Network (Paul and Jan Crouch), Christian Broadcasting Network (Pat Robertson) and the now defunct PTL Network (Jim and Tammy Faye Bakker).

NRB (National Religious Broadcasters) describes itself as a non-partisan, international association of Christian communicators whose member organizations represent millions of listeners, viewers and readers, and its mission to advance biblical truth, promote media excellence, and defend free speech. NRB claims that survey data reveals that 141 million people in America alone listen to, or view, the programming of Christian broadcasters at least once a month, more than the number of people who attend church in that same period. The dark clouds on NBR's horizon are calling historic Christian teaching, such as demonizing homosexuals, feminists, liberals, Muslims and abortion providers, as hate speech, demanding they hire Christians who don't support 100% of their agenda in key staff positions, and the "Fairness Doctrine."

The airwaves belong to "We the people" but our elected officials have given them to broadcasters for free. Sometimes in return the officials ask broadcasters to make public service announcements. In 1949, lawmakers feared that the three main television networks—NBC, ABC and CBS—could set a biased public agenda. The Fairness Doctrine mandated that broadcast networks devote time to contrasting views on issues of public importance to level the playing field. Congress backed the policy in 1954 and later the FCC called the doctrine the "single most important requirement of operation in the public interest."

In 1969 journalist Fred Cook sued a Pennsylvania Christian Crusade radio program after a radio host attacked him on air. In a unanimous decision, the Supreme Court upheld Cook's right to an on-air response under the Fairness Doctrine. In 1974, when Florida tried to hold newspapers to a similar standard, the justices agreed that the Fairness Doctrine didn't apply to newspapers that don't require licenses or airwaves, since theoretically every citizen has a right to publish his own newspaper, and only publishers have freedom of the press. In 1987 the FCC abolished the policy that the public broadcast license-holders had a duty to present important issues to the public and to give multiple perspectives, opening the way to what has become pervasive propaganda from ads to news.

Accuracy in Media, the "experts" from corporate think tanks, the "Religious" Right media and other groups attacked journalists who viewed public schools, social and secular media, the economy favorably. Public schools were a mutual enemy as were the "liberal" media, and "secular" was a four letter word to the "Religious" Right.

Reagan, a lightweight B-grade actor, worked better on the smaller TV screen where he looked bigger, and giving brief introductions to a following program suited him. James Lake, press secretary of the Reagan-Bush campaign, said Ronald Reagan was "the ultimate presidential commodity...the right product."

One former White House aide admitted, "He's an actor. He's used to being directed and produced. He stands where he is supposed to and delivers his lines, he reads beautifully, he knows how to wait for the applause line."

With thousands of religious broadcasting outlets at his back, and the small screen for a sail, Reagan launched his attack on three fronts with a ridiculous tale. A woman in Chicago "has 80 names, 30 addresses, 12 Social Security cards and is collecting veteran's benefits on four nonexisting deceased husbands. And she is collecting Social Security on her cards. She's got Medicaid, getting food stamps, and she is collecting welfare under each of her names. Her tax-free cash income is over $150,000." It was the Big Lie, a lie so big and malicious that people believed it because no sane and moral person would publicly say that if it weren't true, and no honest reporter would pretend it wasn't a lie.

It was a contemptuous slur and it was aimed at three targets—all blacks, poor mothers and children, and all the poor. The government is the problem because it takes your hard-earned money and gives it to "Them," the indolent "strapping young buck," and insolent, bloated welfare queens.

It was also a lie many wanted to hear. In the South it was code for a huge, black woman driving up in a new Cadillac, after parking her unlimited kids somewhere, to pick up the hard earned money of white men. Christians who knew that Jesus commanded them to feed the hungry and care for the sick heard it as a workable rationalization for ignoring Jesus and spending their money on their own worthy obese selves. For those who hated and feared women for their lust that made men weak, it was code for rapacious women who wanted to act like men and should be locked up since there was no way to curb their fecundity without abortion or family planning, which were verboten.

That portrait of the "welfare queen" hid the dirty picture in the attic; the real insolent, bloated welfare queens who flew to Washington in their private jets to exchange stuffed envelopes with Reagan over coffee.

It was a salvo in the War on Women that would attempt to strip women of their rights to economic, political and personal freedom. The day of his inauguration Reagan invited leaders of the birth on demand movement into the Oval Office and asked them what they wanted. They wanted the removal of Dr. Ward Cates, the scientist and physician who headed the Abortion Surveillance Unit of the CDC. Dr. Cates resigned from the government. His colleague, Dr. David Grimes, left the government a few years later. Women lost experts of a legal medical procedure but the "Religious" Right got their blood debt.

At the same time Reagan's new Secretary of Health, Education, and Welfare, Richard Schweiker, spoke at a birth on demand rally and declared that the Reagan Administration would be "pro-life" as though women's lives were worthless. Schweiker instituted the "squeal rule" requiring school authorities to notify parents if their children sought contraceptives at school clinics. Reagan began the global "gag rule." Workers at family planning clinics receiving federal funds could not speak to women regarding abortion even if their lives were in danger from pregnancy. Physicians, nurses, counselors were forbidden to use their professional skills to save women's lives. Reagan opposed stem-cell research, sex education, family planning, and a national response to the epidemic of HIV/AIDS. Appointments to health policy jobs went to people who were fanatics on birth on demand.

After Reagan's election political and "Religious" Right media aided the administration in silencing critics by appealing to their editors and publishers. Editors, columnists, reporters have only the freedom the publisher grants them. Ordinarily, it is not a problem. Editors and columnists, opinionaters learn quickly what is out of bounds and self-censorship drives the agenda.

Reagan's relationship with the "Religious" Right was symbiotic. Like W. Bush he seemed to believe in a literal Armageddon and Gog and Magog from the apocalyptic vision of the Hebrew prophet Ezekiel, found in the biblical book of Ezekiel. There would be a climactic war between good and evil in Israel. The "Religious" Right supported Reagan's MIM complex because an end-time war of Good (us) against Evil (Soviet Union) would fulfill biblical prophecy. Jesus would return, Jews would accept him as their Messiah or volunteer for eternal punishment. They believed the UN was the tower of Babel because it opposed the slow but steady Israeli acquisition of Palestine in defiance of God, and because in the UN, the USA was not exceptional. Falwell publicly stated, "To stand against Israel is to stand against God." No Palestinian father or mother had a right to protect their child on the way to church, mosque or school, even in their own land.

Believing that Scriptures written hundreds of years ago were meaningless until you were born to decipher them requires a certain self-regard and Reagan and the "Religious" Right had it. Reagan believed that the end could occur in his lifetime. Some people in their waning years find it unpleasant to believe the world will continue to exist without them and wouldn't mind if their end marked the end of everything. Usually they are people who have no children or grandchildren. But that belief made it easy to ignore the environmental damage to the earth and climate change. What did pollution of water, air, the food we eat, global warming matter if it was all going to end soon? "Since Reagan's election, our government has catered to the needs of corporations that refuse to accept the destructive consequences of their actions," Jane Smiley later wrote.

Reagan's Hollywood hedonism, his life of comfort and privilege, resonated with the "Prosperity Gospel" preachers. His conviction that greed was a virtue gave credence to preachers who had once railed about conspicuous consumption, egotism, vanity and pursuit of worldly goods, but now preached that money and earthly pleasures were God's reward to those whom the Almighty preferred. Every dollar given to God, through the preacher, would be rewarded five-fold, ten-fold or more or God was a liar because that's what the Holy One had said. No preacher ever explained why they were chosen for prosperity when others such as the prophets Elijah, Jeremiah, John the Baptist, even Jesus and his apostles had not been blessed with luxury. Neither did they explain how God received the money sent through the preacher, but some of the preachers boasted of diamond rings on their fingers, luxury cars in their garages, race horses, private jet airplanes. Anything secular celebrities had religious celebrities had. The poor and desperate looking for a ray of hope from out of their slavery to debt happily and hopefully threw their last dollars at the preacher's feet.

For centuries Christians had believed that the reward for a godly life, for being the "elect" or chosen, was poverty on earth and riches in heaven. The ethics of the prosperity gospel was get it while you can. It was a new and pernicious heresy.

Reagan, pandering to bigots, said that the Voting Rights Act that made it more difficult to prevent blacks and others from seeking representation in government was "humiliating to the South." He said there was no "racism" in America, which made racists feel better. He supported apartheid in South Africa, calling South Africa a country that was "essential to the free world" because of its minerals. He vetoed Congress's attempt to place sanctions on the racist government. Congress overrode his veto.

Reagan's cynicism regarding race was perhaps best illustrated by naming Clarence Thomas to the Equal Employment Opportunity Commission. (EEOC) According to The Atlantic (2/87) Thomas was openly critical of affirmative action, opposed busing, believed the Supreme Court declaration that the segregation of public schools was illegal was based on the assumption that any all-black school had to be inferior to an integrated school, and claimed that blacks would be fine in their own schools. Thomas wanted to strengthen black colleges and universities rather than push white schools to admit more blacks.

Personal Note: Thomas does have a point there but how is it going to happen? And it presumes that personal contact means nothing, that having friends at Harvard is no more important to business or political success than friends at Grambling.

Anyone who experienced separate but equal knew that black schools were planned and operated to be inferior and that it would take federal funding and federal policing to make all-black schools equal. In the South that probably would have meant guerrilla warfare. Thomas's son attended an integrated private school in the Washington suburbs because Thomas wanted the best education for his son

Although I didn't believe it at the time, I was repeatedly advised, "It's not what you know, it's who you know. The most important thing you get out of college is personal contacts." I didn't belong to the right organizations or court the stellar personalities. But at that time for coeds going to college for an Mrs. was not the joke it has become. Women from small towns had limited choices in selecting a life-mate. Limited to a high school education, moving to a large city did not put them in a choice workforce. Some secretaries did marry their bosses but many did not. College gave women a much wider range of possible life mates.

I am sorry to see the decline and closure of some black colleges, most of them private colleges because state schools would not admit them. Those schools have a place in the history of America and I hope that those who attended those schools will write their story so that they will not be forgotten.

According to Atlantic, Thomas agreed with Reagan that civil-rights leaders encouraged discontent to justify their own "rather good positions." He asked where Malcolm X said, "black people should go begging the Labor Department for jobs? He was hell on integrationists. Where does he say you should sacrifice your institutions to be next to white people?" Thomas seemed to favor a black ghetto rather than a melting pot, a small black nation inside a large nation of mixed races. How would that work without black autonomy?

The EEOC can investigate a charge and seek a settlement with the employee. Most people who have been discriminated against lack the resources to hire a lawyer to subpoena evidence, take testimony, and file suit on their behalf. A class action lawsuit gives individuals more power and lawyers more of an incentive to take a case. Thomas did not like class action lawsuits. If a number of women or blacks or elderly had been discriminated against and could show a "pattern and practice" of discrimination that would aid their case. Thomas did not want to see a "pattern and practice" of discrimination. He wanted every woman or black who believed they had been a victim of discrimination to come to the government and prove his or her allegation. He wanted the burden to be on the individual, and the remedy to be back pay and a job only. "Anyone asking the government to do more is barking up the wrong tree," Thomas said.

He didn't understand that a worker had to take off work to file a complaint and had no way to prove it without the power of subpoena. Later, he and some other "justices" demonstrated their ignorance that an employee would require more than 30 days to discover a pattern of discrimination that occurred over decades. Without a lawyer an employee wouldn't know where to start and would have no power to start, but no lawyer would take a case for a percentage of 30 days back pay.

> *Personal Note:* I had my own bout with EEOC while Thomas was in charge. I had my evidence, part of it an evaluation document on which an evaluator had marked "too old." That seemed like age discrimination to me, but not to EEOC. Too old wasn't necessary negative. It was on an evaluation, I explained. But it didn't say "too old" was negative. I had assumed that an evaluation that stated an employee was "too young" would be negative. However, if one were above the protected age "too old" was not negative.
>
> I had the same problem with a dean, evidence from a general publication that quoted the administration as saying the university was looking for "bright young people" and "making it attractive for older faculty to leave." I might read it as saying that the administration preferred younger faculty but "someone else might read it another way," the dean said.
>
> I was in a meeting where every tenured member of the department recommended tenure for a junior faculty member. A different dean from the one in the previous paragraph said he was not recommending tenure because the recommendations were not "positive enough." The process required each tenured faculty member to discuss

the strengths and weaknesses of the candidate for tenure but any mention of weakness was seen by the administration as not positive. The decision for tenure was made at the top and evaluations of the tenured faculty were a meaningless ritual but there was no way to prove that without a lawyer, subpoenas and depositions.

Thomas made it EEOC policy to ignore class-action suits because he didn't want to see blacks treated as numbers. In "fiscal year" 1980 (October 1, 1979, to September 30, 1980) the EEOC settled 32.1% of the cases that it closed. For the first half of 1986 the rate was 13.6%. The proportion of cases in which the EEOC found "no cause" for a lawsuit increased from 28.5% to 56.6% over the same period. Twenty-two percent fewer cases were filed in court in 1985 than in 1981. The decline pleased Thomas. He had heeded complaints that white managers felt that there were not enough qualified minority candidates.

Personal Note: As a member of a department I was part of the hiring process for new faculty. Although the university advertised itself as an "equal-opportunity employer" the department of which I was a member never hired a minority candidate other than white women. Search committees always returned with the same message—the best minority candidates would go to a better university and the others were below our standards.

Thomas publicly criticized civil-rights leaders who "bitch, bitch, bitch, moan and moan and whine" about the Reagan Administration. He saw protests against apartheid in South Africa as less important than efforts at home to improve education for blacks and end poverty and drug abuse among them. However, he made no effort to do any of that, and it's possible he didn't know that the Reagan administration was behind the drug abuse.

Before Thomas the EEOC had brought headline class-action lawsuits against major companies such as General Electric. The agency had caused changes in hiring practices, as well as getting back pay for the victims, multimillion-dollar settlements, and goals and timetables to govern future hiring. Thomas focused the EEOC on cases brought by individuals, fewer class-action suits, less use of goals, timetables, and quotas to remedy discrimination, fewer attempts to stop employers from giving tests, setting standards, or recruiting in a way that caused disproportionately low numbers of blacks, women, and other minorities to get jobs.

The media of the "Religious" Right and corporations served Reagan well. The Pentagon raid on the Treasury was not recognized until David Stockman published his memoirs in 1986, and even then the news media largely ignored the story. Defense Secretary Caspar Weinberger and his deputy Frank Carlucci tricked Stockman, the budget director, shortly after he took office. The three agreed to a compromise of 7% increase in military spending. Carlucci suggested that the increase begin with the 1982 budget that was $80 billion bigger than the 1980 Carter budget that Reagan had criticized.

Fred Hiatt, *Washington Post,* who uncovered the $600 coffee pots and toilet seats, and the $100 tools that could be purchased for a dollar at hardware stores, explained why the theft of taxpayers' money didn't gain traction in the media. "There's a symbiotic relationship in this town between government officials and outside critics and news stories, and until something is recognized within those circles as a problem, the one or two stories that may get done on an issue tend to run inside the paper."

Reagan began his presidency by illegally selling arms to Iran, a violaltion of the US and UN embargo because Iran was a state sponsor of terror. The still underreported evidence indicates that the agreement occurred before Reagan was president, and perhaps even the first sale of illegal weapons to Iran was shipped by Israel before Reagan was president.

Personal Note: Evidence—According to Robert Parry, Consortium News, 8/29/08: In a PBS interview, Nicholas Veliotes, Reagan's assistant secretary of state for the Middle East, said he first discovered the secret arms pipeline to Iran when an Israeli weapons flight was shot down over the Soviet Union on July 18, 1981, on its third mission to deliver US military supplies from Israel to Iran. "And it was clear to me after my conversations with people on high that indeed we had agreed that the Israelis could transship to Iran some American-origin military equipment...I believe it was the initiative of a few people (who) gave the Israelis the go-ahead. The net result was a violation of American law."

In May 1982, Israeli Defense Minister Ariel Sharon told The *Washington Post* that US officials had approved the Iranian arms transfers. "We said that notwithstanding the tyranny of Khomeini, which we all hate, we have to leave a small window open to this country, a tiny small bridge to this country," Sharon said. In 1996, during a meeting in Gaza, Yasir Arafat told Carter, "You should know that in 1980 the Republicans approached me with an arms deal if I could arrange to keep the hostages in Iran until after the elections."

In a letter to the US Congress, Dec. 17, 1992, former Iranian President Abolhassan Bani-Sadr said he first learned of the Republican hostage initiative in July 1980. A nephew of Ayatollah Khomeini, then Iran's supreme leader, returned from a meeting with an Iranian banker, Cyrus Hashemi, who had close ties to William Casey, Chair of the Reagan election campaign, and to Casey's business associate, John Shaheen...Bani-Sadr said the nephew "told me that if I do not accept this proposal they (the Republicans) would make the same offer to my rivals." The nephew said that the Republicans "have enormous influence in the CIA," Bani-Sadr wrote. "Lastly, he told me my refusal of their offer would result in my elimination." Bani-Sadr said he resisted the GOP scheme, but the plan was accepted by the hard-line Khomeini faction.

In 1993, in a press conference former Israeli Prime Minister Yitzhak Shamir said he had read Gary Sick's book, *October Surprise*, arguing that the Republicans had intervened in the hostage negotiations to disrupt Carter's reelection. One interviewer asked, "Was there an October Surprise?" "Of course, it was," Shamir responded. As many as two dozen other Iranian, European and Middle Eastern officials made similar assertions of GOP interference. But in January 1993, after a year-long investigation, a special House task force concluded that "no credible evidence" existed to support allegations of a Republican dirty trick.

After the collapse of the Soviet Union, a report of Russian spies revealed that they had seen the same US and Iranian people at a secret Paris meeting as reported by the French secret service that provided security for the meeting. The House Task Force ignored the report.

Iran-Contra special prosecutor Lawrence Walsh also came to suspect that the arms-for-hostage trail led back to 1980, since it was the only way to make sense of why the Reagan-Bush team continued selling arms to Iran in 1985-86 when there was so little progress in reducing the number of American hostages in Lebanon. (Final Report of the Independent Counsel for Iran/Contra Matters, Vol. I, p. 501)

"Watergate might have been petty compared with Iran-contra, but its dramatic arc was complete—climaxing with a President reduced to madness and fleeing the White House." (*New York Times* 6/4/93) Was Reagan mad? In Ron Reagan's memoir, *My Father at One Hundred*, the son wrote that he saw symptoms of Alzheimer's disease in his father while Reagan was still in the White House. He repeated the story on ABC's 20/20 (1/14/11).

In 1986, CBS's White House correspondent Leslie Stahl said goodbye to Reagan before moving to another assignment. In her book, *Reporting Live*, 2000, she wrote that Reagan didn't seem to know who she was, that she and other reporters suspected that Reagan was "sinking into senility" years before he left office, that White House aides "covered up his condition," and the "free" press chose not to report it. Was that wise? The most dangerous man in the world with the deadliest weapons in the world was mad and the Republican administration and the corporate media chose not to report it?

Special Prosecutor Lawrence Walsh, a lifelong Republican appointed Deputy Attorney General by Eisenhower, was appointed Special Prosecutor because of his loyalty. Walsh had proved his conservative credentials by defending G.M., A.T.&T., I.T.T., and pharmaceutical firm Richardson-Merrell. Hundreds of lawsuits claimed that Bendectin, an anti-morning-sickness medication made by Richardson-Merrell, had caused catastrophic birth defects. Walsh won the lawsuit, but the drug was discontinued a few years later. Forgotten were hundreds of dead and severely deformed babies, shattered families trying to cope with anger, frustration, guilt, and ruinous medical expenses because of "preexisting conditions." (*New York Times* 6/29/97)

Walsh soon saw that official Washington had reached a consensus. Notwithstanding his appointment as independent counsel, the goal was that as little as possible be exposed regarding the rat's nest of lies and bloodshed at the heart of Iran-contra. The cover-up strategy was delay, delay, delay while Republican lawmakers and the compliant media complained that the investigation took too long and was too expensive.

Added to the withholding of pertinent documents was the fog of forgetfulness in which Reagan enveloped himself. Known as the kind of President who left the details—perhaps even the thinking—to others, Reagan's inability to shed any light on the crime, while not entirely plausible, was at least in character. Walsh concluded that he was dealing with an Administration "with no feeling for the rule of law," that Reagan-Bush operatives would resort to any subterfuge—even patently illegal—to keep the facts of Iran-contra hidden. (*Ibid*)

Contrary to common sense, Oliver North and John Poindexter had been given immunity before they testified, allowing them to lie with impunity. Bush saved himself from impeachment by pardoning Secretary of Defense Caspar Weinberger, National Security Council adviser Robert McFarlane, assistant Secretary of State Elliott Abrams, who'd pleaded guilty to withholding information, and three former C.I.A. officials, Duane (Dewey) Clarridge, Alan Fiers and Clair George. Weinberger's personal notes said Bush endorsed the arms shipments to Iran. Some believe Bush's pardon of him was to avoid being called as a witness in Weinberger's trial rather than to avoid his own indictment. It's hard to see how Bush could testify at Weinberger's trial without incriminating himself.

The Tower Commission report, a quick whitewash commissioned by Reagan as a pre-emptive strike against the Senate hearings, wrote Iran/contra off as a rogue operation, by well-meaning superpatriots without sanction or even knowledge from above. Tower was one of the Republicans involved in interrupting the Vietnam peace talks.

Iran/contra figure, ex-CIA officer Donald Gregg, testified that he was unaware of North's contra resupply operation despite the discovery of a vice presidential office memo describing a planned meeting with Rodriguez about "resupply of the contras." Gregg failed a polygraph test when he denied knowledge of the contra supply operation. He also failed when he denied participating in the alleged secret CIA-GOP operation to undermine President Carter's Iran hostage negotiations and secure Reagan's election. (Robert Parry, *Trick or Treason*)

There is much more evidence. It is off limits to the corporate media but readers who wish to know more should read *Secrecy and Privilege* and *Neck Deep* by Robert Parry, *Walsh Iran/Contra Report*, and Walsh's *"Firewall: The Iran/Contra Conspiracy and Cover-Up."*

As if to acknowledge criminal intent, W. Bush rewarded Dick Cheney, David Addington, John Bolton, Elliott Abrams, John Poindexter, John Negroponte, Robert Gates, and others, for their part in the Iran/contra crime by placing them in his administration. Late in W. Bush's administration Elliott Abrams convened a reunion to review their success in evading both jail and disgrace. According to Seymour Hersh, they concluded that with help from Israel, Iran, Saudi Arabia and the contras their illegal operation had been successful in subverting the Constitution, defying Congress and stonewalling the media; however, they agreed, it would have worked far better if the CIA and the military had been kept out out of the loop and the whole thing had been run out of the Vice President's office.

That seems monumental information by one of America's best known reporters, but it had no traction in the media. Journalists who dared file critical reports on the US-backed Salvadoran army or the drug smuggling contras who occupied no territory and mostly attacked villages to kill, rape and steal had been called on the carpet, and some had been summarily dismissed. Daniel Ortega who was elected president, was voted out of office in the next election, and has since been elected president of Nicaragua again. Rev. Miguel d'Escoto, the former foreign minister of Nicaragua's Sandinista government was elected president of the United Nations General Assembly. (6/23/08)

The sales and shipments through Israel continued when Iran took more hostages, even after Hezbollah (Arabic for God's Party) armed with much of the materiel sold to Iran, blew up the US Embassy and a Marine barracks in Lebanon. Perhaps unknowingly, Israel and the US were creating another monster.

> *Personal Note:* Reagan sent the Marines to Lebanon, on the verge of a civil war where their mission was "presence." The Marines asked to be sent to the front lines where the Lebanese army was. Their request was rejected. They were sent to a former hotel at the Beirut airport that was impossible to defend. They were ordered not to assume a defensive posture, carry loaded weapons or fire until they were attacked. Some Marines had been killed, some wounded but they couldn't pursue their attackers. It was Reagan's "Bring it on" moment. When a suicide bomber drove a speeding truck full of explosives toward the hotel the two Marines on guard did not have time to load their weapons. When the truck exploded at the hotel it was the single greatest one day loss of Marines since D-Day on Iwo Jima.

Of course, no one was responsible although the Marines, particularly those on guard were faulted. Judge Royce Lambert later wrote that the Marines "were more restricted in their use of force than an ordinary US citizen walking down a street in Washington, D.C." Mission accomplished, Reagan declared he would not withdraw the Marines from Lebanon as it would signal weakness, then Reagan ordered them to cut and run. As a former Marine I give some financial support to the expanding Marine Heritage Museum at Quantico. I almost quit when I saw that Reagan was an honorary member. Reagan said some good things about the Marines but as usual his words and his deeds didn't match.

Other Marines with Army, Navy and Air Force units invaded Grenada, that had no army, navy or air force. The reasons for the undeclared war changed daily. Communists were building an airfield to enable Soviet bombers to attack America from close range, but the airfield was for commercial use only. The invasion was to prevent a Communist takeover, although most US casualties were caused by "friendly fire," and the fleet had to steam past Cuba, a Communist nation with an army, navy and air force, to attack a small island. The invasion was to rescue US students who were trying to get their M.D.s in a less arduous and academic environment. The students, who didn't know they needed rescue, said later that their only danger was being shot by the US military.

Nevertheless, the media that had called Carter's attempt to rescue the Iranian hostages a debacle because two helicopters collided killing eight Americans, ignored Reagan's debacle that resulted in the deaths of more than 30 times as many Marines. A day after the senseless deaths of Marines, Reagan invaded Grenada and that was the story that was reported, although Reagan had censored the press that did not know about the invasion until military personnel told them the story to write—it was Reagan's "finest hour." It was America's time to beat its chest and crow.

Reagan's deputy chief of staff, Michael Deaver, was suspected of dreaming up "the Grenada operation after observing how the 1982 Falklands war had boosted British P.M. Margaret Thatcher's sagging popularity. One Reagan press aide later confirmed in an interview for Mark Hertsgaard (*On Bended Knee: The Press and the Reagan*

Presidency by Mark Hertsgaard) that 'there were a lot of discussions by some White House people about what the British had done in the Falklands.'"

Deaver said he did not "engineer" the invasion but that he supported it because, "It was obvious to me it had a very good chance of being successful and would be a good story." Deaver believed the government had to control to the maximum extent what Americans were told and especially what they were shown about it. (ibid) That was a lesson the Bushes would take to heart. Find a defenseless or near defenseless nation, make a brutal attack on it, "manage perception" and celebrate American exceptionalism.

"America is standing tall," Reagan crowed. But not the dead Marines who were political fodder. Most of the world condemned a criminal war for political purposes but most Americans never knew that because the US media was less brave and less honest. At least about America.

Even after the Iran/contra crime was revealed the US media were slow to release it and the news was cautious. The investigation by the congressional subcommittee chaired by Senator Kerry was criticized for wasting time or money. Without subpoena power the committee was unable to do a thorough job but they did discover that in 1984 General José Bueso Rosa and coconspirators planned to assassinate Honduran President Roberto Suazo Córdoba financed by a $40 million cocaine shipment to the US. The FBI intercepted the shipment and Bueso was arrested.

Bueso was involved in the CIA's contra operations. Declassified email messages reveal that Oliver North led an effort by US officials to get Bueso "pardon, clemency, deportation, reduced sentence." Bueso got a short sentence in "Club Fed," a white collar prison in Florida. The Justice Department declared the Bueso conspiracy the "most significant case of narco-terrorism yet discovered."

The Kerry report in 1989 noted that Oliver North, then on the National Security Council staff at the White House, and other senior officials created a privatized contra network that attracted drug traffickers looking for cover. The group headed by North ignored repeated reports of contra drug smuggling and worked with known drug smugglers such as Manuel Noriega to assist the contras. John Lawn, DEA director, testified that North leaked a DEA undercover operation, jeopardizing agents' lives, to aid Reagan in an upcoming

Congressional vote on aid to the contras.

The Kerry Committee concluded that "senior US policy makers were not immune to the idea that drug money was a perfect solution to the contras' funding problems...In each case (of drug smuggling) one or another agency of the US government had information regarding the involvement either while it was occurring or immediately thereafter."

Oliver North stated on the Hannity & Colmes talk show that Kerry "makes this stuff up and then he can't justify it." Kerry's staff was accused of obstructing justice. Newsweek mocked Kerry as a "randy conspiracy buff." When a reporter asked about the report at a White House press conference, a *New York Times* reporter told him to ask a "serious question."

Even the more damning and detailed reports of the Inspector General of the CIA showing that at least 50 contra entities smuggled cocaine into the US with the knowledge of the CIA and sometimes the support of the Justice Department received the, ho-hum, "everyone knew that" treatment. Few in the news media cared to know how they had been snookered.

When Swift Boaters attacked Kerry for his heroism in Vietnam to take the spotlight off Bush's cowardice, the news media pretended they didn't know it was vengeance because Kerry refused to back off the truth of contra smuggling despite their threats.

Information regarding contra drug smuggling with protection from the Reagan administration is too vast to cover here. The best sources are the report of the Senate Foreign Relations subcommittee on terrorism and narcotics, chaired by John Kerry, and the CIA Inspector General's Reports at the National Security Archives (nsarchive.org). Also valuable is *Lost History* by Robert Parry.

> *Personal Note:* I earned two degrees and taught for four years at Baylor University. The president of my alma mater, Kenneth Starr, wrote an excellent essay, "Morality, Community, and the Legal Profession" (Wyoming Law Review, 2005). Mr. Starr mentioned the collapse of Enron, WorldCom, Tyco, HealthSouth. He spoke of Bush's "torture memorandum." Then he asked, "Where were the lawyers? Both outside lawyers and inside lawyers." Mr. Starr expressed belief in a "lawyer's duty in community," and stated, "If potential wrong doing is afoot, you do not sit on the information." That is very impressive.

However, it does raise some questions. Reagan appointed Starr to the US Court of Appeals for the District of Columbia Circuit where he served from 1983 to 1989. The court has the responsibility of directly reviewing the decisions and rule-making of many federal independent agencies of the US based in D.C. This often gives the judges of the D.C. circuit a central role in affecting national US policy and law. In 1989, Herbert Walker Bush appointed Mr. Starr as Solicitor General. The solicitor general, directly below the attorney general, represents the Justice Department before the Supreme Court.

Reagan's attorney general, William French Smith freed the CIA from legal requirements that it report drug smuggling by CIA assets, the contras in Central America and Islamic terrorists in Afghanistan. That was already too late. Declassified documents show that the CIA knew that ADREN, a Central American rebel group, made a drug shipment to Miami in July 1981 using Honduran businessman, Alan Hyde. But the CIA did not inform the DEA, FBI, or other law agencies. A 1984 US Defense Department report described Hyde as "a businessman making much money dealing in 'white gold,' i.e., cocaine."

According to the reports of the Inspector General of the CIA, in 1982 the CIA sent a "contractor," known as "Ivan Gomez," to run the Costa Rica-based contra operations. "Gomez" had been working in his family's drug-money-laundering business. "Gomez" directly participated in illegal drug transactions, concealed participation in illegal drug transactions, and concealed information about involvement in illegal drug activity. CIA officials protected "Gomez" from law enforcement and congressional oversight even after he left the agency in 1988.

In 1983, fifty drug traffickers were arrested near San Francisco. Contras in Costa Rica claimed in a letter to the federal court that $36,020 seized from a drug defendant belonged to them. CIA headquarters protested planned depositions of contra figures in Costa Rica. Assistant US attorney Mark Zanides was told by CIA counsel Lee Strickland that the CIA would be "immensely grateful" if the depositions were dropped. They were. The money was returned to Zavala. CIA headquarters sent a cable to the Costa Rica station about the CIA's role in derailing the depositions: "We can only guess as to what other testimony may have been forthcoming." There is far more about the Justice Department, the CIA, and contra smuggling of tons of cocaine into the US in the Inspector General's report. (nsarchive.org)

In 1988, the politicization of the Justice Department became so bad that six Republican senior officials, including the deputy attorney general and the chief of the criminal division, resigned in protest. Where were the lawyers inside and outside the government? Where was Mr. Starr? Is it possible that Mr. Starr did not know? Still does not know? After lying repeatedly to US citizens, W. Bush publicly confessed to authorizing torture. That is a war crime, a violation of the Constitution and the Convention Against Torture. Where is Mr. Starr? Where are the lawyers? The inside and outside lawyers? The ABA? The lawyers that have taken oaths to uphold the Constitution?

All that Americans got out of Iran/contra was arming an enemy, arming terrorists, tons of cocaine that blighted our youth and hundreds of smugglers who learned routes and techniques with the help of the CIA. And being found guilty of international terrorism by the International Criminal Court. The Reagan administration demonstrated its contempt for law by refusing to even appear in the court that the US had been instrumental in creating. The US had to withdraw from the court to prevent Reagan, Bush and others from prosecution and possible imprisonment.

Archibald Cox, Watergate Special Prosecutor who was fired by Solicitor General Robert Bork, said, "Whether ours shall continue to be a government of laws and not of men is now for Congress and ultimately the American people." The American people believed we continued to be a government of laws but they were wrong.

Reagan's economic plan combined cuts in social spending and deregulation with reduced taxes for the wealthiest Americans. The federal government also sent less money to the states and counties that had to raise taxes, including property and sales taxes, increase fees for licenses, and add new taxes to support college and hospital districts, etc. That burden fell disproportionately on the working poor and small business. Peter Milius, *Washington Post*, said, "This was a program that by its nature militated against poor people and for rich people." When told there were hungry people in America, "Sure there are," Reagan replied. "They're on diets." The protected class laughed all the way to a five course meal accompanied by Scotch cocktails, French champagne and German wine.

Later, David Stockman, Reagan's budget director, confessed that "supply-side economics" was intended mainly to cut taxes for the top bracket, a lie to justify transferring large amounts of money to the rich, the people Reagan was most comfortable with. The deficit hit what was then a peacetime high of 6% of gross domestic product. The millionaires and mudsills increased.

Although Reagan is remembered for his tax cut to the rich, according to Harvard Professor and Nobel Laureate Paul Krugman, Reagan's 1981 tax cut was followed by 16 months of rising unemployment. (*New York Times* 6/15/09) Reagan raised taxes 11 times. Contrary to myth and Reagan's professed beliefs, he grew the government more than anyone before him, nearly tripled the size of the deficit, and federal spending ballooned as he threw money at the military/industrial/media complex. While preaching "free trade" he imposed a 100% tariff on some Japanese electronic imports, established quotas on sugar imports, and created the largest steel tariff in US history. The number of homeless doubled, the deregulated Savings and Loan industry collapsed taking the savings of the lower middle class and small business owners with it. And they were the ones who had to pick up the tab.

Krugman further revealed that despite the high price of oil due to the embargo the average economic growth rate of the Carter administration was slightly higher than the growth rate under Reagan, blessed with cheap oil caused in part by Reagan's partnership with terrorists. Louis Bayard wrote that Reagan "left the percentage of national income diverted to federal taxes virtually unchanged between 1981 and 1989—even as states went scrambling to offset cuts in federal assistance." The federal debt tripled, reaching 63% of the economy.

The health misery index rose as the costs of medical care rose more than inflation. Reagan gave employees and employers less incentive to participate in employer-sponsored insurance. People took on themselves the risks of health and high medical costs. Hendrik

Hertzberg of The New Yorker wrote that Reagan "undermined environmental, civil-rights, and labor protections, neglected the AIDS epidemic, and packed the courts with reactionary mediocrities. He made callousness respectable."

More to the point for families and children, the per capita income for the bottom 90% fell by .3% while the income of the top 1% increased by 55%. The bottom 40% of householders paid out more of their income in federal taxes in 1988 than they did in 1980. According to the Hinckley Institute of Politics, (3/28/12) Between 1983 and 2004, in large part because of tax cuts for the wealthy and the defeat of labor unions, of all the new financial wealth created in the US, 43% of it went to the top 1%. Ninety-four percent of it went to the top 20%—meaning that the bottom 80% received only 6% of all new financial wealth generated in the United States during the strong economic years of the '80s, '90s, and early 2000s. By the early 2000s, CEO pay averaged 367 times the pay of the average worker. In 2007, the ratio between CEOs and factory workers was 344:1, while in Europe it was about 25:1.

US corporations had long had factories and operations in other countries to use cheap labor, increase profits and reduce taxes. Their representatives in Congress, who had been elected by the people, decided corporations could increase profits if moving jobs overseas were subsidized by taxpayers. It was a win/win situation for lawmakers and for corporations that gave tips for such favors.

After an appropriate period of time, a few journalists attempted to set the record straight. In (*Free Lunch: How the Wealthiest Americans Enrich Themselves at Government Expense, and Stick You With the Bill*) David Cay Johnston, reported that from 1980 to 2005 the national economy, adjusted for inflation, more than doubled, but the average income for the vast majority of Americans actually declined, wages driven down because Reagan granted amnesty to 3 million illegal immigrants plus their families, a multiple of 3 million. The standard of living for the average family improved only because wives and mothers were forced into the workplace to help feed the family.

Ketchup was the vegetable in federally funded school lunches, trees caused smog, a movie actor who never left the safe shores of the US delivered Jews from concentration camps, German SS troops were war heroes, drug-dealing thugs in Central America were "the moral equivalent of our Founding Fathers," Communist Sandinistas were a 48-hour drive from Texas, "small government" meant the big, bloated but ineffective administration that Reagan grew; "the arms race" was the race of the best armed nation in the world to see how much money could be thrown at the military/industrial/media complex, "the Evil Empire" was going to be gifted with our Star Wars defense once it worked. (about 56 minutes into the Reagan-Mondale presidential debate)

> *Personal Note:* The Star Wars missile defense hasn't worked yet but it's still in the budget. Strangely, Republicans claim that Reagan won the Cold War (he didn't) but no Republican presidential candidate has followed up on Reagan's pledge to give our missile defense to Russia and I know of no reporter who has asked a Republican president or presidential candidate their stance on that pledge. I don't even remember it being mentioned in news stories about the Reagan presidency.

America, that sold weapons to a state supporter of terror, that armed terrorists that blew up a US Embassy and a Marine barracks killing more than 240 Marines, that armed and supported death squads in El Salvador, that threw money and arms at drug smugglers in Nicaragua and studiously overlooked their smuggling, that sold weapons and agents necessary for the production of Weapons of Mass Destruction to Saddam Hussein, that was found guilty of international terrorism, that turned against its own citizens to feed gluttonous corporations, was the "city on a hill."

That was the beginning of "non-reality" based thinking with the assistance of the media that was becoming rapidly collectivized. That was the famed "recovery." The cesspool of corruption, the explosion of a Marine barracks and the trash fires of the homeless were mourning in America. Former New York Governor Mario Cuomo said that rather than turning America into a "shining city on a hill," Reagan turned America into a "tale of two cities." But the story of only one of those cities was reported by the media.

Those who wanted to protect children and families soon realized that to gain representation in government they had to first regain representation in the media. In Mark Hertsgaard's book, *On Bended Knee: The Press and the Reagan Presidency*, Benjamin Bradlee, executive editor of the *Washington Post*, is quoted as saying, "We have been kinder to President Reagan than any President that I can remember since I've been at the Post." David Gergen, former White House director of communications, confirmed shortly after leaving the administration in January 1984 that President Reagan and most of his advisers had come to believe that the basic goal of their approach to the news media—"to correct the imbalance of power with the press so that the White House will once again achieve a 'margin of safety'"— had finally been attained. Tom Brokaw, anchor and managing editor of the NBC Nightly News, said that Reagan got "a more positive press than he deserves."

Leslie Janka, deputy White House press secretary who resigned in protest of press censorship during the invasion of Grenada, said, "The whole thing was PR. This was a PR outfit that became President and took over the country. And to the degree then to which the Constitution forced them to do things like make a budget, run foreign policy and all that, they sort of did. But their first, last, and overarching activity was public relations." ABC News Washington bureau chief George Watson said, "Today as never before our reporters are part of the town's elite, which seems a reasonable factor in explaining why there is less of an adversarial tone in the coverage."

Jody Powell, Carter's press secretary, believed that other administrations would copy the strategy of news management, learn that the press's bark was worse than its bite and that the American people would be the poorer for it. "If you as much as say to the administration, which is what the press is doing, 'Look, you can do this and there's not a damn thing we can do about it,' they're damn sure going to do it. It's too much of a temptation for frail mortals to bear."

Reagan, under investigation for his Iran/contra crimes, chose Robert Bork for the Supreme Court. When special prosecutor Arhibald Cox subpoenaed Nixon's White House tapes, Nixon tried to fire him, but as special prosecutor Cox worked for the Justice Department and could not be fired by the executive branch. Nixon ordered Attorney General Elliot Richardson to fire Cox. Richardson resigned rather than violate his oath of office. Nixon ordered Deputy General William Ruckelhaus to fire Cox. Rucklehaus also resigned. Nixon ordered Solicitor General and Acting attorney general Robert Bork to fire Cox and Bork did so, an act that was later found to be illegal. Apparently, Bork agreed with Nixon that "when a president does it that means it's not a crime."

In *Takeover: The Return of the Imperial Presidency and the Subversion of American Democracy,* Charles Savage reported that in 1987 Dick Cheney and David Addington wrote that it was "unconstitutional for Congress to pass laws intruding" on Reagan's authority.

It's obvious why Reagan, under investigation for Iran/contra crimes, wanted such a man as Bork on the Supreme Court. Reagan had been saved from impeachment because of obstruction of justice by those loyal to the party rather than their country or their oath of office. Contrary to common sense, Oliver North and John Poindexter had been given immunity before they testified, allowing them to lie with impunity. Bush saved himself from impeachment by pardoning Secretary of Defense Caspar Weinberger, National Security Council adviser Robert McFarlane, assistant Secretary of State Elliott Abrams, who'd pleaded guilty to withholding information and three former C.I.A. officials, Duane (Dewey) Clarridge, Alan Fiers and Clair George. Weinberger's personal notes said Bush endorsed the arms shipments to Iran. Some believe Bush's pardon of him was to avoid being called as a witness in Weinberger's trial rather than to avoid his own indictment. It's hard to see how Bush could testify at Weinberger's trial without incriminating himself.

Bork also held some unusual opinions. He believed that the First Amendment right to free speech was limited to explicitly political speech and did not apply to any other other "form of expression, be it scientific, literary or that variety of expression we call obscene or pornographic." He believed that antirust laws hurt consumers. He supported poll taxes if states desired them, called the Civil Rights Act "a principle of unsurpassed ugliness," and stated a wish to roll back previous civil rights decisions by the Supreme Court. He called the Supreme Court decision giving couples the right to family planning "utterly specious," believed that the "equal protection clause probably should be kept to things like race and ethnicity" and not to gender discrimination, believed citizens had only the right to privacy given by legislation rather than acts of the Supreme Court such as the right to abortion. He believed that Congress could override Supreme Court decision by super-majority vote rather than by legislation.

Personal Note: I agree with Bork on one issue. He believed the Second Amendment gave the right to citizens to participate in a government militia. I don't see any other way to read the Second Amendment that requires "a well regulated militia." The Constitution Article 1, Section 8 gives Congress much power over the militia, including "provide for calling forth the militia to execute the laws of the Union, suppress insurrections and repel invasions; to provide for organizing, arming and disciplining the militia..." Article 2, Section 2 of the Constitution states that: The president shall be commander of the army, the navy, and the militia of the several states. What other militia can the Second Amendment be referring to? What other militia has a history of executing the laws of the union, suppressing insurrection and repelling invasions?

To decide otherwise, "justices" had to ignore the militia acts written by the first Congress and signed by the first president, George Washington. The first act mandated that all eligible males enroll in the militia and report for muster and training. The second militia act mandated the weapons and equipment each militia member must possess.

Even if they knew nothing of the militia acts, "justices" should have known a tiny bit of history such as: President Washington called forth the militia and personally led them in response to the Whiskey Rebellion. When the South Carolina legislature passed an act nullifying the federal tariff, Andrew Jackson, who commanded militia in the Battle of New Orleans, as president sent the US Navy to Charleston to assert federal power to enforce the law. When the governor of Arkansas called up the National Guard to prevent the integration of Little Rock High School, Eisenhower nationalized the Arkansas National Guard. Guardsmen who had prevented the integration of the school began protecting the black children who integrated the school.

When the Second Amendment was written each state required a militia for protection. There were no US forts or military camps scattered across the nation. There were no highways, trains or airplanes to move federal troops quickly to protect states. An enemy, Canada, was on the northern and northwestern border, the French had colonies in the south and Spain had colonies in the southwest, and Indians, sometimes hostile bands, roamed the continent. One by one the state militia changed their name to the National Guard. Were there truly "justices" who did not know that?

The idea that the Second Amendment gives individuals the right to take up arms against the government is foolish beyond ignorance. The Constitution declares that Congress has the power to call up the state militia to "suppress insurrection," and the state militia, the National Guard is equipped with artillery, tanks, airplanes and helicopters. What equipment do the pretend militia have? Assault rifles? Fifty caliber sniper rifles? Neither will stop a tank or an F-16.

Bork was outspoken against women who claimed gender discrimination. He was particularly offended by work-related and other accident victims driving up the cost of business. He once wrote that "juries dispense lottery-like windfalls," and compared the civil justice system to "Barbary pirates." (*New York Times*, 6/14/07)

In 2006, Bork was invited to speak at the Yale Club and fell stepping up to the dais, "injuring his leg and bumping his head." Nevertheless, he was able to make his speech and leave under his own power. Afterwards, Bork "filed a suit that is so aggressive about the law that, if he had not filed it himself, we suspect he might regard it as, well, piratical." Bork claimed actual damages for his fall "in excess of $1,000,000," plus punitive damages, and that the Yale Club pay his attorney's fees.

The *Times* imagined what Bork the legal scholar would ask Bork the plaintiff. Was it "reasonably foreseeable" that without stairs and a handrail, "a guest such as Mr. Bork would be injured, why did Mr. Bork try to climb up to the dais? Where does personal responsibility enter in? And wouldn't $1 million plus punitive damages amount to a lottery-like windfall?" (ibid)

The corporate and "Religious" Right media supported Bork, just as they had attacked Special Prosecutor Walsh. After the Senate rejected Bork as a Supreme Court justice, there was an immediate reaction by the media to portray him as a martyr. If you look up Bork in a dictionary you will find something similar to: verb -obstruct (someone, especially a candidate for public office) through systematic defamation or vilification. Origin: 1980s: from the name of Robert Bork, an American judge whose nomination to the Supreme Court (1987) was rejected following unfavorable publicity for his allegedly extreme views." Such was the power of the Right media. That may be what your children and grandchildren will read in their schoolbooks.

If anyone thought it would be better for We the people in the H.W. Bush administration, the illusion was quickly wiped away. Bush's nomination to the Supreme Court for the seat once occupied by Thurgood Marshall was equally appalling. The selection of Clarence Thomas revealed to blacks the government's opinion of them. The process of his appointment revealed to women their place in the federal government.

It seemed a calculated insult to women and other minorities to reward a man for his lack of performance in a regulatory office and they were quick to say so. Their congressional representatives in Congress did likewise. Fearing that the American Bar Association would give Thomas a low rating the White House pressured the ABA for a good rating while also discrediting the ABA as partisan. The ABA did rate Thomas as qualified, although with a low level of support for a Supreme Court nominee.

An FBI interview of Anita Hill, who had worked with Thomas at EEOC, was illegally leaked and Hill was called to testify. David Brock, a right-wing bomb thrower, described Hill as "a little bit nutty and a little bit slutty." She was called to testify at Thomas's confirmation hearing and swore that Thomas's conduct toward her was sexual harassment or at least "behavior that is unbefitting an individual who will be a member of the Court." She was aggressively questioned by some senators who had made excuses for Oliver North when he was testifying about his role in the Iran/Contra crime. Instead, some agreed with Thomas who called the hearing "a circus" and a "national disgrace."

That was true enough but Thomas's description of his treatment— "it is a high-tech lynching for uppity blacks who in any way deign to think for themselves, to do for themselves, to have different ideas, and it is a message that unless you kowtow to an old order, this is what will happen to you. You will be lynched, destroyed, caricatured by a committee of the US Senate rather than hung from a tree—" better described Anita Hill's treatment than his own. Despite receiving preferential treatment unlike most blacks Thomas has always seen himself as a victim.

David Brock, a Reagan psychophant who admired Robert Bork, became part of the "Arkansas Project" to smear Bill Clinton, was involved in the character assassination of the Gingrich era, and broke the "Troopergate" scandal that was the basis for the Paula Jones suits against President Clinton. Later the troopers confessed they had lied and when Jones got her chance to testify that Clinton had harassed her she named a time and place when Clinton was speaking to a public audience at the same time but another place. The media gave the facts the usual "ho-hum, everyone already knew that," but the Republicans made their point.

April 24, 2005, Andy Shaw of ABC News asked former representative Henry Hyde if the impeachment of Clinton was "payback." "I can't say it wasn't," Hyde responded. "But I also thought that the Republican Party should stand for something, and if we walked away from this, no matter how difficult, we could be accused of shirking our duty." Hyde did say that he regretted spearheading the impeachment because it brought to light his own extra-marital affair that broke up a family and was much closer to being an "affair" and involving what most people consider as "having sex." When asked about how his affair was different during the investigation, Hyde said he had gotten away with it.

Brock came to believe that what he was writing was lies and what he had become was a hypocrite. In his confessional, *Blinded by the Right*, Brock revealed that a judge illegally gave him access to the FBI interview so that he could savage Hill, but he came to believe Hill told the truth and that Thomas lied, claimed that Thomas frightened another witness into refusing to testify, and cited the right-wing press and the "richly endowed think tanks" for the poisonous political climate that was destroying the nation. The book was published in 2002, after the time permitted for a lawsuit for slander had run out.

Bork reminded citizens that they were not only losing their voice in their government and the media, they were losing their power through the law. The weapon of choice was the ill-named tort "reform" to take away the little power of the law that citizens had. The power grab was supported by so many in the media with stories of frivolous lawsuits that "frivolous" and "lawsuit" became one word. And there were frivolous lawsuits, although it was difficult to tell which suits were frivolous.

A man whose wife died of complications for treatment for a cancer when the autopsy showed the tumor was benign, was joined by other victims of alleged medical malpractice at a rally in Florida. They protested a campaign by doctors and insurance companies to blame the victims of malpractice by attempting to limit the compensation that juries can award. (*PublicCitizen* November/December 2002)

As governor of Texas, W. Bush fought for and signed legislation limiting lawsuits. He repeatedly voiced a strong belief that most lawsuits were frivolous and that citizens were too litigious. It scared business out of Texas. Overhauling the civil justice system to give businesses a break was a campaign theme. When Bush's car was damaged by a rental car while Bush's daughter was driving Bush sued the rental car company. (*Express-News* 8/17/2000) Many lawyers thought Bush's insurance company should take care of it and that for Bush to sue seemed hypocritical. Not so, said Bush's corporate sponsors. Like Bork, they and Bush believed access to the courts was for the powdered princes like themselves.

Bush's tort reform also tied a corporation's responsibility to an accident victim's monetary value. A corporation would bear less accountability to the family of a mother and homemaker who died than the family of a businessman who died. (*Express-News* 7/23/2000) You could always get another mother.

WalMart was punished more than 60 times in six years by judges for hiding evidence or obstructing justice, showing the relative power of a corporation and a citizen. Some of those who had sued spent more on the lawsuit than they could recover in damages. In the summer of 2002, WalMart began settling customer lawsuits they had fought for years. (Bloomberg 7/30/02)

A Latino artist painted a series of "gallo" paintings that to him symbolized the Mexican American culture. "Corazon de Gallo" means people who are brave. The Gallo winery sued for trademark infringement because wine bibbers couldn't tell a bottle of wine from a painting. After a battle of five years, a settlement allowed the artist to use a Spanish word. (Express-News.net 11/1/02)

When the University of North Carolina assigned the Quran as summer reading, pundits such as Bill O'Reilly, fundamentalist Franklin Graham and fundamentalist groups such as the Family Policy Network sued the University to block the assignment. A federal appeals court allowed the students to read the book. (*Express-News* 8/31/02)

A federal judge accused the W. Bush White House of making purposefully misleading arguments in defending V.P. Cheney's energy task force against two lawsuits. The general counsel of Judicial Watch said that the judge's opinion showed that the arguments of the Bush administration were frivolous and were made for the sake of delay. (Associated Press 7/13/02)

A family store in Elizabethtown, KY, was named Victor's Secret after the owner Victor Moseley. Victoria's Secret, a 750 store chain, sued for trademark infringement, won two rounds in court and hoped the Supreme Court would protect their good name. (Associated Press 4/16/02)

Billy Bob's Beds sued Bubba's Beds in another city because the stores' names were too similar. (*Express-News* 11/13/02)

A developer filed a $24 million suit on a citizen who claimed that the developer received a city waiver to bulldoze trees. Such suits are called SLAPP suits, strategic lawsuits against public participation brought by corporations against citizens who write, protest or petition private acts against public welfare. The aim is not to collect damages but to stifle free speech and intimidate protesters. Corporations have money, lawyers and time; citizens and grassroots organizations don't. At least twenty states have passed anti-SLAPP laws. The Texas legislature has failed at least five times to pass such a bill protecting the free speech of Texas citizens. (*Express-News* 1/6/03)

Some of the stories were lurid, others humorous but rarely reported were the dull facts. According to government data, although insurance premiums rose sharply, malpractice payouts to patients were flat from 1991 to 2001. Insurance experts found that the spike in premiums was caused by the drop of investment income by the insurance companies in the Bush economic turndown. And the government had to race to the rescue of the insurance companies.

In Houston a patient operated on for a herniated disk lost most of his blood and bodily fluids and suffered brain damage before his blood supply was replenished. The doctor, known to be addicted to prescription sedatives including Vicodin, had previously twice operated on the wrong leg. The severely brain damaged patient had been awarded $40.6 million. An appellate court threw out the award and sent the case back for retrial because in the mid-90s the Texas Supreme Court ruled that a hospital cannot be held liable for negligence of its doctors unless it acted with malice. Hospitals have confidentiality privileges on records and meetings of doctors making those documents unavailable as evidence. Even with those documents malice would be hard to prove, even if the doctor was a known addict.

Maybe the hospital gave the doctor operating privileges to save money. (*Houston Chronicle* 1/10/03)

Government data also show that from 1990 to 2004, 5.5% of doctors accounted for 57.3% of all malpractice payouts. About 1 in 10 doctors who had made three or more malpractice payouts had ever been disciplined. From 2001 to 2004 there was a drop in the number of payouts, and the 2004 number was only 5.5% higher than in 1991. Total payouts from 1991 to 2004 adjusted for inflation rose from $2.1 billion to $2.3 billion. The median size of payouts from jury verdicts adjusted for inflation grew from $125,000 in 1991 to $146,000 in 2004, an average annual increase of 1.2%. (*Public Citizen* May/June 2005) That was not the story that most citizens read.

A doctor in Pennsylvania paid 24 claims between 1993 and 2001 totaling more than $8 million. One was for operating on the wrong part of the body; another was for leaving a "foreign body" in the patient but the doctor was never disciplined by Pennsylvania authorities. (Health Research Group April 2003)

There is no legal limit on the number of hours a doctor can work in a 24-hour period and 70% of surgeons do not believe that fatigue affects their performance in the operating room. (National Academy of Sciences' Institute of Medicine) Most doctors don't count medical mistakes as critically important, but the Institute of Medicine estimated in 1999 that nearly 100,000 Americans die in hospitals every year as a consequence of errors, many of which could be prevented. A study by Auburn University suggested that two prescriptions out of every 100 filed in community pharmacies have errors, 60 million mistakes a year. (*Express-News* 1/6/03)

> *Personal Note:* Doctors are no better at policing themselves than lawyers, televangelists or CEOs.

It's easier to get information about a mechanic you want to check your car than it is to get information about a doctor you choose for a dangerous and expensive procedure. For that reason Pubic Citizen created "Questionable Doctors Online" containing information about doctors who have been disciplined by state medical boards and other agencies for incompetence, misprescribing drugs, sexual misconduct, criminal convictions, ethical lapses and other offenses. National Practitioner Data Bank is the most complete database containing state medical board sanctions and hospital disciplinary actions and medical malpractice awards, but neither you nor your doctor are allowed to see it. Your insurance company can.

Another dirty trick was portraying arbitration as an inexpensive and impartial alternative to the court. Corporations often write mandatory arbitration clauses into contracts because arbitration is much more expensive for plaintiffs and it is controlled by defendants. When plaintiffs prevail, the monetary rewards are typically much lower than jury awards because companies will provide arbitrators with future business. When plaintiffs lose there is no appeals process. Some plaintiffs run out of money because of the fees and are forced to drop their claim.

The power grab was supported by scare stories of doctors who were going to quit practice because of malpractice insurance, presumably to teach science in high schools if they hadn't socked away enough money to retire. Doctors who were retiring and had already paid for their condo on the beach or in the mountains, or their cruise around the world claimed they were retiring because of the cost of malpractice. Although the facts showed that 5% of doctors caused 50% of malpractice lawsuits and the rare but headlined pay-outs added slightly less than 1% of the cost of healthcare, it was the 1% where citizens had some power over powerful health insurance companies, doctors unions, and hospitals.

The facts were rarely reported, doctors, hospitals and insurance companies paid lobbyists to explain their position to politicians looking for campaign funding, and paid for newspaper ads and TV commercials that were called information. Most citizens were reluctant to sue their doctor and their hospital, especially in small towns where there were no other choices if they or a family member subsequently needed care. Citizens, some of them misinformed, voted away their right to redress corporate wrongs. The stories of doctors being paid by drug companies to prescribe new medications that were no better but were more expensive than the one they had been taking, stories of hospitals over-treating or overcharging patients, sometimes with the help of insurance companies began to reappear in the media.

As late as August 6, 2012 *The New York Times* reported HCA, the largest for-profit hospital chain in the nation with 163 facilities, "had uncovered evidence as far back as 2002 and as recently as late 2010 showing that some cardiologists at several of its hospitals in Florida were unable to justify many of the procedures they were performing." A nurse's complaint led to evidence that "unnecessary—even dangerous—procedures" drove up costs and increased profits at some HCA hospitals. According to internal reports, cardiologists "made misleading statements in medical records that made it appear the procedures were necessary." You can only hope that injured patients haven't been robbed of their legal rights to redress by such doctors and hospitals and their political enablers.

Collectivization of the media continued. Today, six corporations control 90% of what we hear, read and see, General Electric controls Comcast, NBC, MSNBC, Universal Pictures, *Focus,* and *Features.* News-Corp owns Fox, the *Wall Street Journal* and the *New York Post.* For Disney it's ABC, ESPN, Pixar, Miramax, and Marvel Studios. Viacom owns MTV, Nick,Jr., BET, CMT, and Paramount Studios. Time-Warner—CNN, HBO, *Time Magazine,* and Warner Bros. CBS—Showtime, Smithsonian Channel, NFL.com, "Jeopardy," and "60 Minutes."

Theoretically, that could mean that the head of ABC or NBC has control of what is shown on their network; but practically, Disney or General Electric decides who the head of ABC or NBC is. Everyone in the TV network knows that all employees will keep in mind the aim of the corporation which is provide a return on shareholder value.

Clearly the media did not represent children and families and before families could gain representation in government, they had to gain representation in the media.

That did not happen until the government created the internet. That gave a small thin voice to the people. But the voice got stronger and citizens learned they could get news about the US from English-language foreign newspapers and television that US corporations could not control. Even the International Herald Tribune, the global edition of *The New York Times*, reports stories about the US outside the US that it does not publish inside this country. Some citizens learned to be their own publisher writing news that was too small or too important for the corporate media to report.

The reaction was swift. As We the people gained a voice in the internet we lost voice in government. The joke of the dead voter who arose from the cemetery to vote was resurrected. It was not as grotesque, as imaginative, or as suitable for shooting range targets as the welfare queen getting rich off dead husbands or the indolent black man buying steaks with food stamps, but it was as useful. The federal government, state governments, US attorneys, state attorney generals, and the news media were desperately searching for the illegal voter, almost as mythical as a person rather than a governor or a corporation CEO who was a "welfare queen."

So busy and loud was the government that many people still do not know that in Florida more than 50,000 legally registered black voters were illegally blocked from voting in the 2000 presidential election. A voice in their government, the right to fair representation that so many black citizens had worked for despite police dogs, police truncheons, water cannons, mass arrests; a voice that some had died for was taken from them by Republican state officials and five in the US Supreme Court for whom a decent name cannot be found.

After the presidential election mess in Florida, a consortium of media hired an independent firm to count all the votes in Florida as the Florida Constitution required and the Florida Supreme Court ordered. The report of the vote count was to be announced September 14. That was three days after 9/11. When neither the report or an announcement was made, media figures knew what happened. Bush had lost. Five "justices" of the supersillyous Court had participated in a coup. That news was reported in most countries around the world but in the US the media pretended they didn't notice the date for the announcement had passed.

The Supreme Court justices knew that Bush would lose the election if all the Florida votes were counted. They knew about the dirty tricks of the Florida Republicans and that if none had worked, Bush would have been buried in a landslide. They also knew if Bush wasn't president, the Reagan/Bush secret papers would be released. No matter how dishonorable it was to them, to their oath, to their office, to the Constitution, to the United States, five of the "justices" believed they had to stop the vote count that the Florida Constitution and the Florida Supreme Court required. They really didn't have to voluntarily foul themselves to live in infamy. The Republican-controlled Florida legislature had already voted to appoint their own electors to decide the election. If the Supreme Court refused to thwart the will of the people, they would.

It was a shocking story, historically a bigger disaster than 9/11, but today many Americans believe Bush won the election. The Supreme Court has never sworn or even declared that on some pretext it is unable to explain it won't stop a future vote count. Since the election of

2000, with its dirty tricks, its disenfranchisement of more than 50,000 legally registered black voters, no American citizen who is eligible to vote can be certain that he or she will be allowed to vote or that if so that their vote will be counted. Faith in America requires faith in a faithless Supreme Court.

In the 2004 presidential election millions of voters voted on electronic voting machines that were easily hacked, and a few million of them voted for every candidate on the ballot except the candidate for the White House. The Harris County (Houston, Texas) assistant voter registrar who decides who gets to vote and who doesn't is a paid Republican political consultant with Harris County Republican candidate clients whose names appear on the ballots he handles. In the 2008 election 70,000 voter registration applications were rejected. In comparison, Dallas County rejected only 1,800 applications during the same period. (*Houston Chronicle* 6/12/09)

Although massive searches for illegal voters still go on, few have been found, far fewer than the voters turned away from the polls in Harris County. The stories of the dead voter have their uses. They encourage citizens to demand voter I.D. The party line is, "Everyone has a driver's license, so what's the big deal?" How many young black voters in major cities have driver's licenses? How many young Latino voters in major cities have driver's licenses? How many elderly citizens in retirement villages and assisted living apartments have current driver's licenses? Some college students have been turned away from polls because their student photo I.D. was not accepted. Who is being targeted?

Who is being misinformed? Glenn Greenwald reported in *Salon* (9/6/08), "Half of Americans now say Iraq had weapons of mass destruction when the United States invaded the country in 2003—up from 36% last year, a Harris poll finds." (*Washington Times* 7/24/06) "Nearing the second anniversary of the Sept. 11, 2001, terrorist attacks, seven in 10 Americans continue to believe that Iraq's Saddam Hussein had a role in the attacks." (*Washington Post* 9/6/03) The same poll in June showed that 56% of all Republicans said they thought Saddam was involved with the 9/11 attacks. In the latest poll that number actually climbs, to 62%." (*USA Today*/Gallup Poll 10/6/04) In the latest Harris Poll (7/21/06) "64% agree that Saddam Hussein had 'strong' links to al Qaeda", 49% of Americans think the president has the authority to suspend the Constitution...Only a third of Americans understood that much of the rest of the world opposed our invasion (of Iraq). Another third thought the rest of the world was cheering our invasion, and a third thought the rest of the world was neutral." (Rick Shenkman 6/08)

According to Greg Toppo in *USA Today* (2/2/05), one in three US high school students said the press ought to be more restricted, and even more say the government should approve newspaper stories before readers see them. The survey of 112,003 students revealed that 36% believe newspapers should get "government approval" of stories before publishing. Asked whether the press enjoys too much freedom, not enough, or about the right amount, 32% said too much and 37% said it had the right amount. Ten percent say it has "too little."

Some voters still blame Obama for the bank bailouts, although the legislation was proposed by the Bush administration and signed by Bush. If you criticize voters faith in lies the media respond that Democrats should get their own message out.

How dangerous is that misinformation? Whose purpose is served by it? Thomas Jefferson said, "If a nation expects to be ignorant and free... it expects what never was and never will be."

After Reagan's death the media lauded him for his "myth-making" as though fabrication were better than fact. That explains somewhat the member of the W. Bush administration who criticized a reporter for being stuck in "reality-based" thinking. "We're creating our own reality," the member smugly explained. And so they did.

Declassified documents in the National Security Archive (nsarchive.org) reveal the confidence of the Bush administration that they could "manage perception." And they did with the media slavishly parroting no warning before 9/11, Saddam Hussein behind 9/11, WMD in Iraq, a few bad apples, we don't torture, government propaganda shown on news media as though it were their own, journalists on the federal payroll.

Paul Krugman wrote in his *New York Times* column (3/ 7/08) that the *Times* did not permit its reporters or columnists to say that George Bush lied when he said there were no warnings of the 9/11 attack and that no one imagined airliners being used as missiles. Reporters had done their job. A *Time* magazine cover story entitled "The Hunt for Osama" reported that intelligence sources "have evidence that bin Laden may be planning his boldest move yet—a strike on Washington or possibly New York City." (*Time* 12/21/98)

Intelligence did its job. More than three years before the 9/11 attack on the United States, U. officials warned Saudi Arabia that Osama bin Laden "might take the course of least resistance and turn to a civilian (aircraft) target," according to a declassified cable released by the National Security Archive December 9, 2005. The State Department cable was not mentioned in the report of the 9/11 Commission which investigated how US intelligence failed to detect planning for the terrorist attacks, using civilian airliners, on the World Trade Center and the Pentagon.

American aviation officials were warned as early as 1998 that Al Qaeda could "seek to hijack a commercial jet and slam it into a US landmark," according to previously secret portions of a report prepared last year by the Sept. 11 commission. The officials also realized months before the Sept. 11 attacks that two of the three airports used in the hijackings had suffered repeated security lapses. Federal Aviation Administration officials were also warned in 2001 in a report prepared for the agency that airport screeners' ability to detect possible weapons had "declined significantly" in recent years, but little was done to remedy the problem, the Sept. 11 commission found. But screening measures at two of the three airports used by the hijackers—Logan in Boston and Dulles near Washington—were known to be inadequate, the commission found. (9/11 Commission)

Yet, no one in the corporate media reported incompetence or dereliction of duty. That had to wait until Katrina. Until then there was collective amnesia in the media as everyone tried to forget the inability of the US to protect itself from 19 hijackers armed with box-cutters, although the White House knew they were coming.

Much of the media adopted George W. Bush as their candidate in 2000. The story line was Bush was a straight-shooter. During Reconstruction the Republican government ran the Southern states. Texas rewrote its Constitution to weaken the power of the governor, giving the lieutenant governor the power of appointments. Bush served as governor while there was a good but powerful lieutenant governor, Bob Bullock.

In what was called "funeralgate," the director of the agency overseeing funeral homes began an investigation after more than 240 complaints. A large funeral corporation being investigated was also a Bush campaign funder and wanted Bush to stop the investigation. Bush pressured the agency to stop the investigation and when the director refused in order to do her sworn duty Bush fired her. The director sued for unlawful termination. To avoid deposition Bush gave a sworn affadavit that he subsequently contradicted in front of reporters. The others involved in the lawsuit also contradicted Bush's sworn statement. The director sued Bush for perjury and obstruction of justice. As a candidate for the Republican nomination for president, Bush had his attorney general, now Senator John Cornyn, to settle out of court using taxpayers' money. Cornyn also settled charges against himself for influence peddling and sealed the records. The corporation faced civil charges in California and civil and criminal charges in Florida. Although those stories were headline, network news and TV magazine stories Bush was never connected to them.

> *Personal Note:* I wrote at least a dozen letters to the editor
> of Texas newspapers. None was published. That was a story
> that was not to be told. It is still a secret.

Bush's successes were slight. His father gave him an oil business that ran aground despite a large infusion of cash as an investment from Harvard University. Bush sold his stock before the corporation collapsed and was charged with insider trading. His father's political muscle stopped the investigation and the day after the investigation was stopped, a letter was "discovered" from the company's lawyers warning all the officers, including Bush, that the sale of stock could be considered inside trading. Young Bush was confident he could ignore such warnings.

Bush's records during the Vietnam War were even worse. Bush, who verbally supported the war, received an appointment to the Texas Air National Guard, not to be confused with the Air National Guard. Faced with a written order for a flight medical exam, Bush left the unit, never obeyed the written order, and never returned to flying duties.

> *Personal Note:* One of the problems with the all-volunteer
> military is that few journalists understand military life,
> military organization, military order, or the way that things
> are done in the military. Bush did not serve in the Air Force
> or the Air National Guard. He did not land an airplane on
> an aircraft carrier. Although Bush twice promised to turn
> over all his military records he never did. However, enough
> were collected before they became Top Secret to show that

after Bush got his wings he could not land an airplane, not even a simulator, and had to return to two-seaters with an instructor pilot. Carrier qualification is a special qualification that a minority of Navy pilots have and a mere handful of Marine pilots.

In the Marines if you were AWOL after 30 days you were considered a deserter. I had a relative who went AWOL from the Navy because he was homesick. He was absent less than a week when he was picked up by MPs and he spent time in a Navy brig with Marine MPs. He told me some lessons he learned from the Marines. Most of them concerned appearing aggressive toward Marines.

I did not have the eyesight and maybe not the intelligence to be a military pilot but I do have a private license and when I was actively flying I had to periodically take flight physicals. They were similar to military flight physicals, except that military flight physicals were more rigorous and when Bush was in the Texas Air National Guard there was mandatory drug testing.

Phil Donohue had the most popular show on MSNBC but he opposed a war on Iraq, although his corporate boss, GE, was a military contractor. He was asked to include a pro-war commentator every time he had an anti-war commentator, and then two pro-war commentators, and finally, his show was canceled. Jessica Yellin, now a CNN correspondent, who was at MSNBC during the run-up to the Iraq war said that she felt pressure to report favorably on the war. Katie Couric said the same.

A leaked British memo of an emergency meeting between Bush and Blair stated that both had agreed that WMD would not be found in Iraq. Nevertheless, Bush said he was making war on Iraq and Blair agreed to go along. Parliament and the British media demanded to know if the memo were authentic. Blair's confession that the memo represented what was said at the meeting with Bush forced him out as Prime Minister. That was headline news around the world except for the US. *The New York Times* did bury a short paragraph about it on an inside page of a MEGO story. Former National Security advisor Zbigniew Brzezinski read from that story at a congressional hearing with reporters in the room. As far as I have been able to discover that story was buried by the corporate media and White House officials to repeat the Big Lie that everyone believed Iraq had WMD when not even Bush nor Blair believed it.

It was the same trick they used when the media consortium figured out how to eke out the fact that Bush lost the election without reporting that Bush lost the election. They buried the lead, the only new information, in a long boring retelling of hanging chads and pregnant chads. Following the release of the news the White House and their media allies repeatedly stated that Bush had won.

After W. Bush made war on Iraq, Fred Barnes wrote in the Weekly Standard, "Stronger countermeasures will be needed, including an unequivocal White House response to obstructionism, curbs on filibusters, and a clear delineation of what's permissible and what's out of bounds in dissent on Iraq." Freedom of the press and media representation by We the people were blown away by Shock and Awe. So was our congressional "representation."

The final blow to fair representation in the media was the absurd decision by whatever scurrilous name you choose for the "justices" that corporations have right to free speech. That's more extreme than Robert Bork's view that freedom of speech applied only to political speech. A homeless veteran or a single mother have the same right as a corporation—with a PR department, research department, think tank, lobbyists, publicists and commentators posing as experts—to as much free speech as they can buy.

"In this point of the case the question is distinctly presented whether the people of the United States are to govern through representatives chosen by their unbiased suffrages or whether the money and power of a great corporation are to be secretly exerted to influence their judgment and control their decisions." Andrew Jackson

Personal Note: Could it have surprised anyone that Scott McClellan, W. Bush's White House spokesman and long-time friend, ridiculed the idea that it was a "liberal" media that were the "complicit enablers" of W. Bush's crimes?

A homeless veteran or a single mother also have the same access to politicians or to justice as they can pay for. Some Arab Americans have sent money to charities in their native land. After 9/11 some of those charities were declared to have links with terrorist and the Americans were arrested, tried and jailed. What could be wrong with that?

Chiquita International, the brand chosen after United Fruit became notorious, and its Colombian Banadex subsidiary made monthly payments, totaling $1.7 million, to the United Self-Defense Forces of Colombia (AUC). Even though Chiquita's outside lawyers insisted that payments stop in 2001, Banadex continued to write checks to the AUC, though Chiquita executives later decided that cash was a better idea. The AUC, often described as a "death squad," was named as a "Foreign Terrorist Organizations" on the US Department of State website in September, 2001.

Allegedly, the company funded two other Colombian groups on the US terrorist lists, the National Liberation Army (ELN) and the Revolutionary Armed Forces of Colombia (FARC), and used its company-controlled ports to smuggle weapons into the country for the AUC. An Enquirer's expose found that in 1997, authorities seized more than a ton of cocaine from 7 Chiquita ships. A 2003 report by the Organization of American States stated that a Banadex ship may have been used to ship 3,000 rifles and 2.5 million bullets to the "terrorist" groups. The chief prosecutor's office in Colombia said that it would ask the US Justice Department for more information about the case. One Banadex legal representative has already been convicted of arms smuggling. A leading Colombian lawmaker asked publicly, "How much more does the US government know about payments to the paramilitaries?"

According to US court documents Chiquita told the Justice Department in April 2003 that it was funding the terrorist groups and continued to make the payments for 10 months. Reportedly Chiquita has agreed to pay $25 million in five annual installments if none of its executives are jailed. What about President Bush's policy that anyone financing a terrorist organization should be prosecuted as vigorously as the terrorists? Apparently, that doesn't apply to corporate citizens. According to some, Coca Cola and Drummond Coal have even clearer links to terrorists in Colombia. And is there any reason to suppose that Chiquita's behavior will change? (Anne Howard 4/3/07)

Can a democracy endure when neither the government nor the media are honest with the people? When new-made citizens such as global corporations wipe their feet on We the people as mudsills?

"I am more than ever convinced of the dangers to which the free and unbiased exercise of political opinion— the only sure foundation and safeguard of republican government—would be exposed by any further increase of the already overgrown influence of corporate authorities." —Martin Van Buren

The Battle for Workers' Rights

There has always been class warfare in America, a war by the ruthless and greedy, often with the help of the government, sometimes with the help of the church, against those least able to fight back, the old, ill, mentally and physically disabled, women and children. And new immigrants.

Child labor, including indentured servitude and child slavery, have existed throughout American history. As industrialization moved workers from farms and home workshops into urban areas and factory work, children were preferred because factory owners viewed them as manageable, cheaper, and less likely to strike. Growing opposition to child labor in the North caused many factories to move to the South. (Child Labor Public Education Project)

In 1832, New England unions condemned child labor. Massachusetts required children under 15 working in factories to attend school at least 3 months a year. 1842 Massachusetts limited children's work days to 10 hours. Other states passed similar laws but most of the laws were not consistently enforced.

In 1837, one-fifth of the workers in Pennsylvania cotton mills were under the age of 12 and worked 11 to 14 hours a day, averaging 72 hours a week.

By the law of supply and demand, when business and industry demanded cheap labor the government opened the doors to supply immigrants. The transcontinental railroads were build by companies on the government's payroll with the attendant corruption. Railroad companies were paid by the mile so they took roundabout routes. They were paid more for difficult track-laying so they chose difficult routes endangering workers and delaying completion. Some of the companies bought timber companies or coal mines that sold their products to themselves jacking up the prices. The railroad/mining trusts promised immigrants wages and houses, loaded them in freight trains and shipped them to mining camps. They lived in houses owned by the company with the rent taken out of their wages, they were paid in scrip that could be used only at the company store where prices kept the workers in servitude.

In 1853 a fundamentalist group called the "Know Nothings" grew fearful of immigrants, especially Irish Roman Catholics. During the 1856 presidential campaign, a Republican newspaper warned that "Roman Catholics, whose consciences are enslaved...regard the King of Rome—the Pope—as the depository of all authority." Other Republicans claimed that the Democrats were an unholy trinity of "the Pope, a whisky barrel, and a (N-word) driver." The Know Nothings waved Bibles but they did nothing to resolve the nation's major issues.

"If any man tells you he loves America, yet hates labor, he is a liar. If any man tells you he trusts America, yet fears labor, he is a fool. All that harms labor is treason to America." Abraham Lincoln

Irish, fleeing famine in Ireland, weren't welcomed in America. Signs offering jobs stated: No Irish. Franklin B. Gowen, president of the Philadelphia and Reading Railroad and the Philadelphia and Reading Coal and Iron Company, did welcome them, sending freight train loads of them to the mines. English and Welsh miners who viewed the Irish as inferior did not welcome them. In Schuylkill County, Pennsylvania, more than 5,000 children ages seven to sixteen worked in the mines for one to three dollars a week. Old and injured miners picked up slate at the "breakers" where coal was crushed. "Breaker boys" breathed air thick with coal dust that blackened their lungs and shortened their lives.

There were frequent fights between the Irish and the others, sometimes murders, and most judges, lawyers, and police were Welsh, German or English. Few Irish found justice in the courts.

In 1869, a mine fire killed 110 coal miners. The mine owners had refused to install emergency exits, ventilating and pumping systems, and sturdy scaffolding. In Schuylkill County 566 miners had been killed and 1,655 had been seriously injured in seven years, a tragedy and financial disaster for their survivors. There had been fifty unsolved murders in four years in Schuylkill County, and growth in the Workingmen's Benevolent Association (WBA) that was founded 1864 to demand safe mining conditions. The WBA opposed violence and militancy.

Due to prejudice in the organization, the Irish decided to form their own group for protection, the Ancient Order of Hibernians (AOH) open only to Irishmen and sons of Irishmen. They wanted justice and were willing to punish those who mistreated workers. According to some the OAH was a cover organization for the secret Molly Maguires. Others believe there was no such organization in the US. There were Molly Maguires in Ireland who resisted English occupation and to the English and Welsh in America, any Irishman could be called a "Molly Maguire."

In 1871, the Philadelphia and Reading was the largest company in the world. Franklin Gowen, president of the company that owned two-thirds of the mines in the area had organized mine operators into the Anthracite Board of Trade and he wanted a showdown with the unions. The Panic of 1873 was one of America's worst depressions and in December, 1874, the coal operators announced a 20% pay cut.

January 1875, the miners went on strike. In March a leader of the union was murdered. A mine boss shot into a group of miners wounding several. Vigilantes shot into a miner's meeting killing one miner and wounded several others. By 1877 an estimated one-fifth of workers in America were unemployed, two-fifths under-employed, and only one-fifth worked full-time. November 1877, Harper's Monthly Magazine reported miners with no time for lunch because they were required to have their car loaded with coal when the driver came for it or lose one of the seven car-loads they were required to produce each day. This was the basis for the song, "You load 16 tons and what do you get?/Another day older and deeper in debt/St. Peter don't you call me 'cause I can't go/ I owe my soul to the company store."

"There is an evil which ought to be guarded against in the indefinite accumulation of property from the capacity of holding it in perpetuity by corporations. The power of all corporations ought to be limited in this respect. The growing wealth acquired by them never fails to be a source of abuses." James Madison

Franklin Gowen, reputedly "the wealthiest coal miner in the world," and other mine owners said they could not afford to pay living wages. Gowen had a Pinkerton spy working for him and the Coal and Mine Police worked for all the owners. The Pennsylvania Legislature authorized "all corporations, firms, or individuals, owning, leasing, or being in possession of any colliery, furnace, or rolling mill within this commonwealth" to hire private police forces to protect their property. The coal companies used them to break strikes, paying a dollar each for commissions to whomever the owners hired. The owners hired gunmen and other ruffians. In 1875 Allan Pinkerton recommended vigilantes "... prepared to take fearful revenge on the MMs (Molly Maguires)." Three men and two women were attacked by masked men. (Coal and Iron Police, Wikipedia; The People Versus the Private Army, historymatters.gmu.edu)

Gowen sent the press fearful stories of terror, assassinations, arson by the Molly Maguires. It was the era of "yellow journalism" and local and national press compared the Molly Maguires to the Ku Klux Klan, reported that both used "floggings, lynchings and tar-and-feathers," referred to the Mollies as ruthless murderers, and claimed that when the AOH could not get the mine owners or legislators to make changes, the Mollies responded with violence. Strikes and violence in other states were blamed on the Molly Maguires.

For the strikers conditions were worse than black slaves had faced even in the last days of the war. Infants and the elderly starved to death, but the nation was unsympathetic. Workers who appealed for help were told to go back where they came from by those who had come earlier. Newspapers did not want their workers organized and churches were openly hostile, using the same rationale as Southern clergy used to support slavery. Ephesians 6:5-8, "Servants, be obedient to them that are your masters according to the flesh, with fear and trembling, in singleness of heart, as unto Christ." Even in America the employer was the ruler of the employee.

In 1875, the Coal and Iron police arrested more than 60 strikers on suspicion of being Mollies, breaking the strike. But the mine owners revenge was not complete. A series of trials failed to discover any Molly Maguires but the press continued to call the accused by that name. Gowen had himself appointed special prosecutor and most of the accused were charged with "conspiracy." Being a member of the OAH was evidence enough for prison. Twenty of the prisoners were sentenced to hang. State militia with fixed bayonets surrounded the prisons and the scaffolds to prevent the condemned being saved by a mob.

The accused had been so vilified by mine owners and the press that before they were hanged, they were excommunicated by the Catholic Church and denied a Christian burial. Later, a judge is alleged to have pointed out that a private police force arrested the hanged men, and private attorneys for the coal companies prosecuted them. The state provided only the courtroom and the gallows. Today the state of Pennsylvania considers the hangings "inappropriate." To workers and union members alike the "Mollies" are heroes. (Pennsylvania Center for the Book; Molly Maguires wikipedia)

Nevertheless, opposition of many churches to unions has persisted. In 1886, three hundred Dutch Reformed workers at the Pullman Works crossed picket lines to help break a strike. The Christian Reformed Church declared that no member of the church could be a member of the Knights of Labor. Generally Protestants opposed unions because they appealed to selfishness and the love of power and undermined the God-given authority of the employer. The unions were also accused of supporting a liberal agenda—compulsory education, equal pay for equal work, equal rights regardless of one's origin or skin color, and opposition to child labor and capital punishment. The Knights of Labor accepted black members and preached tolerance.

As late as 1927 the newly formed Protestant Reform Church published a pamphlet stating, "The stand against labor union membership by the Christian defended in this pamphlet is principled. It is a stand based on Scripture's condemnation of unionism's constitutional nature. It is also a stand that is well aware of the actual spiritual condition and conduct—the ungodliness—of the unions, which every member willingly joins and for whose constitution, condition, and conduct every member makes himself responsible before God the Judge."

Fr. John Ryan published *A Living Wage* in 1906 and served as the author of the US Bishops' Program of Social Reconstruction that established the Catholic Church as pro-union. Free markets and self-reliance were not enough. Workers needed rights such as a minimum wage and insurance for the sick and elderly. Most immigrants were Catholic and repenting its actions against the "Molly Maguires" the Church supported labor organizing with statements such as: Unions are indispensable for the universal common good. Unions are rooted in the right of free association. Unions protect the right to fair wages and benefits. Remuneration is the most important means for achieving justice in work relationships. A fair wage was one that provided workers and their families the means to a material, social, cultural and spiritual life. Unions contribute to the solidarity of all through meaningful decisions that affect the common good.

In the 1930s more than 150 Catholic labor schools taught rank and file workers how to form and run unions. Things changed when employees tried to form unions at Church owned schools, hospitals and other institutions. In 1949 Cardinal Spellman used seminarians to break a strike by gravediggers. Communism was the weapon of choice and Spellman said the workers had been influenced by Communist agitators and that he was proud to be a strikebreaker. Other church leaders said nothing about workers' rights or opposed them, sometimes hiring "union avoidance" professionals such as lawyers and consultants to thwart workers' rights by delaying legal action, spying on unions, framing the debate in newspapers as wounded employers under attack by hoodlums.

Rebounding from the Panic of 1873, the 1880s were a period of rapid economic growth. 1881 The first national convention of the American Federation of Labor passed a resolution calling on states to ban children under 14 from all gainful employment. 1883 Led by Samuel Gompers, the New York labor movement successfully promoted legislation prohibiting cigar making in tenements, where thousands of young children worked in the trade.

1883 Miners produced so much silver that it was no longer profitable to owners. Because of good prices and good weather farmers bought more land. Farms in South Dakota were mortgaged at 46% of their value, Kansas 45%, Minnesota 44%, Montana 41%, Colorado 34%. Because of over production, food prices fell. In 1890, the "Billion Dollar Congress" passed a pension bill for all Union veterans who were unable to work whether it was service related or not and expanded benefits to veteran's parents, widows and children. Congress also passed the McKinley Tariff that raised the prices on durable goods and lowered the price on exports, especially harmful to farmers as wheat and cotton exports were a major source of income. The Billion Dollar Congress also required the government to buy more silver with Treasury Notes that could be redeemed in silver or gold. Investors in England and Europe sold their investments in the US in return for gold. Speculators in America traded their silver for gold depleting gold supplies.

In 1886, Jay Gould owned the elevated rail lines in New York City, the Union Pacific, the Missouri Pacific, the Missouri Kansas & Texas (Katy), almost 12% of the tracks in the US, and the Western Union telegraph service. Determined to break the power of the union, Gould fired a foreman breaking an agreement and workers went on strike. Gould hired Pinkerton guards, strikebreakers, and appealed to the governor and the governor sent Texas Rangers and the state militia (National Guard). The government's use of police and military as strikebreakers provoked the desperate workers to violence, alienating the public, and unions never fully recovered in Texas.

Also in 1886, factory workers in Chicago went on strike to get a shorter work day. Police were used to protect strikebreakers and fights broke out. One person was killed and others injured. Chicago had become an industrial giant with thousands of German immigrants working at starvation wages. Attempts to organize were met with repression and violence. The immigrants had a German-language newspaper, the Arbeiter-Zeitung that presented a workers view in contrast to the corporate press that extolled corporate virtues.

Chicago also had socialists and anarchists, some of them militantly revolutionary. The anarchists called for a peaceful demonstration protesting police brutality. The demonstration was disrupted by a bomb thrown into a group of police, followed by gunfire. The press blamed the anarchists. Union members believed the police opened fire in defense but shot each other in the confusion. Others blamed the Pinkerton guards who had previously used lethal violence. News of the bombing and gunfire became national and international news with sensationalized stories and graphics. Eight anarchists were tried, seven were convicted, four were hanged, one committed suicide and the others were pardoned. By associating socialists and anarchists with union members the press succeeded in creating fear of unions.

Collectivization was good for corporations as they built gigantic Trusts to control commerce and the economy, threatening the government. The Philadelphia and Reading Railroad (P&R) had expanded into coal mining, iron making, canal and sea-going transportation and shipbuilding to become in the 1870s the largest corporation in the world. In 1893, the P&R went bankrupt, followed by the Northern Pacific, the Union Pacific, the Atchison, Topeka & Santa Fe, plus 15,000 companies and 500 banks. Many depositors had lost their savings in the panics of 1873 and 1884 and hurried to the banks to withdraw their money. The US Treasury's gold reserve fell below the legal limit. The Secretary went to New York to beg banks to give up gold in exchange for paper notes. Four times between 1894 and 1896, the Treasury issued bonds to obtain coins.

"The fortunes amassed through corporate organization are now so large, and vest such power in those that wield them, as to make it a matter of necessity to give to the sovereign—that is, to the Government, which represents the people as a whole—some effective power of supervision over their corporate use. In order to insure a healthy social and industrial life, every big corporation should be held responsible by, and be accountable to, some sovereign strong enough to control its conduct." Theodore Roosevelt

Employers cut jobs and wages. Unemployment plus the loss of savings in banks meant that the comfortable middle class could not pay their mortgages losing their homes to the banks that had lost their money. A populist "Army of the Commonweal in Christ," labeled "Coxey's Army" by the press, marched on Washington to demand jobs. Coxey and other leaders were arrested for walking on the Capitol grass. President Cleveland had to borrow $65 million in gold from J.P. Morgan. A wave of strikes and violence swept over the country as workers complained of 16 hour days and demanded companies cut rent on company houses and the price of goods at company stores.

Collectivization that was good for corporations was bad for laborers because organization gave workers some control over their lives. A single laborer was helpless because any complaint or attempt to organize could be taken as a personal insult and lack of respect for the employer. The worker could be thrown out of his house with his wife and children with no job and a debt he could not pay.

1890 Employment of children under the age of 12 was prohibited from working underground as miners.

1892 A lockout at the Homestead Steel Works turned violent as 300 Pinkerton detectives hired by the company arrived at the mills by barge. Workers picketing the plant greeted the Pinkerton's with violence, fighting for their families, and the confrontation turned into a pitched battle killing seven Pinkertons and eleven union members. Court injunctions crushed the union, safeguarding the steel industry from organized labor for decades.

"As a result of the war, corporations have been enthroned and an era of corruption in high places will follow, and the money power of the country will endeavor to prolong its reign by working upon the prejudices of the people until all wealth is aggregated in a few hands and the Republic is destroyed. I feel at this moment more anxiety for the safety of my country than ever before, even in the midst of war. God grant that my suspicions may prove groundless." Abraham Lincoln

The American Railroad Union supported a strike at the Pullman Palace Car Company and 125,000 workers on 29 railroads refused to run trains that contained Pullman cars. Richard Olney, son of a manufacturer and banker, had been appointed US Attorney General in 1893 and used the law to oppose the working class. Olney told district attorneys to issue injunctions against the strikers, and ordered federal marshals to protect trains. He persuaded President Cleveland to send

US troops to end the strike that interfered with delivery of US Mail and violated the Sherman Antitrust Act that was supposed to have prevented overweening corporate power.

Union busting dates at least to the 19th century when a rapid expansion in factories and manufacturing capabilities caused a migration of workers from agricultural work to mining, manufacturing and transportation industries. Conditions were often unsafe, women worked for lower wages than men, and children were employed for long hours. Because employers and governments did little to address these issues, labor movements were formed to seek better wages, hours, and working conditions. (Union busting, Wikipedia; History of union busting in the US, Wikipedia; americanrightsatwork.org; huffingtonpost.com/2011/06/28)

"We stand for the rights of property, but we stand even more for the rights of man. We will protect the rights of the wealthy man, but we maintain that he holds his wealth subject to the general right of the community to regulate its business use as the public welfare requires." Theodore Roosevelt

The repeated depressions caused by banks and big business convinced many in the middle class, including the churches they attended, that the poor were not entirely to blame for their poverty. The church and state that workers believed were their protectors had instead protected and aided the syndicates that collectivized for political and financial power in order to oppress them. The public demanded banking reform and regulation of business, but their attention span was short and the press sensationalized violence and vandalism occurring near strikes blaming everything on union leaders.

Floods of immigrants weren't the only competition workers faced. Convicts, orphans and other poor children worked for wages below the subsistence level. The Texas State Federation of Labor officially organized in January 1900 to support compulsory education, the income tax, state-owned utilities, the eight-hour day, equal pay for equal work, and opposition to the use of convict labor and of child labor from state orphanages in competition to free labor.

1900 States varied regarding child labor standards and enforcement. American children worked in large numbers in mines, glass factories, textiles, agriculture, canneries, home industries, and as newsboys, messengers, bootblacks, and peddlers. (Child Labor Public Education Project)

Shortly after 1900, there were few effective employers' organizations that opposed the union movement. By 1903, these organizations started to collectivize to exert influence on industrial relations and public affairs.

For nearly a decade a union called the Western Federation of Miners had grown in power, militancy and radicalism because of dangerous working conditions, employer-employee inequality, the imposition of long hours of work, and an imperious attitude on the part of employers. The union had been outraged by employers' use of labor spies in Coeur d'Alene. The mine owners had organized to increase work hours to ten per day with no increase in pay. The miners won a referendum for an eight hour day with 72% of the electorate but employers and politicians ignored it. The miners went on strike and to break the strike, the owners hired detectives to work as spies. Two mines settled and were operating.

Strike breakers were brought in by the owners but the striking miners met the trains and persuaded the workers not to take their jobs. There was gunfire at the Frisco Mine. The owners said the strikers shot first. The miners said the guards shot first. The miners rolled a barrel of gunpowder into one of the mine buildings. It exploded killing one company man and injuring others. The miners fired into a building where the guards had taken cover and killed another man. More than 60 guards surrendered.

A fight broke out at a nearby mine and 130 strikebreakers were ordered out of the area. The mine owners turned to the governor who declared Martial law and sent in the Idaho National Guard to "suppress insurrection." Federal troops arrived and confined 600 miners without formal charges. Some were sent to prison for violating injunctions and some for obstructing the US Mail.

In the early decades of the twentieth century, the numbers of child laborers in the US peaked. Child labor declined as labor and reform movements grew and labor standards improved, increasing the political power of working people and other social reformers to demand legislation regulating child labor. Organizations led by working women and middle class consumers, such as state Consumers' Leagues and Working Women's Societies, generated the National Consumers' League in 1899 and the National Child Labor Committee in 1904. Goals included anti-sweatshop campaigns and labeling programs. (Child Labor Public Education Project)

"I again recommend a law prohibiting all corporations from contributing to the campaign expenses of any party. Let individuals contribute as they desire; but let us prohibit in effective fashion all corporations from making contributions for any political purpose, directly or indirectly." Theodore Roosevelt

1909 The International Ladies' Garment Workers Union went on strike demanding a pay raise and a 52-hour workweek. More than 20,000 factory workers supported the strike, the largest labor action by women in the nation's history. 1911 a fire at the Triangle Shirtwaist Factory killed 146 women and girls because they were locked in. The oldest was 48, two were 14. Most were unwelcomed Jewish and Italian immigrants. The owners subcontracted work to contractors who hired the desperate paying as little as possible and pocketing a portion of the profits. Subcontractors paid the workers whatever rates they wanted, often extremely low.

Industrial workers real wages declined. Between 1900-1914, adjusted for inflation, wages were less than the average in the 1890s.

1914 Miners at the unsafe Rockefeller Ludlow coal mine went on strike. The miners and their families were evicted from their company owned homes during a Colorado winter. Assisted by unions the miners erected tent cities. The doctors, priests, schoolteachers, and law enforcement were all company employees. Company guards built an armored car, mounted a machine gun and randomly shot at miners and their families. The governor put other company guards in National Guard uniforms and ordered the destruction of the tent camps. The "guardsmen" burned the tents and shot those trying to escape, killing 66. The oldest was 45. The children's ages were 11, 8, 7, 6, 4, 2, 4 months and 3 months. No one was prosecuted.

1914 Henry Ford reduced work hours from nine to eight and raised wages to $5 when the normal minimum wage was $1. He wanted his workers to be able to own a Ford.

To paraphrase John Spargo: In the spinning and carding rooms of cotton and woolen mills, where large numbers of children are employed, clouds of lint-dust fill the lungs and menace the health... In bottle factories and other branches of glass manufacture, the atmosphere is constantly charged with microscopic particles of glass. In wood-working industries...the air is charged with fine sawdust. Children employed in soap and soap-powder factories work in clouds of alkaline dust which inflames the eyelids and nostrils. Boys employed in filling boxes of soap-powder work all day long with handkerchiefs over their mouths.

In some occupations, such as silk-winding, flax-spinning, and various processes in the manufacture of felt hats, it is necessary to keep the atmosphere quite moist. So long as enough girls can be kept working, and only a few of them faint, the mills are kept going, but where faintings are so many and so frequent that it does not pay to keep going, the mills are closed. The children who work in the dye rooms and print-shops of textile factories, and the color rooms of factories where the materials for making artificial flowers are manufactured, are subject to contact with poisonous dyes, and the results are often terrible. Very frequently they are dyed in parts of their bodies as literally as the fabrics are dyed. (*The Bitter Cry of the Children,* John Spargo)

In 1916, Congress passed the first federal child labor law. Not everyone was in favor. Senator Redfield Proctor, Vermont, said, "I have never known any child abuse. Public sentiment would correct it. I have never known an employer but who carefully guarded against any violation of what was right." Senator Thomas Hardwick, Georgia, said, "..what they propose to do with a child who is the sole support of his widowed mother, when they take from him his opportunity to work; what substitute are they going to give? Honest, self-respecting toil is far more elevating than either public or private charity." Senator Nathan Scott, West Virginia declared, "A gentleman...said that he had visited glasshouses (factories) and had seen children— boys and girls—with emaciated forms, with their eyes, as it were, protruding from their sockets, all due to overwork. He spoke of their little bodies being blistered by the hot furnace, and a lot more of that kind of magazine stuff, for it is nothing but stuff." (*Congressional Record,* Dec. 19, 1906; *Discovering American History,* Alan Kownslar and Donald Frizzle)

1916 Andrew Carnegie, one of the richest men in America, testified to the congressional Commission on Industrial Relations, "...thus is the problem of rich and poor to be solved... Individualism will continue, but the millionaire will be a trustee for the poor; entrusted for a season with the great part of the increased wealth of the community, but administering it for the community far better than it could or would have done for itself.... (Soon there will be) no mode of disposing of surplus wealth creditable to thoughtful and earnest men... save by using it year after year for the general good...The day is not far distant when...the public verdict will..be, 'the man who dies... rich dies disgraced.' "

Unlike Carnegie, John D. Rockefeller, richer than Carnegie, who created enduring riches for his family believed in Social Darwinism: "The growth of a large business is merely a survival of the fittest...the working out of a law of nature and a law of God."

The Supreme Court struck down the child labor law because it violated a child's right to contract his or her own labor. 1924 Congress passed a constitutional amendment giving the federal government authority to regulate child labor. The states never ratified it.

1920s Easy money created boom times called "The Roaring Twenties." Harding championed a "return to normalcy" meaning a retreat to lackadaisical government unconcerned with events at home or abroad. Hardings' years in the White House were marked by scandals. Nobody cared because the post-war recession was over, good times were here and most everyone went on a spending spree boosting corporate profits. The spending wasn't from earnings or savings but from easy credit on a new invention, installment plans, that permitted ordinary workers to buy furniture, refrigerators, and the new got-to-haves, radios and cars. Consumerism was born, business and manufacturing surged, selling consumer dreams such as washing machines and pianos. Henry Ford started discount grocery stores putting mom and pop corner shops out of business.

By 1927 Ford had made and sold 15 million Model Ts, prompting the building of roads and highways. Assembly line mass production turned out the goods that consumers wanted. Factory canned foods, ready-made clothing, appliances allowed women to slow down and radio filled homes with entertainment and news—sports, business, and the "Red Menace." Communism was spreading across Europe and Asia as small, weak countries were enveloped into the Soviet Union. Protesting against the government became dangerous if you were labeled anarchist, fascist, communist, socialist or all of them at the same time. Getting the name right didn't matter.

Unions were called tools of communism and opposition to unions was regarded by newspaper, radio and Christian churches as patriotic. Utah promoted an "open shop" where workers would be free to join or not join a labor union. The presiding bishop and the church president of Latter Day Saints gave approval and by 1930 Utah and American industry had become non-union. In some places men and women who were union members were barred from employment.

The number of people living and working on farms peaked at 32,530,000. Farms were small. In towns and on the farm, droughts and high tariffs drove up the price on everything they needed while lowering the price on everything they sold. Farmers needed tractors to replace the horses, mules and stoop laborers. Small farmers with free child labor could no longer compete with large farms that required expensive equipment but needed fewer workers.

According to the Department of Agriculture in 1926 more than one million people left the farm to find work in towns and cities. And some of them left in automobiles as Will Rogers pointed out. Most of the migrants were tenant farmers with little money and basic skills. Their migration lowered wages wherever they went but their work made America the richest nation in the world. The disparity between the richest and the poorest Americans reached a level that it would not reach again in the 20th Century.

"A small group had concentrated into their own hands an almost complete control over other people's property, other people's money, other people's labor—other people's lives. For too many of us life was no longer free; liberty no longer real; men could no longer follow the pursuit of happiness." Franklin D. Roosevelt

Hoover, who replaced Coolidge in the White House, was popular until he vetoed the Veteran's Bonus Proposal. There is always some tension between those who serve their country during a war and those who don't, especially when those who don't, profit by the absence of those who do. Many doughboys returned from World War 1 to discover that someone had taken their job at a wage they had not dreamed of. They left for war with bands playing, flags waving, people cheering and, except for the first to return, came home to find that their country had forgotten them. The American Legion and Veterans of Foreign Wars lobbied for "adjusted compensation." Those opposed called it a "bonus" or "entitlement." Those who had endured the miserable trenches, the constant mud, the shelling, infantry and gas attacks and the unfailing stench of death thought both terms derogatory. This was something they had earned from low pay, hobnail boots, hardtack and bully beef.

A compensation bill was passed by Congress but was vetoed by Harding. In 1924, Congress passed a compensation act. Coolidge vetoed it but Congress overrode the veto. Soldiers were to be compensated at $1.25 a day for foreign service and $1 a day for serving at home. The money was not paid in cash but was used to create a 20-year endowment. Veterans could borrow up to 22.5% of their share. Veterans were not happy with the solution.

1929 the stock market crashed. By 1931, many veterans were in poverty and unable to feed their children. Congress approved a bill to allow them to borrow half of the previously approved compensation. Hoover vetoed the bill because it cost too much and because the bill applied to all the veterans rather than being need-based. Congress overrode the bill but veterans wanted the money quick and in cash to feed their families. About a thousand of them made a "Bonus March" on Washington. Many of them had no home, no job and no money. They vowed to stay until they received what the government had promised them. They slept in empty buildings, government buildings, the Capitol grounds. Their numbers swelled but they remained peaceful.

Congress offered them transportation money to return home. Most took it but more than a thousand remained. They marched down Pennsylvania Avenue chanting: "Mellon pulled the Whistle, Hoover rang the bell, Wall Street gave the signal, And the country went to hell." Andrew Mellon was Secretary of the Treasury who agreed with Hoover that cutting tax rates increased revenue.

> *Personal Note:* That belief has become dogma or superstition despite abundant evidence to the contrary. It has never worked anywhere but it is believed because those who receive the biggest tax cuts are those best able to express their gratitude in speech without words. The top income tax rate was cut from 77% to 24%.

Hoover ordered the army to move the bonus army out of the city. Gen. Douglas MacArthur was in command with Dwight Eisenhower and George Patton among the officers. They forced the veterans out of the city and destroyed the shanty town the veterans had cobbled together for shelter. More than a 100 veterans were injured and a three-month-old baby was killed by breathing tear gas. Many Americans were appalled by the action of the government. Such scenes were not seen again until the civil rights marches for representation in the government. (US History.com)

> *Personal Note:* My father served in the trenches of World War I. He returned to the farm he had left without any

desire to see Europe again. After the Armistice his division, the 90th Texas and Oklahoma Division, marched into Germany. He seemed to hate that march to pacify Germany more than anything that had happened to him during the war although his company suffered such heavy losses in the Meuse-Argonne that it was singled out in a newspaper article.

Perhaps because of that march he liked the Germans and Belgians, meeting so many of them in peaceful situations. Dad hated the French and British. He hated the French because he had to fight for their country but they treated him and his comrades as inferiors. He hated the British because he was Irish. Many times I heard him say that America had fought the wrong war. They should have fought to free Ireland from British occupation.

Most of all Dad hated MacArthur. He regarded MacArthur as a "glory hound" during World War 1. His sympathy was with the Bonus marchers and he saw newsreels of cavalry troops driving veterans out of the city the veterans had fought for. Some of the troops swung batons. Dad believed MacArthur showed his true colors when he left Corregidor, not because he left the besieged island. Roosevelt had ordered that just as Hoover had ordered MacArthur to drive the Bonus Army out of the city. But MacArthur left the Philippines on 4 PT boats, taking his Filipino cook, housekeepers and furniture with him. Left behind were American women nurses and wounded soldiers who would not survive capture.

In 1933 there was almost no organized resistance when Hitler became chancellor of Germany. The churches had been co-opted, labor leaders had been imprisoned and labor unions dismantled, the press and radio were under state control and other political parties had been suppressed. Citizens had no voice in government.

In America, Christians in churches had failed to feed the hungry, house the homeless, care for the sick as Jesus had commanded of his followers. Christians in government did so. Once in office, Roosevelt moved quickly. In 1933, shortly after inauguration he ordered the banks closed until federal examiners found them solvent. The Federal Emergency Relief Act made loans to states and cities to help the poor. He established the Civilian Conservation Corps (CCC) to employ single young men 18-25 years old who had been hobos riding the rails, living in Hoovervilles, and offering to work for food. The Public Works Administration financed programs to construct dams, waterworks, sewers and ships. The Civil Works Administration improved roads, airfields and schools.

1934 The Federal Securities Act required companies that issued securities to provide complete, accurate information to investors, with severe penalties for not meeting those requirements. The Securities Exchange Commission (SEC) had power to enforce rules for the stock market to stop speculation and unfair practices.

1935 The Works Progress Administration put men and women to work rebuilding the infrastructure and employing artists, writers, actors and musicians. The National Labor Relations Act permitted workers the right to organize unions and bargain with employers. The Social Security Act provided unemployment and old age insurance. The Farm Mortgage Moratorium Act allowed farmers to pay rent if they could not keep up their mortgage payments. Taxes were raised on incomes over $50,000 dollars and 75% on incomes over $5 million. Taxes were lowered on small corporations and raised on corporations earning more than $50,000.

The National Housing Act, 1937, was to clear slums and build inexpensive housing for poor families. The Fair Labor Standards, 1938, established a minimum wage, set the maximum work hours at 40 hours per week, time-and-a-half for overtime, and required free, compulsory education for all children. For the first time ages of employment and hours of work for children were regulated by federal law. (*Discovering America*, Allan Kownslar, Donald Frizzle)

Curiously, employers resisted the eight hour day despite evidence that it increased productivity. "In 1848, the English parliament passed the ten-hours law and total output per-worker, per-day increased. In the 1890s employers experimented with the eight hour day and repeatedly found that total output per-worker increased." In 1914, Henry Ford was criticized by the National Association of Manufacturers collective for reducing the work day to eight hours. It took the federal government to force employers to increase productivity when their intention seemed to be to punish workers. (Sara Robinson, *Salon* 3/13/12)

A partisan Supreme Court dismantled most of the New Deal. Roosevelt asked Congress to allow him to make an additional appointment to the court for every justice over 70 and-a-half years. One justice changed his mind and the minimum wage passed. Initially it was 25¢ an hour increased to 30¢ the following year and 40¢ in 1945. The minimum wage has been increased three times in the past 30 years. Each increase was introduced by a Democratic member of Congress. (Washington Spectator)

There were complaints from the privileged class and accusations of socialism and communism. Roosevelt responded: "These economic royalists complain that we seek to overthrow the institutions of America. What they really complain of is that we seek to take away their power. Our allegiance to American institutions requires the overthrow of this kind of power. In vain they seek to hide behind the flag and the Constitution. In their blindness they forget what the flag and the Constitution stand for."

Personal Note: Not much of that applied to me at the time. Farmers were exempt from the minimum wage and maximum hours. Laborers who pulled bolls were paid a penny a pound. Since most farm work paid $1a day, that was living in "high cotton." As a kid I'm not sure that I ever pulled 200 pounds a day but young men did. A hard working boll puller could pull 400 or 500 pounds a day. A man and his wife with five children could earn the bulk of a year's pay pulling bolls, although it kept children out of school. It was hard work and good workers pulled cotton sacks 15 to 20 feet long.

Jean worked longer at pulling bolls than I did because girls did not drive tractors. After her family moved to town she worked after school and on weekends through high school. Her last two years in high school Jean worked in a program called "distributive education." In the morning she took core classes and in the afternoon she worked. During her junior year she worked as secretary for an elementary school principal, Mr. T. G. McCord. Jean had always looked beyond the cotton field but Mr. McCord was the first person to encourage her to look beyond high school.

The act that had the most immediate effect on me was the 1935 Rural Electrification Act that brought electricity to the farm. It took a long time to get to our farm. I remember trying to read and do arithmetic problems by the light of an Aladdin Lamp, the Cadillac of non-electrical lamps. I don't remember reading much by the Aladdin Lamp because natural gas came to the farm. We not only had gas lights, a huge improvement, but gas cook store and gas heaters. We even had a gas refrigerator. I never understood how heat produced cooling but it did. It took most of a day to make ice, and we still had to use lanterns when working outside in the dark, but we no longer had to buy block ice, except for making ice cream. The refrigerator kept milk, meat and cheese cool and fresh vegetables fresh.

Dad built a windmill that produced enough electrical power to charge two wet-cell batteries so we could listen to war news on a radio that had short wave capability. I'm not sure how it operated but I do remember hearing Hitler ranting, probably recorded somehow and rebroadcast. I don't remember listening to music or radio entertainment programs, maybe because it ran down the batteries. I heard town school mates talking about "Jack Armstrong, the All American Boy." I listened to that without much interest but it did allow me to live in part of the world town boys lived in.

After REA came to the farm, one of the first things we bought was a radio. Dad listened to livestock reports on the price of cattle, sheep and hogs but I don't remember listening to much music after we gave up the Victrola. Like most people having a house wired for electricity in that day we thought we needed only one outlet per room and we located the plugs at the same height as the light switches.

The National Labor Relations Act of 1935 permitted companies to influence unions through bargaining, labor relations, and by other means, but employer-controlled unions were outlawed in the United States. Supervisors were forbidden to join unions and an employer could neither assist (as in the event of unions competing to organize the company), nor dominate any labor organization. That meant nothing to me at the time.

During the war years, so many men and women were in uniform that there was a labor shortage at home. That allowed many women their first chance at employment outside the home, and for the first time for some financial independence. At the end of the war, the US military demobilized faster than any military in history. Men suddenly out of uniform and out of a job required readjustment on the part of both men and women. The government provided them with a soft-landing, the GI Bill that offered them unemployment pay and, biggest of all, paid them to go to school. One critic said that "the lazy and 'chisely' types of veterans would get the most benefits, whereas the resourceful, industrious and conscientious veterans would get the least benefits, if any." Another said, "We have 50,000 Negroes in the service from our state and, in my opinion, if the bill should pass in its present form, a vast majority of them would remain unemployed for at least another year, and a great many white men would do the same."

The Constitution offered little to African Americans. It didn't abolish slavery and it gave little protection from racial discrimination. The Civil War freed the slaves but with no land of their own they had to work for the same kind of white men who kept them as slaves, but now only their labor was valuable to their former owners. Employers didn't care whether they were sick, injured or old. No work, no pay.

Blacks were free to search for the best pay and benefits but wages were determined by white men who dared not offer more than others. Any blacks who complained invited visits by men in white sheets who carried guns, ropes and whips. The courts were still in the hands of white men who were angered by any black person who tried to use them to destroy the Southern Way of Life. Free or slave, the blacks were mudsill people, and education and the vote that allowed them a voice in government was dangerous to good order.

After the Civil War three amendments had been added to the Constitution. The 13th Amendment abolished slavery. The 14th Amendment granted citizenship to everyone born in the United States, banned states from limiting citizens' rights, depriving them of due process of law, or denying "any person...the equal protection of the laws." The 15th Amendment prohibited racial discrimination in voting.

Laws are nothing but words unless they are enforced and in the South, after Reconstruction and the withdrawal of federal troops there was little difference between slaves and freed slaves. They lived under constant insults and threats of beating and lynching. Few were allowed to vote unless they voted the way employers dictated. Jim Crow laws required segregation in all public areas, including hospitals, restaurants, hotels, trains and buses, playgrounds, and cemeteries. Signs marked "white" and "colored" dominated the South.

In 1892 a light-skinned black man refused to sit in the "colored" only section of a train. He was arrested and convicted and his case went to the Supreme Court. With only one dissent, the Court ruled that Jim Crow laws had nothing to do with slavery and therefore had no reference to the 13th Amendment and that the 14th Amendment was not intended to enforce social equality.

In the 1930s the NAACP began challenging legal segregation by focusing on graduate and professional school education. In 1936, a federal appeals court ordered the University of Maryland to admit to its law school a black student it had rejected because the state had no separate facility for blacks. Two years later, the US Supreme Court ordered the University of Missouri Law School to admit a black student. The state had no separate law school for blacks, but had offered to send the student to an out-of-state school for blacks. The Court ruled that sending the student to a black school in another state did not "remove the discrimination," which violated the 14th Amendment.

Such rulings allowed blacks to train for professional careers.

1947 Congress passed the Taft-Hartley Act that among other restrictive measures, outlawed the closed shop. One especially hurtful provision permits state governments to outlaw the union shop. That means employees don't have to join the union even after being hired. As a result, at least 23 states have so-called right-to-work laws that make union membership optional and have vastly weakened the labor movement.

"Wherever right to work laws have been passed, wages are lower, job opportunities are fewer and there are no civil rights." Martin Luther King, Jr.

The 1948 Universal Declaration of Human Rights recognized that "everyone has the right to form and to join trade unions for the protection of his interests."

Also in 1948, Truman ended discrimination in the military, establishing equality of treatment and opportunity in the military for all races, religions, and national origins. For the first time military careers at the highest ranks were open to black Americans. In 1949, the Secretary of the Army was forced into retirement for refusing to desegregate the Army. The last all-black units were abolished in 1954. In 1963, the Secretary of Defense required military commanders to employ their financial resources against facilities used by soldiers or their families that discriminated based upon sex or race.

> *Personal Note:* When I was very young, a white family lived on our farm. Dad furnished them a house and well, and allowed them to keep a garden, a cow, a pig, and chickens or guineas as the house was in the trees and bobcats, coyotes, foxes, and hawks feasted on chickens. Guineas lived longer. In exchange Dad had first rights to their labor when needed at the same price other farmers paid, $1 a day except when harvesting cotton. As Roosevelt's New Deal cranked up white families moved to towns where jobs paid better and were more accessible. They were replaced on farms by black families.
>
> Working with black people and taking orders from black men wasn't a problem for me but it was for some southern boys who were accustomed to deference. Showering and sleeping beside black men was different to me but in those early weeks in the Corps, everything was different. One of the benefits of an integrated military is becoming acclimated to those who are different. You may not like some of them but you see them as individuals. You recognize them as human beings and not types. It wasn't unusual for southern boys and blacks to become friends. I often wondered if the boys from the South ever invited their black friends to their southern homes, but I never asked.
>
> Once our battalion was in the field for several days and returned on a pay day. The pay officer had left and most of us had no money to go to town or anywhere else. One company CO, a black captain, borrowed enough money to advance his troops some or all of their pay. That was crucial to married men who had wives, children and bills waiting for them in town. Word of the captain's thoughtfulness

spread through the ranks and you can guess who was believed to be the best CO in the battalion.

After World War II, the University of Texas denied admission to a black student. Instead, Texas opened a separate law school for blacks in three basement rooms not far from the white law school. After five years, the Supreme Court ordered that the student be admitted to the University of Texas.

A federal court ordered the University of Oklahoma to admit a black graduate student. The university admitted the student, but roped him off from other students, reserving a section for him in classes, at the library, and in the cafeteria. In 1950 the Supreme Court ordered the school to end the segregation because under the 14th Amendment the student "must receive the same treatment as students of other races." Blacks could train for a career in law without having to leave their home state.

1954, the Supreme Court by unanimous decision declared that segregation in America's public schools, when authorized or required by state law, violated the Constitution, specifically the 14th Amendment's guarantee of equal protection of the law. For the first time, black Americans could believe the US Supreme Court could be color blind.

In 1955 Utah's predominantly Mormon and Republican legislature passed its version of a "right-to-work" law. Utah became the eighteenth state, and one of the few outside the South, to outlaw union security.

In 1959, Congress passed a law guaranteeing the rights of private employees to form and join unions in order to bargain collectively. In 1962 Kennedy issued an executive order establishing the right of public sector employees—teachers, office workers, police and firefighters—to form trade unions with certain limitations regarding collective bargaining and a special caveat making it "illegal" to strike.

In the 1960s psychologists used psychological techniques to screen potential union supporters, identify hotspots vulnerable to unionization, and structure the workplace to facilitate the maintenance of a non-union environment. Between 1974 and 1984, one firm established by one industrial psychologist trained over 27,000 managers and supervisors to "make unions unnecessary" and surveyed almost one million employees in 4,000 organizations. (Union busting, Wikipedia; unionbustingplaybook.com; *Huffington Post* 6/28/11; *Wall Street Journal* 4/29/11)

The 60s were the years of the Civil Rights and feminist movements. 1961, Martin Luther King Jr., said, "The two most dynamic and cohesive liberal forces in the country are the labor movement and the Negro freedom movement. Together, we can be architects of democracy." And so they were. Both were murdered in the name of Social Darwinism. King was in Memphis to support striking black sanitation workers.

By 1962, the distribution of income and wealth had improved modestly for two decades, the middle class was growing, unions were a powerful force, and even Republicans accepted the New Deal. (Harold Meyerson)

In 1963 Congress prohibited wage discrimination based on gender. Women's earnings rose from 62% of men's in 1970 to 80% in 2004, helping working women support their families. Like many other rights the right to equal pay has never been fulfilled because of lax enforcement and benign neglect by the government and outright opposition from corporate America.

Personal Note: After my first year as a professor we returned to Texas for the summer months because I could not find work in North Carolina and as parents of a baby daughter one of us had to work. The only job I could find in Texas was driving a tractor ten hours a day at $1.25 an hour. The first day I worked the temperature was 110 degrees. At those wages we would have to live with Jean's family. E.E. Holt, Jean's former employer at 7Up Bottling Company in Waco, tracked Jean down at her mother's house. His telephone call was a huge surprise. An office employee had left and the office was in chaos. He wanted Jean to come and organize things. When he had first employed her he asked her if she had ever picked cotton. She said yes. Ted Getterman, Mr. Holt's son-in-law and second in command, told her later that Mr. Holt asked all prospective employees that question. He also said that when Jean answered in the affirmative that he knew Mr. Holt would hire her. Mr. Holt also had picked cotton and he knew that she understood what hard work was.

Mr. Holt offered her a salary higher than I could make. After a brief conversation, we agreed that I would keep our six-month old daughter, write, and in spare time type papers for professors attending a local science institute. It was great to bond with our daughter, we had no problems that required me to call Jean at work, and I was able to write every day. I didn't write anything memorable but I was learning. The downside was that the professors paid 50¢ a page and they wanted the science papers to look good, sometimes requiring that a page be retyped. Other times a light erasure and a typeover was good enough. That was before liquid paper became the world's greatest invention.

Jean made more money than I had been able to make but less than the man she replaced. She talked to her boss but he said the man she replaced had to support a family. Jean pointed out that she was supporting a family and he gave her a raise but not as much as the man who did the same job.

Nonprofit hospital workers were excluded in 1947 with the *Taft-Hartley* amendments. During the 1960s, nonprofit hospital workers wanted to form unions and demand better pay and working conditions. Hospital workers and labor leaders petitioned government and in 1974 the *National Labor Relations Act* was amended to extend coverage and protection to employees of non-profit hospitals.

The civil rights battles were still raging when in 1965 Lyndon Johnson declared, "In a land of great wealth, families must not live in hopeless poverty. In a land rich in harvest, children just must not go hungry. In a land of healing miracles, neighbors must not suffer and die untended. In a great land of learning and scholars, young people must be taught to read and write...To help that one-fifth of all American families with income too small to even meet their basic needs, our chief weapons...will be better better health and better homes and better training and better job opportunities...The cause may lie deeper in our failure to give our fellow citizens a fair chance to develop their own capacities, in a lack of education and training, in a lack of medical care and housing, in a lack of decent communities in which to live and bring up their children..."

Popularly known as "the war on poverty" it was the closest this nation has come to winning a war since the unconditional surrenders ending World War II. It did not end poverty and probably nothing ever will. The poverty rate of about 19% was lowered to approximately 11%. The program gave us Head Start, Volunteers in Service to America, Job Corps, food stamps, work study, Medicare and Medicaid, TRIO programs through the Department of Education including Upward Bound, Talent Search, Equal Opportunity Centers, and student support services; and the Housing Act that banned racial discrimination in housing and subsidized low income housing. Medicare alone saved millions of Americans from slipping into poverty. (Sourcebook, fordham.edu)

1968, in Richard Nixon's acceptance speech as the Republican candidate for the White House, he announced his Southern Strategy, "...it's time to have power go back from the government in Washington, D.C. to the states and to the cities of this country all over America... the first requisite of progress is order...let us also recognize that some of our courts in some of their decisions have gone too far in weakening the peace forces as against the criminal forces in this country...we have been deluged by government programs for the unemployed, programs for the cities, programs for the poor, and we have reaped from these programs an ugly harvest of frustrations, violence and failure...America is a great nation today, not because of what the government did for people, but because of what people did for themselves...let government use its tax and credit policies to enlist in this battle the greatest engine of progress ever developed in the history of man—American private enterprise..."

Blacks, the poor, women, children, the ill and handicapped understood that the government would no longer represent them but white men in luxurious palaces of power. Republicans applauded Nixon's pledge to let power go to states and cities because the major employer in a town has enormous power over the town and the town newspaper. In cities and states it requires more businesses but they are collectivized to hold power over the states and cities. And there is less accountability in cities and states as each has its own bureaucracy to navigate as responsibility shifts from one office to another.

To upwardly mobile blacks, Nixon's statement about "order" meant an attempt to roll back the fair housing laws that permitted blacks to move into white neighborhoods, maybe even the house or apartment next door. Real, scary black men, women and children free to walk through the neighborhood, even at night. "Law and order" became the catch phrase of one of the most unlawful administrations in US history.

Historian Tony Judt believed that the poverty program lost power because of its success. Fewer people feared hunger, sickness and ignorance. Conservatives returned to calibrating the "worthy" and found that too many of them were black. Some who had read the Bible regarded "the poor you will have with you always" as a commandment; others regarded it as an excuse to let them eat cake. As the wife of a future president would say, "They're having the time of their lives." A pundit would write, "Poor people are poor because they make poor decisions. That's the root cause of poverty." (*Washington Times* 4/23/12)

They were poor because they chose to be black and born in the South, born in a neighborhood with poor schools and little access to health care. Or because they chose to be disabled. Or chose to be mentally ill. Or chose to be born in a family with one member who required 24-hour care. Or picked a widowed mother. Or an alcoholic father. There are dozens of bad choices fetuses make, and the best part is that you are not responsible for any of it because they chose it.

"Conservatives say if you don't give the rich more money they'll lose the incentive to invest. Then they say as for the poor, they've lose all incentive because we've given them too much money." George Carlin

In 1971, The Department of Defense partially financed union busting by its contractors. Such activities appear to be illegal, for they conflict with the NLRA. (Confessions of a Union Buster, Martin Jay Levitt)

Taxpayers provide State treasuries the funds for public employee salaries— teachers, police, firefighters, clerks, etc. Out of their salaries public employees pay union dues. At one time state laws did not allow government contracts to provide public money to union avoidance consultants to represent management. One such law, passed in Wisconsin in 1979, was struck down by the US Supreme Court in Wisconsin Dept. of Industry v. Gould in 1986. Labor leaders responded that "federal labor law forces states to hire union busters."

In 1998, Catholic Healthcare West, the largest private hospital chain in California and a major recipient of state Medicaid funds, conducted a campaign against Service Employees International Union at a cost of more than $2.6 million. After the Catholic Healthcare West campaign, the California state legislature passed a law prohibiting the use of taxpayer funds for anti-union activities.

The Center for Cerebral Palsy, a major recipient of New York Medicaid funds, hired a law firm to fight a union organizing drive. In 2002 the State of New York passed a labor neutrality act prohibiting the use of taxpayer dollars for union busting. The law was passed as a direct result of the campaign against the union. In May 2005, a district court judge struck down the labor neutrality law in a ruling that the legal representatives of the Center for Cerebral Palsy described as "an enormous victory for employers."

Reagan had been president of the Screen Actor's union but if anyone believed Reagan wanted unions to empower others they had seen too many movies. His first year in office Reagan fired 13,000 members of the Professional Air Traffic Controllers Organization (PATCO) in a devastating blow to government union members from which the labor movement never recovered. Citizens worried about flying without top air traffic controllers but no one in government seemed to care.

Twenty-five years later the National Air Traffic Controllers Association that was created to replace PATCO again tangled with the FAA over a new contract that cuts wages. W. Bush's two lost wars, his 9/11 bailout of the airlines, insurance companies, and his tax cuts for the rich didn't leave enough money for air traffic controllers without raising taxes. Georgetown University historian Joseph McCartin said that prior to PATCO, it was not acceptable for employers to replace workers on strike, even though it was legal. The PATCO strike eased those inhibitions. Major strikes plummeted from an average of 300 each year in the decades before to fewer than 30 today. "Any kind of worker...was vulnerable to replacement if they went out on strike, and the psychological impact of that...was huge. The loss of the strike as a weapon for American workers has some rather profound, long-range consequences."(NPR.org/8/3/06)

Employers began to take tough stands against unions and replaced strikers with replacements to keep wages low and corporation profits high to the detriment of families.

In 1953, the top 1% of Americans raked in only 9.9% of total income. Most of the rest went to a growing middle class that fueled the greatest economic boom in history that continued through the 60s and into the early 70s. In the meantime private-sector unionization has fallen below 7% from a post-World War II high of roughly 40%. "Already, the economic effects of a union-free America are glaringly apparent: an economically stagnant or downwardly mobile middle class, a steady clawing-back of job-related health and retirement benefits and ever-rising economic inequality." (Harold Myerson)

From 1947 through 1972 productivity increased by 102%, and median household income increased by 102%. As the rate of unionization fell, a gap opened between the economic benefits of a more productive economy and the incomes of ordinary Americans so that in recent decades, all the gains in productivity have gone to the wealthiest 10% of Americans. When labor was at its height in 1955, the wealthiest 10% claimed 33% of the nation's income. By 2007, with a weak labor movement, the wealthiest 10% claimed 50% of the nation's income. In 2009, US corporate taxes had fallen to only 1.3% of GDP, from 4% in 1965.

"Today, wages account for the lowest share of both gross domestic product and corporate revenue since World War II ended. The portion of GDP going to wages and benefits has declined from 64% in 2001 to 58% this year. In Europe the only nations in which labor's share declined were Greece, Spain and Ireland. (Harold Meyerson, *Washington Post* 6/12/12)

In the 60s and 70s, numerous Catholic organizations marched with César Chavez to support the United Farm Workers. In The Compendium of the Social Doctrine of the Church (2004) Unions are indispensable for the universal common good. Unions are rooted in the right of free association. Unions protect the right to fair wages and benefits.

The Compendium states, "Remuneration is the most important means for achieving justice in work relationships." The Church defines a fair wage as such that workers "may be furnished the means to cultivate...material, social, cultural and spiritual life and that of his dependents..." Unions foster solidarity through participation and subsidarity. The Compendium teaches that "The characteristic implication of subsidarity is participation...by means of which the citizen, either as an individual or in association with others, whether directly or through representation, contributes to the cultural, economic, political and social life of the civil community to which he belongs."

Regardless of the Compendium corporations, supposedly with no Catholics in management, moved jobs to "open shop" states. Corporations didn't pay the cost of moving to benefit workers but because it would be harder for workers to start a new union when nonunion workers could enjoy the same pay and benefits that the union had to earn but pay none of the cost, not even union dues. That destroyed worker solidarity and the spirit of working together for a common cause.

Other corporations moved jobs to countries where labor was cheap, plentiful and powerless. Taxes were cheaper and there were no safety regulations or work hours restrictions. Through a generous loophole written in for them, corporations also got a federal tax break for exporting jobs—manna from heaven. It took years for that information to be known and workers to discover they were paying heavier taxes to subsidize the corporations that had taken away their jobs.

Congressional Democrats tried to pass a bill that would cut taxes for corporations bringing jobs back to America. They also tried to pass a bill to close the tax loophole that rewarded corporations for moving jobs out of America. Republicans, who had been shouting for more jobs, blocked both bills. No one was surprised. The elected representatives of the people listened to their lobbyists (p.c. for paymasters).

In 2008, the Bishop of Scranton busted the Scranton Diocese Association of Catholic Teachers by restructuring his school system and refused to negotiate with the union. There are many examples of Catholic schools universities and hospitals that spend large sums of money to employ "union avoidance" firms that boast of their track records in "union prevention in the workplace."

The "Reagan Recovery" was a slide downhill from the Carter administration. According to Congressional Record a comparison of Carter's last years in the White House during an OPEC oil embargo (1977-1980) and Reagan's first years in the White House with an oil glut that dropped oil prices precipitously (1981-83). Gross National Product dropped -59%, industrial production -97%, plant and equipment expenditures -97%, business failures +189%, civilian unemployment +38%, number of unemployed +47%, disposable income -32%, prime rate +35%, federal budget deficit +215%, farm income -326%. But that's not the story you saw, heard and read in the news media.

Reagan's policies also hurt families by turning the war on poverty into a war on the poor. A recession followed Reagan's first tax cut and unemployment jumped to 10%. The federal government plunged into debt from which it has not yet recovered.

Mothers were forced to work outside the home to help feed the family while politicians sniffed self-righteously at feminists who placed infants and children in daycare centers or left them with grandmothers to chase a career in male-only domains.

Carter had told the people the truth: We could not always depend on cheap Arab oil; it cost too much politically and morally. OPEC was not our friend and Americans should do what Americans had always done in hard times, pull together, tighten our belts and find new ways to power the equipment we needed. It wasn't a message we wanted to hear. Reagan lied about America's future and he did more than anyone to threaten it.

Reagan ordered deep budget cuts in Medicaid, food stamps, aid to families with dependent children and other "means tested"" programs that were critical to large numbers of lower-income families. Especially hurt were poor black families while Reagan gave tax credits for segregated schools. He cut back public housing, claiming that the "homeless were homeless by choice." He tried to cut the school lunch program until even some of the "Religious" Right protested. (Eric Pianin and Thomas Edsal, *Washington Post*)

Poor families didn't protest in the media about the cut in food stamps. They didn't lobby Congress. Grocery chains, food packagers, and food producers lobbied Congress. Cutting money for food stamps would cut their profits, hearts of gold and silver complained.

Deregulation and intentional neglect of regulation cost some families their savings, and increased taxes to bail out the deregulated Savings and Loan institutions. Reagan did not understand that hated government regulation served business interests. FDR's regulatory programs promoted fairness in economic competition. Greater transparency helped investors judge the value of securities in the stock market. Separation of commercial and investment banks brought financial stability and the bank insurance program, the FDIC, reassured families that had been burned by bank failures that they could trust banks with their money. Those programs worked for the rest of the century to avoid another depression or deep recession. (Robert Brent Toplin, History News Network)

When Supreme Court chief justice John Roberts was a young government lawyer he proposed reining in the EEOC because its civil rights positions were "totally inconsistent" with Reagan's policies, according to a declassified memo. (Bloomberg, 8/29/05)

By the summer of 1992 Reagan's teflon was wearing thin. Only 24% of Americans said their country was better off because of Reagan, while 40% said it was worse off, and more Americans 48% viewed Reagan unfavorably than favorably, 46%. (Steve Kornacki, *Salon* 8/13/10)

Reagan's magic wand was Communism, and the fear thereof. No doubt Reagan, Cheney, Paul Wolfowitz , John Bolton were scared. They were afraid of everything from union workers to gays and feminists. They ran around shouting "the Russians are coming" like Paul Revere without the horse. They were afraid of horses.

According to William Blum, when Mikhail Gorbachev's close adviser, Aleksandr Yakovlev, was asked whether Reagan's extravagant military spending and "Evil Empire" bombast had any effect on the Soviet Union he replied, "It played no role. None. I can tell you that with the fullest responsibility. Gorbachev and I were ready for changes in our policy regardless of whether the American president was Reagan, or Kennedy, or someone even more liberal. It was clear that our military spending was enormous and we had to reduce it." (William Blum, *Killing Hope*)

Blum, American historian and foreign policy critic, also asserts that George Kennan, former US ambassador to the Soviet Union and author of the "containment policy" said that "the suggestion that any United States administration had the power to influence decisively the course of a tremendous domestic political upheaval in another great country on another side of the globe is simply childish." Instead, extreme US militarization strengthened hard-liners in the Soviet Union. "Thus the general effect of Cold War extremism was to delay rather than hasten the great change that overtook the Soviet Union."

Personal Note: I've had a growing suspicion that the Cold War was unnecessary. Gen. Patton loudly believed that with the destruction of Hitler's regime, the US should attack our Soviet allies. Gen. MacArthur and other hard right ideologues believed we should save nationalist China by using atomic bombs on the Chinese Communist army. Russia has a long history of paranoia since Europe considered it a weak Asian country and Asia considered it a weak European country. Russia fought wars in both Europe and Asia. It is is a huge country with a population of just under 142 million people and the population is in decline. (World Bank)

Jean and I were in Russia a few years ago. We talked to school teachers and families in small towns between St. Petersburg and Moscow. They never had duck-and-cover drills in school. They never had bomb shelters stocked with water and food in sealed containers. (There was one in the basement of our church) They never feared the US. They claimed they had never thought of America as their enemy. Neither of the two great cities had bomb shelters but citizens of Moscow used the subway as a bomb shelter during World War II, the same as citizens of London. St. Petersburg, named Leningrad during Communist rule, was besieged by the German Army for 872 days during World War II and more than a million people died there.

In Moscow we met with three former Soviet generals and a woman military nurse. The generals said they knew America had made the Jeeps and other vehicles and ships they used to defeat the Germans, although their leaders claimed the US had stolen Russia's ideas to make them. They carefully explained that they didn't fight the Germans, they fought Nazis. I don't think any Americans made that distinction. They swore they never thought America would attack them.

Reagan's redistribution of the wealth from those who have little to those who have an over abundance has led to the happy circumstance of the richest Americans taking home a bigger share of total income than at any time since the 1920s, the prelude to the Great Depression. Even Republican economists give Obama credit for averting a second Great Depression but some cling to policies that may make it inevitable.

According to the Hinckley Institute of Politics (3/28/12) "If, following the 1920s, taxes accounted for the decrease in wealth for the very rich, what accounts mostly for the increase in wealth and income for most of the rest? In large part, it was the union movement...Strong union advocacy means higher wages, better benefits, and a rippling effect that raises wages for others. It also brings into focus the disparity between the pay of top executives and average workers... Between 1983 and 2004, in large part because of tax cuts for the wealthy and the defeat of labor unions, of all the new financial wealth created in the US, 43% of it went to the top 1%. Ninety-four percent of it went to the top 20%—meaning that the bottom 80% received only 6% of all new financial wealth generated in the United States during the strong economic years of the '80s, '90s, and early 2000s."

The demise of unions can perhaps be illustrated by one industry. In 1906, Upton Sinclair published *The Jungle* about the life of a meatpacking worker. The lack of sanitation, the disgusting and dangerous jobs of the workers had been kept quiet for years, the way corporations are able to maintain secrecy and lack of regulation until a whistleblower sacrifices himself and his family to tell the truth. The farm-to-butcher process had changed into a collective of meatpacker plants called the Big Five that employed mostly immigrants willing to work at subsistence pay. Readers were horrified and Theodore Roosevelt pressured Congress to pass the first food safety laws, the Pure Food and Drug Act and the Federal Meat Inspection Act.

As immigration slowed and unions gained a tenuous foothold the lot of meatpackers improved. By the late 60s meatpackers had moved into the middle class with a home, refrigerator, radio, TV, maybe a car, the same as workers in the steel and auto industries. In 2005, independent reports by Human Rights Watch (HRW) and the Government Accountability Office (GAC) showed how little had changed in the industry. Meatpacking was still among the most dangerous jobs in the world while regulators pretended benign ignorance.

Meatpacking plants moved from cities into the more rural midwest, 80% of the workforce was foreign born, union membership had declined from 46% in 1980 to 17% in 2005. Wages had declined 30%, and the job remained among the most dangerous in America, almost four times the reported non-fatal injury rate as workers in manufacturing. Underreporting of injuries by employers is believed to be pervasive to keep down insurance costs. And as in Upton Sinclair's day secrecy is carefully guarded.

A report (9/1/11) by a public-interest group, Nebraska Appleseed, interviewed 455 workers in beef packing plants in Nebraska and found that 62% reported injuries in the past year, much higher than that reported by the US Bureau of Labor Statistics. The common complaint was line speed. Workers were required to process six cattle per minute, up to 400 per hour and thousands per shift. Poultry workers process 120 chickens per minute, an increase from 70 ten years ago. Workers were given no bathroom breaks and some reported urinating while standing in the assembly line. Conditions such as speed while using sharp instruments encourages accidents and musculoskeletal injuries from prolonged repetitive movements. Meatpackers report one and a half more repetitive movement injuries than workers in manufacturing.

Those permanently disabled are removed from payroll and replaced by younger, fresher hands.

"Exploitation occurs when the master considers his worker not as a partner nor even as an assistant, but as an instrument out of which he must extract as much service as possible at the smallest possible price. Yet the exploitation of a man by another man is slavery. The worker-machine is nothing more than part of capital like the slaves of the ancients. Service becomes servitude." Frederic Ozanam, Founder Society of St. Vincent de Paul.

According to the conservative/libertarian Cato Institute, in 2002 government officials handed out 50% more of taxpayers' money to the corporate welfare nanny state that to needy Americans. That doesn't include no-bid and cost-plus contracts, tax breaks, tax shelters, tax write-offs, tax loopholes, and tax credits. It doesn't include the $1.4 billion of overcharging and fraud discovered by the Pentagon's Defense Contract Audit Agency. That's the cost of doing business.

It does include the $15 billion in handouts to corporations on the dole in the oil, gas and coal industries. There's a difference between corporate welfare and poor families with hungry children. There is no means-testing of fat corporations. They don't have to skip work to appear repeatedly, shame-faced, hat in hand, to beg that their food stamps or their assistance checks be continued.

The heads of corporations are flown to Washington in private jets, taken by limousine to lunch with lawmakers, other business leaders and media celebrities. Sometimes an appropriate bishop or religious celebrity will join them. There may be time for a golf game followed by dinner. The day of business that began with warm greetings, and filled out with pleasantries, wishes and dreams, will conclude with goodbyes and the exchange of appropriate promises and envelopes.

When was the last time you saw labor leaders lunching with lawmakers, other labor leaders, media and religious celebrities? Your newspaper has a business section and a jobs section. Does it have a labor section of labor news and views? Radio and TV give business reports but labor reports, if any, mention the rate of joblessness, the outrageous money some worker is getting, or some Democrat speaking to a union. Labor is as marginalized in the media as it is in the government.

In 1956 workers in Poznan, Poland went on strike resulting in reforms of the Stalinist government. Hardline Stalinists were removed from government and Soviet officers in the Polish Army were sent home. In 1980 labor unrest led to the formation of an independent, anti-communist union, Solidarity. In 1981, martial law was declared, Solidarity was suspended and most of its leaders imprisoned. In 1982, the government banned Solidarity. In 1983 martial law was lifted but Solidarity existed only in secrecy. In 1988, there were nationwide strikes and in 1989, semi-free elections. Solidarity was elected to power in Parliament. The Communists' comrades-in-arms parties switched to Solidarity and by the end of the year Parliament amended the Constitution to restore democracy and civil liberties. An independent union gave citizens a voice in the government.

If there had been strong unions in America, they might have called for national strikes to prevent the illegitimate coup by five "justices" whose names will live in infamy, that put an undocumented "president" in the White House. If that had happened, it's unlikely that a legitimate president would have neglected to warn defense forces, the CIA, the FBI, the State Department, the Defense Department, the FAA, first responders, the airlines or the public of an impending attack. There would have been no need for two wars that were planned to be lost, no need for lies about yellowcake uranium and Weapons of Mass Destruction, no need for torture to force lies to justify those wars, no need for "bailout" tax cuts that transfered the wealth of the nation to the top 1%. We would still be a lawful nation.

There is a Department of Labor and the US Department of Labor reports that in the last 50 years: Years of presidency: Republicans 28 years, Democrats 22 years, Total Jobs created: Republicans 24 million, Democrats 42 million. Stock Market return: Republicans 109%, Democrats 992%. Stock Market return annualized Republican 2.7%, Dems 11%. Gross Domestic Product: Rep 2.7 %, Demos 4.1%. Income Growth Republicans 0.6%, Democrats 2.2%. Is that what the media reports?

What has trickled down from the federal government to your state is the practice of giving taxpayers' money to prosperous corporations. Every dollar that goes to a global corporation is a dollar that doesn't go to the local economy.

Caterpillar, a maker of heavy equipment used around the globe, shows healthy profits. The corporation has a new plant in North Carolina and North Carolina is picking up much of the cost: $1 million to train workers and a community college commitment to develop a curriculum for them worth $4.3 million. Good Jobs First, a nonprofit research organization reported (12/14/11) "States are spending billions of dollars per year on corporate tax credits, cash grants and other economic development subsidies that often require little if any job creation and lack wage and benefit standards covering workers at subsidized companies." Happily for North Carolina, the Tar Heel State is one of the best in applying job standards to their major subsidy programs. Texas received a C- although it leads the nation in the number of minimum wage workers.

States aren't the only ones that put corporations on the dole. Cities do also, often giving property tax abatements that hurt schools because property taxes are the base of school finances supplemented by state and federal funds. Cities aren't always careful in the drain on natural resources and damage to the environment. "If subsidies do not result in real public benefits, they are no better than corporate giveaways," said Good Jobs First Research Director Philip Mattera, principal author of the report.

Dollars that go to subsidize business undermine the American Dream of upward mobility for parents; but even more they wish it for their children. That dream has faded. "Americans enjoy less economic mobility than their peers in Canada and much of Western Europe," Jason DeParle reported. (*New York Times* 1/4/12) The depth of poverty in the US leaves poor children far behind. Children tend to follow their parent's "educational trajectory" and that increases the importance of family background. Children whose parents didn't finish high school find a steep ladder to climb to a university degree. A study led by a Swedish university found that 42% of American men raised in the bottom fifth of incomes stay there, compared to 25% in Denmark and 30% in Britain that admits to having class distinctions.

Only 8% of American men born at the bottom rose to the top 5th, compared to 12% of the British and 14% of the Danes. "About 62% of Americans raised in the top fifth stay in the top two-fifths," according to the Economic Mobility Project of the Pew Charitable Trusts, and 65% born in the bottom fifth stay in the bottom two-fifths. Reihan Salam, a writer for The Daily and National Review Online, discovered that a Danish family can move from the 10th percentile to the 90th percentile with $45,000 of additional earnings, while an American family would need an additional $93,000.

Nobel laureate economist Joseph Stiglitz wrote, "We've moved from a democracy, which is supposed to be based on one person, one vote, to something much more akin to one dollar, one vote. When you have that kind of democracy, it's not going to address the real needs of the 99%."

In the 19th Century, children had been workers. Slowly they became students training to run a democracy that showed little evidence of equality. Presently they are valued as insatiable mouths, gobbling cheap, over-priced, heavily advertised, quick-to-be worthless fads. They are also prized as commodities. The buying of children as students in privatized schools and inhabitants of privatized prisons approximates the auctions of the poorhouse.

Republican legislators in Texas intend to promote vouchers that can be used for private schools, including religious, for-profit, and on line schools. The state pays a fee for each student each day in school. The advantage of privatization is, in addition to private profit, less accountability and more rewards. If you steer money to a public school you might get a letter of appreciation, maybe even a certificate suitable for framing. If you steer money to a private school, the rewards are more fungible.

The big money is in housing prisoners. Some judges are already in jail for sending convicted children to privately run prisons instead of juvenile facilities. Any time the government and private enterprise engage in commodities, the commodities increase. "Locking up illegal immigrants has grown profoundly lucrative for the private prisons industry, a reliable pot of revenue that helped keep some of the biggest companies in business." (AP 8/2/12) Nearly half of the 400,000 immigrants held annually are housed in private facilities costing the federal government $2 billion a year. Yet the government says it isn't necessarily cheaper to privatize prisons.

The Associated Press tallied up more than 10 years of federal and state records, the scope of the private facilities, their cost and the money the companies spent on lobbying and campaign donations and found "a complex, mutually beneficial and evidently legal relationship between those who make corrections and immigration policy and a few prison companies." A private, profitable gulag, right under taxpayer's noses, largely controlled by three companies: Corrections Corporation of America, The GEO Group, and Management and Training Corp. The growth is not over despite the drop in illegal immigration. The three businesses have spent at least $45 million combined on campaign donations and lobbyists at the state and federal level in the last decade. "Immigrations and Customs Enforcement agents detain men, women and children suspected of violating civil immigration laws at these facilities."

"CCA was on the verge of bankruptcy in 2000 due to lawsuits, management problems and dwindling contracts. Last year, the company reaped $162 million in net income. Federal contracts made up 43% of its total revenues, in part thanks to rising immigrant detention. GEO, which cites the immigration agency as its largest client, saw its net income jump from $16.9 million to $78.6 million since 2000." The average nightly cost to taxpayers to detain an illegal immigrant is about $166, up from $80 in 2004.

"It's a millionaire's business," Pedro Guzman told AP. Guzman, who was married to a US citizen and was "living legally under temporary protected status" spent 19 months in private prisons until he was granted legal permanent residency. "One fundamental difference between private detention facilities and their publicly-run counterparts is transparency. The private ones don't have to follow the same public records and access requirements," AP said. Rep. Hal Rogers, Kentucky, who heads the powerful House Appropriations Committee received about $59,000 in campaign contributions since 2000. Rogers often criticizes ICE for not filling more detention beds.

"ICE has begun providing more oversight as part of the Obama administration's pledge to overhaul the nation's system for jailing immigration offenders. It recently scrapped plans for CCA to build a 1,500-bed immigrant detention center," Associated Press reported.

Personal Note: Jean and I have a relative who works in the National Security Agency.

William A. Clark, a Montana banking and copper magnate in the 19th and early 20th centuries, bought a seat in the US Senate by bribing lawmakers in the days when senators were still selected by state legislatures. After being exposed, he declared, "I never bought a man who wasn't for sale." Barons like Clark who bought political power created a reaction that led to a 1912 state law limiting the flow of campaign cash. Today, the average winning Montana state senate candidate spends about $17,000. "The state's top court upheld its law on the grounds that any reasonable reading of Montana's history would conclude that massive flows of money into politics are corrupting."

Unconcerned with corruption, or perhaps in bed with it, the US Supreme Court struck down Montana's law because it conflicted with the supremely corrupt ruling that global corporations, labor unions and wealthy individuals can buy as many politicians in the three political branches of the government as their money allows. The "justices" said they did not believe political expenditures would give rise to corruption, or even the appearance of it in their eyes. (*USA Today* 6/26/12) How much money does it take to blind a justice?

"You are either in favor of evil or you are in favor of good. You are either on the side of the oppressed or on the side of the oppressor. You can't be neutral." Bishop Desmond Tutu

Be afraid, little children. Be very afraid. One political branch of the government has you in its gun sights.

Jan. 24, 2007, Harry Holzer, Professor of Public Policy at Georgetown University and Nonresident Senior Fellow with the Brookings Metropolitan Policy Program, testified to the House Ways and Means Committee about the economic costs of poverty. "Most arguments for reducing poverty in the US, especially among children, rest on a moral case for doing so—one that emphasizes the unfairness of child poverty, and how it runs counter to our national creed of equal opportunity for all...Our results suggest that the costs to the US associated with childhood poverty total about $500B per year, or the equivalent of nearly 4% of GDP" (compared to 1.3% of GDP from US corporate taxes).

...If anything, these estimates almost certainly understate the true costs of poverty to the US economy. For one thing, they omit the costs associated with poor adults who did not grow up poor as children...our conclusions point unmistakably to several clear options..."

Among the options were "Higher minimum wages and more collective bargaining." This was the opposite direction from which the nation has been moving since 1981.

"In the councils of government, we must guard against the acquisition of unwarranted influence, whether sought or unsought, by the military-industrial complex. The potential for the disastrous rise of misplaced power exists and will persist. We must never let the weight of this combination endanger our liberties or democratic processes. We should take nothing for granted." Dwight D. Eisenhower

The Battle for Education

To save children it was necessary to get them out of fields, factories, mines and place them in schools. Education was the province of the colonies and then the states. Education has been uneven, unequal and often at odds every since.

From the beginning, the Union needed unity, a commonality. Some came to America for religious freedom and tried to deny it to others. Some came for economic opportunity but tried to deny it to others in order to increase their own. Some had come as convicts, slaves, indentured servants, refugees. Early Americans seemed to unite only when they had a common enemy.

Not all colonials fought for independence. Some fought for freedom from the king; others fled to Canada. Much of New England wanted no part in the War of 1812, and threatened to secede if the United States invaded Canada.

Americans didn't have the same language and diversity grew with immigration. They were almost entirely Christians but of different varieties, often competitive, some times hostile to each other.

They had a common book in the Bible and literature, commerce and politics used the Bible for metaphors and picturesque language. Metaphors and language also came from work and merchants, seamen, cowboys and farmers had their own vocabularies making the American language colorful but also making it difficult to understand each other.

The only commonality was the Constitution of We the people and the pledge to promote the general welfare. America needed a common history, something we have not yet been able to achieve. The history and culture of the Indians was destroyed. The blacks were never permitted a history or culture apart from that of the dominant race. Immigrants, if they have not suppressed it, have a family history of their arrival and survival in America.

The first immigrants to New England were middle-class farmers, tradesmen and artisans who believed in free, popular education. Boys had to read in order to read the Bible, write in order to communicate and cipher in order to do business.

1642, the Massachusetts Bay Colony required parents to teach their children the three Rs, and in 1647, required settlements of 50 or more families to hire a schoolmaster. Needing educated clergymen for their churches they established the first college in what was to become the USA.

In the Virginia Colony there was limited education. Wealthy planters depended on imported school masters, and there were "field schools" to teach children "within riding or rowing distance the three Rs." (*History of the American People,* Samuel Eliot Morrison)

There was also the second oldest college in America, William and Mary, second only to Harvard with plans dating back to 1618. It would have been the first college but building was delayed by an Indian uprising that killed 347 colonists. A 17-year old George Washington received his surveyor's license from the school and returned as the first American chancellor. Thomas Jefferson, John Tyler and James Monroe received undergraduate degrees from William and Mary. The Christopher Wren Building is the oldest college building in the US.

In 1778, a school master at Hartford, Noah Webster, best known for his dictionary, wrote, "America must be as independent in literature as she is in politics, as famous for arts as for arms." The first efforts were mostly school books, including Webster's own bluebacked speller. School children needed new arithmetic books since coinage had changed from pounds to dollars, new geography books to keep up with the changing colony/nation, literature and art to inspire patriotism because those who knew America best would love it most.

The "foreign" vote has been important since 1820 but New York City public schools were unable to keep up with immigration until after the Civil War. Upstate New York was well furnished with Protestant academies and colleges.

1821, Boston opened a free high school and in 1828 a free girls school. Ohio had free public schools by 1830 and in 1836 sent a seminary professor to Europe to study their education systems. He returned with plans for dividing education into elementary, grammar and high school.

In 1831, after talking to Charles Carrolton, the last survivor of the signers of the Declaration of Independence, Alexis de Tocqueville observed, "This race of men is disappearing after providing America with her greatest men. The people become educated, knowledge extends, a middling ability becomes common. Outstanding talents and great characters are more rare. Society is less brilliant and more prosperous."

In Pennsylvania Germans did not want free schools for fear of loss of their language and culture. The free public school law in 1834 was optional but they still opposed it. Free public eduction was often sold as insurance against radicalism and by 1837, about 42% of the children were enrolled.

Most of the early colleges were formed by religious groups. Michigan established a state university in 1837, Missouri in 1839, Wisconsin in 1849. Cities offered vocational courses and night schools. Free public libraries, supported by taxes were established, the first in Peterborough, New Hampshire in 1833. Improvements in printing made possible the penny newspapers in the 1840s.

1837, Horace Mann became chairman of the Massachusetts board of Education and brought a version of German education into the public school system. 1839, the first American teacher's college was formed. In 1852, Massachusetts passed a truancy law with punishment.

Indiana adopted a free public school system in 1848 but it was several years before attendance was enforced. In the 1850s, a court ruled that local authorities did not have the right to raise taxes for the maintenance of the schools. That closed most of the high schools.

In 1855, Massachusetts enforced integration of all its schools. In northern New England where there were few blacks, they were admitted to the schools without hesitation. In urban centers, reformers and blacks favored separate schools to give the children "more congenial companionship." Segregation was not required in New York until 1900.

Whereas in New England free popular education was desirable for citizens of a democracy, in the South, compulsory education scarcely got going before the Civil War. At the time of the war, illiteracy of native-born Southerners was about 20%. "The University of Virginia, that Jefferson saw as the crown of a free public school system became the seminary of the privileged class." (*History of the American People*) Literature of the South had to glorify the Southern Way of Life and defend slavery. An abolitionist was little better than an escaped slave and scarcely safer. There was little free speech. Even churches supported slavery.

Despite slavery and limited education, natural science was not feared in the South as much as it is today but was privately pursued for personal satisfaction. Andrew Jackson was role model of southern upward mobility. Born of immigrant parents he became a successful lawyer, a wealthy owner of land and slaves, a famous warrior and president of his country. He was also role model for distrust of "intellectuals." Southerners sometimes favored free education for white children but in general distrusted intellectuals. The uneducated and willfully ignorant were suspicious of highly educated outsiders and "foreign" thought.

Fear and suspicion of intellectuals is as alive today as it has ever been and has become pervasive through "Religious" Right media and their right wing allies. A Harvard education is highly suspicious, a trained scientist is untrusted unless he is in the pay of a major chemical or oil corporation, an experienced traveler is shunned unless he/she is career military.

Southern politicians were ill-educated, middle class or poor, feared blacks although they owned none, and held "foreign" ideas in contempt. Confident of their righteousness and their homegrown ability they intended to denigrate the inferior blacks and marginalize them forever.

In Spanish Texas there were mission schools for the Indians but the indifference or hostility of the Indians and the difficulty of getting supplies accomplished little. A non-mission school operated in San Fernando de Béxar (San Antonio) as early as the 1740s, but it failed. In 1802, legislative proclamations compelled parents to send their children to school. Settlements and military posts with sizable populations were to provide salaries for teachers, That effort also failed. Sometime after 1812 a public school was established at San Antonio to be supported by public funds, but it didn't last.

The Constitution of 1824, ratified by the new Republic of Mexico, delegated control of education to the states and the state of Coahuila and Texas provided for the establishment of elementary schools in principal towns in the state but no money. In 1830 six primary schools were projected; at least one of them opened in Nacogdoches, but, overall, education in Mexican Texas never materialized. Incidentally, the flag of the Constitution of 1824, that had been rejected by the dictator Santa Ana, flew over the Alamo.

In 1836, the Texas Declaration of Independence cited the failure of Mexico to provide education as a justification for rebellion. However, after independence, the Republic of Texas did no better. In 1838, President Mirabeau Lamar of the Republic of Texas advocated setting aside public land, of which Texas had plenty, to support public schools. In 1839, Texas set aside three leagues of land for each Texas county. Wealthy Texans sent their children to the US for education, and there were private and "field schools" but the Republic did not establish a public school system.

> *Personal Note:* My alma mater, Baylor, claims to be the oldest college in Texas in continual existence, having been chartered by the Republic of Texas.

After being granted statehood by the US, the 1845 Texas State Convention advocated public education and designated at least 10% of tax revenue for the schools. In 1854, the governor signed the bill setting up the Texas public school system. In 1858, the citizens of New Braunfels voted for a tax to support a "free" school.

After the Civil War, the Freedmen's Bureau founded the first black schools in the South and supported four black colleges: Howard, Hampton, Atlanta and Fisk. The Bureau brought in teachers from the American Missionary Association to teach in black schools but unreconstructed rebels burned some of the schools and chased off white teachers from the North. Education spoiled blacks.

George Peabody, a Massachusetts born financier, set up a trust fund of $3.5 million to promote primary education in the South with no racial strings. In 1886, Gen. Samuel Armstrong, colonel of a black regiment in the war, raised funds to found the Hampton Normal and Industrial Institute in Hampton, Virginia, to provide blacks with both mental and manual training. Booker T. Washington was an early graduate.

Gen. Clinton Fisk founded Fisk University, a black college, in Nashville in 1865. The Freedman's Bureau supported the school. William Marsh Rice, of Houston, a Texas Unionist was so badly treated during the war that he left Texas never to return but founded Rice Institute in his hometown. Henry Ward Beecher, famous preacher and brother of the author of *Uncle Tom's Cabin,* and Bishop Potter raised funding for Washington college in Lexington, Virginia, of which Robert E. Lee was president.

The present Texas Constitution, 1876, allotted 52 million acres for school purposes. An ad valorem tax was later added along with free textbooks. Later laws granted cities and towns more freedom regarding the operation of the schools and today there are more than 1,000 independent school districts in Texas.

Getting children out of sweatshops was not the same as getting them educated. America was largely rural, public schools were mostly one or two rooms and the teachers were women, dooming education from the beginning as "woman's work" and therefore on the lower rung of states' concern. The curriculum varied. In rural areas boys studied agriculture and girls learned "homemaking." Math was essential in both subjects but in cities rapid counting of change was more important than keeping records of when crops were planted and when cows became "fresh." The founders' idea of education to train citizens to live in, work in, and maintain a democracy was not on the horizon. There were times when we have almost reached that goal but each time there has been repression.

In 1911, a rural high school law permitted creation of rural high schools in Texas. State support for teacher salaries improved education of farm and ranch children. (*Handbook of Texas*)

Personal Note: As the product of a Texas rural school, let me describe it to you. The best equipped schools were in cities, towns, villages, in a descending order. In rural areas there were one-room and two-room schools and children walked to school from farms or ranches, some of them across fields. No one rode a horse or a bicycle to the school I attended when I was there, although on a really bad day a parent might drive a child to school. The worst walking-to-school weather I remember were sandstorms from the north and the school was north of our house. The wind almost blew children down and the sand stung your eyes, clotted in your nostrils and burned exposed skin.

I was too young to be in school for the blizzard that struck one day in April. All the roads in several counties were closed by snow, a train was stalled between Paducah and Quanah, and school children in Quanah, unable to get home, spent the night in the courthouse.

Dad drove to school to get my brother and sister. At the school he found his best friend whose car was stuck in the snow. His friend had walked to the school for refuge but suffered a frostbitten nose. Somehow arrangements were made that the children and teachers, and Dad's friend, would spend the night at our house. I don't know how they all got to our house but Mother took them in. There were no telephones in the country and parents had to trust that the teachers and neighbors would protect their children. I believe I could do the same today.

In the 30s, my older brother, sister and I attended a two-room school with two teachers, the lower four grades in one room and the upper four grades in the other. Each room had a gas light, three windows on the south side that I remember as being large, and a gas heater. It was what history books call "a field school." The school was surrounded by fields. The nearest building, other than the two-hole and three-hole outhouses, was my uncle's house a half-mile away. My cousins walked to school down the railroad track. Our house was a mile away and we had a dirt county road to walk on. The two-hole outhouse was for boys and the three-holer was for girls.

The school was called Midway because it was midway between the Chillicothe and Tolbert schools. Chillicothe was a village and Tolbert was a community with an all-purpose store and gas station, two churches, a cemetery and a school. Midway had two dedicated teachers and a close-knit community around the PTA. PTA was the first word I learned to spell, a family joke. Before I started school I learned to spell p.i.g and when I demonstrated my spelling talent, Dad asked if I could spell PTA. I couldn't. But I learned. Everyone went to PTA; it was our community. At the next PTA meeting, I demonstrated my skill at spelling by challenging the students to spell PTA. They already knew.

The day before school began the PTA gathered at the school. The women cleaned the inside of the school and the girls' outhouse. The men cleared the school yard of weeds, painted and repaired the buildings, swings and seesaw, the only playground equipment we had.

Other PTA meetings included watermelon feasts, ice cream suppers, Easter egg hunts, Thanksgiving and Christmas performances, student declamation, skits, poetry recitation and rhythm band performances. Our instruments were limited to a triangle, a small drum, a set of cymbals and sticks but we sometimes beat out a recognizable rhythm.

I wanted to ring the triangle but I never graduated from sticks.

Each year we had to memorize an assigned number of lines of poetry and recite them to the class. If we were good we had to recite the poem at PTA. Teachers don't have time for that any more but memorization was good practice. I still recite some lines from those poems but no longer the entire poem. It also gave us an idea of the scope, breadth and rhythm and rime of poetry. "Captain, O Captain." "Sunset and evening star and one clear bell for me/ and let there be no moaning at the bar when I put out to sea." "Once upon a midnight dreary while I pondered weak and weary."

I won a third place white ribbon in first grade declamation in a county-wide contest, in front of the largest crowd in the biggest auditorium I had ever seen. My parents were certain that destiny called. My brother had won a "best baby" contest but that was before I was born so that didn't count.

In second grade I believed I would do better but there was one word in the declamation that I had a hard time remembering. "Brayed." A donkey "brayed." Sure enough, when it was my time to declaim I couldn't remember "brayed." I paused hoping for the word to appear before me or my mother to whisper it without anyone else hearing. In desperation, I inserted a word that I knew was wrong but it would allow me to finish my declamation and get off the stage. The donkey mooed. I won some laughs but no ribbon.

I know now that one of the purposes of PTA was to educate parents about social skills such as hygiene and etiquette, bits of local and Texas history, and simple math problems, science questions and locating nations on a geography chart. "If you have a glass full of water and you put ice in it, what happens and why?" I remember Mrs. Wilson asking. I had no idea. Students were supposed to solve the problems and answer the questions, but parents learned.

Most of the children were from share-cropper families. Some lived in houses with dirt floors. I never visited any that had running water. The children had to fetch water from a cistern or well or adults hauled water from a creek or river. Because we were subject to water-borne diseases we had to take a typhoid shot the first day of school each year.

My family had running water but only in the kitchen. I remember Dad taking water samples from our well to the Farm Bureau in Vernon. They sent it to Texas A&M for analysis. Our water was always good. Like the share-cropper kids, we bathed in a big metal wash tub, and usually with homemade lye soap. Daily bathing was out of the question.

There was no janitor so the teachers arrived early or stayed late to clean the school. We waited outside regardless of the weather until the Superintendent, who taught the upper four grades, came outside and rang her bell. We formed two lines, one for the upper four, one for the lower four, and marched inside, hanging our coats on nails and placing our lunches on shelves in the cloak room.

For my first day of school, Mother and Dad bought me a metal lunch box that had a container in the lid for soup or a drink. In the bottom was the usual sandwich and piece of fruit if it was in season. Most of the lunches were in sacks that became increasingly greasy over the school year or in metal syrup buckets that had holes punched in the lid so that you "didn't sweat your biscuits." Of course, I wanted one of those.

While still in line our teacher inspected us for scrofula, spotted fever, mumps, measles and chicken pox. She checked our faces, ears, hands and fingernails to see if we had washed before school, our teeth to be certain we had brushed and had no swollen or bleeding gums or rotted teeth. She checked our hair for cleanliness, combing and head lice. Farm children get head lice from cattle and it can spread quickly. If we passed inspection a gold star was placed next to our name on a chart on the wall. We were proud of those gold stars.

Most of the children wore clean, neat, patched, and often, hand-me-down shoes and clothing. Some children came to school barefooted. Many of the girls wore dresses made of flour sacks. I didn't like the worn and patched two-strap overalls that most of the boys wore, preferring to be belted around the waist. I don't remember us wearing patched clothes but we wore the same outer garments all week, at least my brother and I did.

Some children came to school without breakfast, some without lunch. They begged for overripe or mashed bananas, scraps or anything we found unappetizing. Some stole lunch sacks and were switched on the back of their legs with a thin branch they had to retrieve from a tree near the school grounds. It was a sacrifice they made willingly because they were hungry.

Some years later after we were bused to Chillicothe, a road grader accidentally cut the gas line to our house. Mother tried to fry us eggs holding a skillet over candles. It was a slow process and we were going to miss the bus but luckily a friend of Dad's came by. He was going to town and he would take us.

I learned four lessons from that accident. Don't send hungry children to school. It is my observation that young people and adults who skip breakfast rarely come from poor families.

Be on time. One of us watched for the school bus that passed on a county road over a mile away. When we saw it we grabbed our coats, books and walked or ran down our quarter-mile dirt road to the county road, depending on the speed required to catch the bus. Some days it was too cold to stand in the wind waiting for the bus, but it was a disgrace to make the other kids wait because you were late.

That lesson was reinforced by the Marines. One time, and one time only, I was late for formation. I was in the ranks when my name was called but not when roll call began. As a consequence, for a week my platoon had an early reveille and 30 minutes of rifle drill before the others had to show up. No one said much because they didn't have to. I knew they were punished for my lack of enthusiasm. I am usually early to events.

Be grateful for what you get, especially when someone does the best they can. The bread wasn't toasted and the eggs were a bit runny but no one complained.

School is important. My paternal grandfather was murdered when my father was eight-years-old, leaving Dad, his two older brothers and their mother to hang on to Grandfather's farm. The only school was three miles away and uphill. When the weather was good they worked on the farm. When it was bad they went to school. Some days they hopped a freight train pulling the hill into Chillicothe. Uncle Frank, the older of Dad's brothers, went back to school and finished high school when he was grown. We concluded that Dad had about a six-grade education but he was a reader. We subscribed to the Chillicothe Valley News, a weekly, the Vernon Daily Record, and the Sunday Fort Worth Star-Telegram and Denver Post.

Mother had two years of high school and had a few times been asked to substitute when a teacher was ill. She was also a reader and every two weeks we went to the Carnegie Library in Vernon and each checked out two books. One of the books had to be something that someone else in the family wanted to read. It gave us a broad education. It was understood that we would go to college. I don't know when that understanding happened but I always knew I would go to college. We all did. My brother and I did postgraduate work.

When students passed into the upper four room the teacher, Mrs. D.T. Wilson took us to her home in Chillicothe. She had a bathtub. She had an indoor toilet. She had reproductions of paintings on the walls. She demonstrated the proper way to set a table with knives, forks and spoons, cups in saucers, cloth napkins. She allowed us to turn on and turn off her radio. That was before REA came to the farms. It was all a little frightening and most frightening of all to me—she allowed us to make a telephone call. Required it, actually. Since most of us didn't know anyone to call we just talked to the operator. She was nice but to me it was most unpleasant and I've since never liked talking on a telephone.

Later Mrs. Wilson took the girls to her home for a longer demonstration of hygiene and what would now be called sex education. Many of them would not finish grade school or would end their education with graduation from grade school. She did not want them to go ignorant into a world more complex and confusing than any of us could imagine.

We had small classes; my cousin Ann and I were two-thirds of the first grade. We had a blackboard in each room. We had textbooks furnished by the state. We studied Texas history, and unlike some Texas schools, we were taught that there were native-born Texians, Latinos, who fought alongside white immigrants at the Alamo and San Jacinto. We heard the upper three grades recite. Much of what I learned in school came from listening to the other grades recite. I think that's a fair evaluation of most rural schools.

We learned a bit of Spanish. I don't know why but we spoke a bit of Spanish, that none of us had ever heard before, and learned a Mexican song and a Mexican dance. We also had a pinata filled with candy. I don't remember the occasion but someone broke it and we grabbed the pieces of candy that fell to the ground. Our teacher gathered them and divided them among us. We were in north West Texas, 500 miles from Mexico. Most of us had never seen a Latino. We had seen Indians. They were a few miles away in Oklahoma.

Each room had a flip chart although the only thing I remember was a colored drawing of a human being with the skin pulled away revealing the innards. I hated seeing it, especially during lunch which we ate at our desks. One of the hungry boys sometimes kissed the exposed organs to prompt those like me with queasy-stomachs to give up our meal.

We had field trips to the county library and the county jail. Parents drove the whole school, 30 plus pupils, to Vernon so that we could catch the train to Chillicothe sixteen miles away. It was the first train ride for most and the last train ride for some. For most of us Vernon, population about 10,000, was the biggest city we had ever seen, and the courthouse was the largest building. When we visited our grandparents in Graham, my uncle who worked at the Possum Kingdom Dam gave us a tour of the dam. When I returned to school I tried to describe the dam to a friend, telling him that it was taller than two of our school buildings stacked one on the other. He refused to believe it.

We had a field trip to the black funeral home in Vernon. I've never been sure of the purpose for that trip. At the time I thought it was to show us an educated, well dressed and well mannered, middle class black family. Most of us knew blacks only as field laborers. A black family lived on our farm so I had a better informed and more tolerant view toward blacks.

We had visiting lecturers. The one I remember best was a former convict who wore his striped suit, showed the thick wooden paddle with holes bored into it that was used to punish prisoners, and a model of "Ole Sparky," the electric chair, with a colorful description of how it worked. I don't know of any of us who went to the penitentiary. It was big enough for us to sit in although none of us volunteered. We had an outdoor basketball court drawn in the dirt with a stick, and, I presume, a regulation basket at each end of the court. None of us became college or professional basketball players either.

What we lacked was a library. Other than textbooks there were no books or magazines in the school. There were a few copies of paintings that we had to memorize that I didn't like even then. The first actual painting by an artist whose name I recognized was at the McNay Institute in San Antonio when I was a postgraduate student. I stood in front of an El Greco. It was real. I could see the actual paint that the artist had mixed, the brush strokes that he had made. That was as awesome as the first time I saw the ocean or a real elephant or sputnik. Those born after TV became ubiquitous may have a hard time understanding how powerful it is being in the presence of something you know only through pictures. Grand Canyon, Niagra Falls, Victoria Falls, the Great Wall, Manchu Pichu, Angkor Wat, rain in the Sahara, sunrise on the Gobi Desert, painted dogs in Botswana and leopards in the Serengeti.

Once Jean asked me to stop at a cotton field beside the highway. She got out of the car and pulled up a cotton plant that had open bolls. She put it on display in the library of the middle school where she was librarian. The children asked what it was. They had never seen cotton before it was thread. In New York City, you cannot see stars at night.

I have walked on the seven continents but nothing on earth has ever been as awesome as Carlsbad Caverns when I was 6-years old. The bottomless pit was a bottomless wonder that stretched my mind, and the total darkness with only the sound of dripping water was impossible to imagine or reproduce,

Midway had no scientific or technical equipment, not even a telephone or a typewriter. But Midway opened for us a world of wonder. Despite its shortcomings I believe it was a good school. All the schools I attended were good schools. I could have gotten better training at other schools, but perhaps it would have different training rather than better.

That was for white children. There was no rural school for the black children who lived on our and other farms. They had to walk four miles from their house to a school in Chillicothe unless they cut across fields and that was not always advisable. The black school in Chillicothe had only six grades. For more education they would have to walk twelve miles to a high school in Vernon. My mother taught reading to the black children on our farm while their mother ironed our clothes. Busing or hitchhiking was not available to black people unless they were picked up by some white person who knew them.

Mrs. Wilson was killed in a car wreck, the rural school was closed, and for 7th grade I was bused to Chillicothe, the nearest school but in another county. The school seemed huge to me. There must have been 20 students in the 7th grade, all of them in the same room. There was a school cafeteria that served unappetizing but healthy food. Each pupil received a glass of grapefruit juice each school day courtesy of the federal government. I don't remember a library or scientific equipment.

For the 8th grade we were sent to the high school to reduce overcrowding. The high school had a science lab in the basement and all I knew about it was that it often emitted noxious fumes. I never stepped inside it but I assume they had a microscope. There was a library at the end of study hall with a dictionary and a few donated books. Mostly there were copies of National Geographic that I viewed with interest, amazed at the variety of cultures and exciting places I barely dreamed of visiting. I don't remember ever checking out a book from the library or reading one in study hall. I attempted to play football and basketball and there was a gym but only one coach/teacher so we were limited in sports and sports equipment. There was no band but there were girl cheerleaders and a pep squad of girls.

Because of my father's health we moved to Vernon and I spent my senior year in Vernon High School. There were more students in my senior class than the whole high school in Chillicothe. They also had better equipment in everything from sports to science to arts. They had a band. It was a band I had heard once when they visited Chillicothe High for a performance. They also had good, dedicated teachers and one semester a creative writing class that I attended.

For some reason I was invited to speak to an assembly at the black high school, perhaps because I was reared on a farm and knew black people in a way that was not possible for white people who lived in town. Not knowing what I was supposed to say I attempted an inspiring and religious message, probably the same thing they had heard in church. I didn't feel they were properly appreciative but what I noticed most is that they used the textbooks that we at the white school had discarded. The same seemed to be true of the desks and other equipment. I didn't feel good about my visit to their school and I met no black students.

Black schools received a third of the funding of white schools and black teachers were paid much less than white teachers. Nevertheless, after the 1954 desegregation decision, San Antonio was one of the first school districts to comply and Texas was one of the leaders in desegregation. In 1964, Texas accounted for about 60% of the desegregated schools in the South. In 1989 63% of black students attended predominately black schools. That is exactly the national average. (*Handbook of Texas*)

The fight over who was to be educated goes back to the beginning. Education was not seen as a universal good. Many of those with the wealth to give their own children a good education were unconcerned about others. Some saw no reason for women and girls to be educated. As with slaves, educating women would lead to discontentment and rebellion. The less they knew the more dependent they were.

Women had to fight for the right to read, write and do sums. They had to fight for a right to high school and college education, sometimes without the support of their families. They had to fight to get into professional schools and then had to fight to perform their profession. Nevertheless, the hardest battle was the right of blacks to an education. In the South, some states had made it illegal to educate a slave. Some owners needed an educated slave and secretly trained him. Some owners were Christian enough to allow slaves to be educated if they desired.

The core of Southern identity was not Christian or American or even Southern, but "not-black." Whatever fate held for them, they would never be black. It was a gift from God.

White men might seed black children but they themselves would never be be black. That was why Southern women had to be protected from black people, especially males, even male children like 14-year old Emmett Till who was tortured to death for not giving deference to a white woman. Imagining a black hand on white skin was more than they could bear. A white woman who gave birth to the child of a black man blackened herself. That was the justification Southern lawmakers made in defeating a lynch law. What about rape?

The most contentious battle over education was in 1954 when the Supreme Court outlawed "separate but equal." San Antonio was one of the first districts to comply. School districts across Texas began the process of integration, though some segregation continued well into the next decade. In 1970, the 1954 decision was extended to Mexican Americans, for whom segregation had not been universal. Changing school-district boundaries, reassessment of extracurricular activities, and increased busing of students to other schools were some of the measures taken to enforce integration.

Unlike Texas, few states acted to enforce the law. Most did nothing or actively rebelled against the law requiring the federal government to again enforce the law with state militia (National Guard) or the US Army. The fight wasn't restricted to the South but it was most violent, most brutal in the South.

When the Supreme Court announced their decision, many evangelical churches supported it. In 1954, before becoming fundamentalist, the Southern Baptist Convention declared the Supreme Court's decision was "in harmony with the constitutional guarantee of equal freedom to all citizens, and with the Christian principles of equal justice and love for all men." However, when church members declared resistance, supported the Ku Klux Klan and enlisted in White Citizens' Councils, the churches maintained a dignified silence or pledged allegiance to the God-ordained "social order," code for The Southern Way of Life. It's funny how white can turn to black and absolutes like "the Christian principles of equal justice and love for all men" fade in the face of opposition.

The Southern Way was Bible-backed just as slavery had been. It was a religious belief that churches and schools forced on all citizens across the South. Some individual Southern Baptist Churches did take a stand. Most of them suffered the consequences. My Baptist hero, Will D. Campbell, took a stand and was fired as chaplain at the University of Mississippi. Nevertheless, he joined other white preachers and pastors to march alongside black preachers and pastors, and to protect black school children who were entering white schools and black women who were released from jails late at night after taxis had stopped service.

Most churches in the South did nothing, inspiring church members to do the same. Many churches began church schools to protect their children from the heresy of equal justice and love, and the degradation of a black presence. Perhaps the Mississippi Supreme Court expressed it best. "Large numbers of people, in this broad land, are steeped in their customs, practices, mores and traditions. In many instances, their beliefs go as deep or deeper than religion itself." It was their religion itself.

McCarthyism was well and alive and anyone opposing the racial tranquility of segregation and its code of etiquette was a pinko, a fellow traveler or a confessed Communist and could expect threats, harassment, arson, beating or death. Many states required oaths of loyalty by its employees including teachers and professors, and many citizens lived in fear, not of government control, but of lack of control by the federal government.

The nation has always needed a common history but has never had one.

In the North, public school students read the story of Southern Rebellion in their textbooks, in the South they learned the War of Northern Aggression, in Texas we studied the War Between the States. "Civil War" was not a common expression in my experience until after the unity caused by World War II. In 1935, W.E.B. DuBois pointed out that one of the lessons in public school textbooks about Reconstruction was that "all Negroes were lazy, dishonest and extravagant." (*Black Reconstruction in America 1860-1880*)

Personal Note: When I first learned of the War Between the States, I came home and told my parents that I would have fought for the freedom of the slaves. I could tell my parents were not entirely in agreement with my opinion and mumbled something about "not that simple." My paternal grandmother, who died at the age of 90 the year I was born, had a brother who died in a Union uniform. My father, who had never demonstrated a Yankee sentiment, had an uncle who was a Yankee soldier. My mother's grandfather was a Confederate veteran. I remember seeing him dead but not alive. His body, in a coffin, was in the house waiting for burial and I stood on tiptoe to look inside the open box. Mostly, I remember the black suit and my brother telling me that my great grandfather's leg had come off. I had failed to see it. I thought he meant the leg had come off in the coffin and I wasn't tall enough to see it.

Why did my parents have Confederate sympathies, especially my father whose mother was born in Vermont and whose father was part of an Irish immigrant family that had settled in Connecticut? I confess that when I see a film in which the Civil War is a part, emotionally I hope this time the South will win. Part of that is an inclination to root for the underdog. I also root for the defenders of the Alamo. Part of it is the romance of The Lost Cause. The rest of it is being baptized in the Southern Way of Life.

I consider myself Southwestern, with an accent on western. I have known from the beginning that slavery was evil. Nevertheless, I breathed the Southern air of defeat and resentment, and a nostalgia for a Southern Eden that never existed. I breathed it in church, in school, and in the newspapers and books I read. Southerners had fought and died for a Glorious Cause. Slavery, and its ugliness that brutalized white and back equally, were covered with liveried servants carrying silver tableware while happy darkies sang in the background. Southerners who owned no slaves fought and died for white supremacy, regardless of accomplishment, as the heart of the South. In defeat it also became the soul of the South.

If, after the Civil War, the South had admitted their defeat and heresy, and confessed their sin of bigotry and oppression, there might have been redemption. If they had made a conciliatory gesture instead of denying blacks their right to equality, to freedom, denying and delaying representation in government, in the press, in business, in sports, in education, it might have been possible to write a common history.

Instead, the South let their defeat, their guilt and shame fester until it rots the nation with race hatred, gender hatred, sectionalism, intolerance and spite. The South has risen again. Only this time the Republicans are on the wrong side.

Martin Luther King and LBJ saved America from a revolution. We should also thank Malcolm X, Emmett Till, Rosa Parks, and hundreds of unknown black women, men, and children who endured hatred and shed blood for America. Soldiers in Vietnam were learning guerrilla warfare and blacks were bringing it home. Instead, they came home to see a little light at the end of a long, dark tunnel and once they had seen the light there was no way to deny them dawn.

When white adults yelled insults, curses and spat at black children who had been blocked from a school building by National Guards's bayonets, Thurgood Marshall spoke to the Supreme Court. "Education is not the teaching of the three Rs," he said. "Education is the teaching of the overall citizenship, to learn to live together with fellow citizens, and above all to learn to obey the law...I do not know of any more horrible destruction of the principle of citizenship than to tell young children (in Little Rock) that those of you who withdrew, rather than to go to school with Negroes ...'Come back, all is forgiven, you win.' Therefore, I am not worried about Negro children in these states...I worry about the white children in Little Rock who are told, as young people, that the way to get your rights is to violate the law and defy the lawful authorities. I am worried about their future. I don't worry about the Negro kids' future. They have been struggling with democracy long enough. They know about it."

Mr. Marshall was right to be worried about white children who saw their political and religious leaders defying the law. He was also right about the higher purpose of education. That was something that many in the South, but also in other parts of the country, could not accept. We have seen the fruit, the ghettoization of America. Enclaves of rich whites crouch behind gated and restricted housing areas and contribute money to those who justify their way of life. Poor whites drive pickups with gunracks and the Confederate battle flag on their rear window. They yell insults at women and anyone who is not white enough to please them. They collect weapons and explosives. When they are mad enough or drunk enough they shoot strangers and drag black men to death.

Parents who did not believe in living together with fellow citizens and could afford to shield their children from foreign ideas, sent them to private schools to avoid the black hand, the "amalgamation of the races." Churches opened schools to give refuge to those whose image of physical whiteness and mental purity was threatened.

Then another bomb fell. Segregated schools were not tax-exempt. Churches that had once hated sin now hated taxes that punished them for sin.

Unable to express their spite and venom against blacks they attacked the schools that most black children attended, the public schools. Ten years after Brown, (1964) 98% of blacks in the South attended totally segregated schools. In 1954 there were 16 white, non-sectarian private schools in Louisiana; in 1964 there were 69 white non-sectarian private schools.

A new sin, taxes, joined the old hated sins—blacks, women, gays. It wasn't enough that the hate-filled "Religious" Right control information and thought in their private and home schools. They fought paying taxes to public schools that did provide information and challenged thought. They supported politicians who promised not to raise their taxes, who supported prayer in public schools, the teaching of an authorized history of American exceptionalism, and science without evolution or sex education.

Personal Note: One year in Chillicothe the Bible was taught as an elective and I signed up for it. The first semester was taught by my Baptist pastor and I loved it. The second semester was taught by the Church of Christ pastor and I didn't like it. I didn't complain, but someone must have. It was never offered again.

I never had a sex education class. I learned about reproduction in college Biology class but human reproduction was inferred from mammal reproduction. A few years ago I was at Baylor to speak to a group. A friend of mine was speaking at Truett Seminary at the edge of the campus. While waiting for him to speak I picked up a seminary newsletter to read. In it, a seminary student wrote a plaintive letter explaining that although he and his wife were college graduates they knew nothing about sex and it was threatening their marriage.

Inspired and exasperated by that letter I wrote a satire, "For the Love of Agape and Eros," about a religious sex shop that provided specialty sex toys for different religions. It's a serious subject. I understand why it's difficult for parents to talk to their children about sex. Why public schools and churches and other religious organizations leave sex education to male magazines and XXX-rated films I don't understand.

Clinton's Surgeon General, Joycelyn Elder, was forced to resign after she publicly promoted sex education in public schools, including masturbation. Evidentially that is something about which misinformation and no information is better than being informed.

The Civil Rights Act prohibited discrimination on the basis of sex as well as race in hiring, promoting, and firing. Johnson ordered all executive agencies to require federal contractors to "take affirmative action to ensure that applicants are employed and that employees are treated during employment without regard to race, color, religion, sex, or national origin." That was the first use of the phrase "affirmative action" and words that should have been applauded became code for "discrimination against white men."

Personal Note: I benefitted from affirmative action in every job I had except the Marine Corps. So did every white man of my and earlier generations. Now, the government was telling us that we would no longer be given preference. I once worked in a venetian blind company where I was paid more than the two black women who trained me. That no black person could apply for the jobs I had as a college professor didn't bother me, baptized in the Southern Way of Life. Receiving higher wages than the black women who trained me did. I saw them every work day. They were fellow but less-valued workers.

All over America employers had to make a pretense of giving equal opportunity to African Americans and other minorities, including women, creating elaborate reasons why you didn't hire them, and filing lawsuits if some female or nonwhite person received a job you wanted. All over America white men were losing control over women. Except in churches where they were kept in their special place.

The way to marginalize blacks was to push them into public schools and then reduce financing for public schools in order to support charter schools, private schools, for-profit schools, and on line schools. According to the National Association of School Nurses, 5% of students in 2009 had a seizure disorder, another 5% had ADHD and 10% had mental or emotional problems. According to law public schools are required to accept them and any with physical disabilities. Those are children who are not likely to be accepted in charter schools or private schools, even religious ones.

When the government wanted certified teachers in every school, Texas created alternative certifications and most of those teach in poor neighborhoods. Republicans are also pushing for on-line education where you can buy diplomas or degrees for the benefit of their corporate sponsors.

Public school systems are supported by a combination of local, state, and federal government funding. Texas deliberately and knowingly passed a bill that reduced property taxes and replaced them with a business tax that doesn't come close to making up the difference. Last year was the first year since Depression/Dust Bowl years that Texas cut school spending, $4 billion dollars. Schools closed. Teachers were laid off. Those who return to school will find larger classes and more paperwork that does nothing to improve education but does feed the vultures that devour funds that taxpayers intended to help children. (John Young 7/4/12)

It frustrates teachers who can go to charter schools where such nuisances are not required. Teachers with alternative certification will replace them. Good students get bored by testing and preparation for testing that they don't need and that they won't have to do in charter, private, for-profit or on-line schools. That leaves other students learning limited answers to limited questions, but not wonder, not excitement, and not critical thinking. The result is that black children, poor children and those with disabilities will return to separate-but-equal education that a once truly Supreme Court outlawed.

A study done by Stanford University found that charter schools on average perform about the same or worse compared to public schools. That wasn't the point. Getting blacks out of white schools was the point. A report from UCLA's Civil Rights Project (2/4/10) found that charter schools are more racially segregated than traditional public schools. In Ohio, a bill was introduced to allow for-profit businesses to open up their own taxpayer-financed charter schools. The plan would also reduce oversight, and eliminate many of the requirements the state places on public schools.

Superior white students will attend charter schools and tax-payer supported private and for-profit schools. Texas is not a poor state but Republicans so fear taxes, especially taxes on business, that they will doom Texas to be left behind. Mexico, across the river, and not a rich country offers free education. Maybe students from Texas, New Mexico and Arizona can go to school there.

Texas still insists it knows best how to treat its children and requires no federal assistance. The Texas Republican party does not want critical thinking taught in its schools, especially regarding science. "We support objective teaching and equal treatment of all sides of scientific theories. We believe theories such as life origins and environmental change should be taught as challengeable scientific theories subject to change as new data is produced. Teachers and students should be able to discuss the strengths and weaknesses of these theories openly and without fear of retribution or discrimination of any kind." How are they to do that without critical thinking? The answer, of course, is found in religion. All you need is belief in a literal, fundamentalist Bible.

For some, home schooling was preferable to schools where masturbation might be mentioned, or evolution, or questions about genocidal wars against the Indians, land-grabbing wars such as the War against Mexico and the Spanish-American War. In home schools children could be sheltered from the questions, the corruption and the sin of the outside world. Home schools showed mixed results educationally but with children holding firm belief in the rightness of their parents' opinion.

The National Household Education Surveys Program that provides data on the educational activities of the US population found that in 2003 parents chose home schooling because of concerns about the school environment, to provide religious or moral instruction, and dissatisfaction with the academic instruction in other schools. From 2003 to 2007, the parents desire to provide religious or moral instruction increased from 72% to 83%. There is little there to suggest that learning to live together with fellow citizens is high on the lesson plan. Religious training is, and in the South that means the Southern Way of Life.

Since most religious and moral instruction occurs in homes, why is it necessary to home school unless it's to shelter children from other religious and moral ideas? Pro-life Texas prefers abstinence only sex education, although that contradicts their principle by increasing abortions. In most public schools sex education is optional and parents can save their children from it. It's troubling to think that these students will go into college, the business world, the military with little knowledge of human reproduction and STDs. We can only pray their parents teach them well.

Home schooled students do not have the testing requirements of public school students. While much of that testing is useless, expensive in time and money and seems designed to put taxpayers' money in the right private pockets, I thought testing skills were one of the important lessons to learn in education. Some students look better on tests than they are and some look worse. Even students who don't go to college will find testing skills are important in life.

While there is bonding with homecomings in high schools and colleges, alumni magazines and news letters, home schooled children have no such ties. They will not have taken part in student elections, group activities such as intramural sports, debates, artistic projects, and other competition. What will be their sense of community? Will home schooled children have a fixed view of life with others? Will they be involved in civic projects? Will they be separatists? Loners? Should a military draft or universal service be adopted, how well will they perform? It's too early to know those answers but the questions are important.

Personal Note: As far as I know I never had a home schooled student. A colleague did and said the student was very bright but believed he was the only one in the class. He did not work well in group studies or projects and he tended to require a lot of the class's time. That is only one example and is meaningless except as one example.

The propaganda behind "school choice" is that it gives parents a choice of where they want their children to go to school. In rural Texas there is rarely a choice. There isn't much of a choice in Texas cities either. San Antonio has some very rich schools in upper-middle class neighborhoods with excellent facilities, better paid teachers, and students who have access to cars. They can go to any school anywhere in the city that will accept them. That is not a choice of black and latino students. Rich schools are going to first accept the neighborhood children. If there are openings, they will go to students who have excellent test scores, superior athletic ability or those with cars because Texas cities do not have good public transportation systems.

San Antonio is largely black on the southeast side, latino on the southwest side and whites, the minority, everywhere else. There are blacks and latinos in other parts of the cities and they go to the neighborhood school but would have little reason to choose a majority black or latino school. "School choice" will transfer money from the poor black schools to the richer public, charter, private and for-profit schools.

In 1959, to prevent school integration in Prince Edward County, Virginia, the Board of Supervisors refused to fund public schools and the schools closed. White students went to private schools; black children stayed home. It took five years for the Supreme Court to order the public schools to re-open. School segregation is increasing across the country. In 2004, 73% of black students nationwide attended schools where minorities were the majority, compared with 66% in 1991, according to the Civil Rights Project at the University of California at Los Angeles.

Who is going to save the Union this time?

Another problem is the loss of religious freedom. "A biology textbook used by a Christian school in Louisiana that will be accepting students with publicly-funded vouchers in the fall says that the Loch Ness Monster in Scotland is real." (*Washington Post* 6/26/12) It isn't just any monster. It's a dinosaur and that proves that evolution is a big lie and Genesis is correct. No doubt that school was chosen by parents to reinforce the parents' religious faith. It's not education.

New Living Word in Ruston has no library. Students spend most of the day watching TVs. Each lesson consists of an instructional DVD that intersperses Biblical verses with subjects such as chemistry or composition. At Eternity Christian Academy in Westlake first through eighth grade students sit in cubicles for much of the day and move at their own pace through Christian workbooks, such as a beginning science text that explains "what God made" on each of the six days of creation. "We try to stay away from all those things that might confuse our children," a teacher said.

That is not education and it is not science or critical thinking. It is religious belief and it is a violation of a student's religious rights. How far is that from teaching that life begins at conception? That is also a violation of a student's religious rights. It contradicts a fundamentalist's literal interpretation of the biblical story of creation and it contradicts the long-held belief of evangelical Christians that life begins at birth.

It is the enshrinement of the Southern Way of Life, poorly educated and uneducated citizens fearful and suspicious of those who have different opinions, better educations, scientific methods and "foreign" ideas. It is the worship of the state-given right to injustice and inequality.

"The purpose of education is to make the young as unlike their elders as possible." Woodrow Wilson

The Federal Government and Public Health

In 1793, Philadelphia, the capital of the country and the largest city in the US with a population of 50,000, was struck by yellow fever. A doctor warned the government of an epidemic. The federal government had no authority to act. Congress was not in session. President Washington had left on vacation and for the laying of the cornerstone of the new Capitol to be built in the city of Washington. The US post office stayed open. Treasury Department employees worked throughout the epidemic. Alexander Hamilton, Secretary of the Treasury, was infected but survived to die in a duel with Aaron Burr.

The mayor asked the city medical society for advice. The society recommended that burials be private, streets and wharves cleaned, gunpowder exploded in the street to increase oxygen, and for everyone to avoid contact with the sick. Because hospitals did not admit patients with infectious diseases the "Guardians of the Poor" moved those infected out of the city to occupy outbuildings on an estate. Vice President John Adams occupied the main building which he had rented.

Those who could left the city before neighboring communities erected road blocks and quarantines. Port cities like New York and Baltimore quarantined refugees and goods from Philadelphia but sent food and money. Other cities, Springfield, New Jersey; Chester, Pennsylvania; Elkton, Maryland offered refuge. In 1706 Philadelphia had appointed "Overseers of the Poor" who collected a poor tax and distributed it among the indigent. Later those duties and the Alms House passed to "Guardians of the Poor." To combat the fever epidemic, Philadelphia mayor Matthew Clarkson organized those who remained, forming committees to help Guardians of the Poor visit the sick, feed those who couldn't feed themselves, carry the sick to the hospital and the dead to burial, and find a home for the increasing number of orphans. Two volunteers managed the fever hospital that was described as "a human slaughter house."

There were rumors of greed, stories of landlords throwing sick tenants into the street, four men demanding $40 for carrying a coffin down the stairs, nurses exacting high fees as the sick over-bid each other, and nurses stealing from those they served. Some charged that the epidemic had been caused by blacks; others that it was a judgment from God, perhaps because of frivolous entertainment. A census after the epidemic revealed that the majority of victims were poor who lived in houses on alleys.

Yellow fever returned to Philadelphia in 1797, 1798, and 1799. Other major ports were struck by yellow fever, 1794 Baltimore; 1791, 1795, 1798, New York City; 1798 Wilmington. Because epidemics recurred in ports and because the epidemics started near the wharves citizens began moving away from water. Those who could vacated the cities during the fever season. However, there were those whose occupations required that they work in the wharves, the ports and on the sea.

The life of a seaman was hazardous not only because of work-related accidents and the perils of the weather and the sea but also because of exposure to diseases at the ports where the ships anchored, and the close quarters in which the men lived and worked. One man with contagion could infect everyone on board while at sea and far from aid.

For that reason the fifth US Congress wrote into law "An Act for the relief of sick and disabled seamen" in 1798 requiring the Department of the Treasury to "provide for the relief and maintenance of disabled seamen." The act required that funding come from merchant seamen and mandated that to work as a merchant seaman a sailor had to pay a monthly fee into the Marine Hospital Fund. President John Adams, who had signed the Declaration of Independence, signed the bill that created several government hospitals at sea and river ports across the US.

This was the first publicly-funded health care and disease prevention federal agency in the US. Although public health care is sometimes derided as "socialism," the bill was written by the fifth US Congress. President John Adams, the second president, who had been the first vice president and a signer of the Declaration of Independence, signed the bill. Thomas Jefferson, credited with writing the Declaration of Independence was vice president and president of the Senate. The Speaker of the House was the youngest man to sign the Declaration of Independence pledging their lives, their fortunes and their sacred honor. These were the founding fathers of this nation. It is clear that public health was their concern and intention.

Following the Civil War there was a dispute about the Marine Hospital Fund. A prominent Army surgeon, Dr. John Woodworth led an investigation of the Marine Hospital Fund, finding it inadequate and disorganized. In 1871, the Hospital Fund was reorganized as the Marine Hospital Service, under the direction of Dr. Woodworth who required his physicians to be a uniformed mobile force to work where they were needed. This later became the Public Health Service Commission Corps using the Navy fouled anchor and the medical caduceus as the seal used today by the Public Health Service.

Dr. Woodworth's office was the forerunner of today's Surgeon General of the United States. The Marine Hospital Service was the forerunner of the present Department of Health and Human Services, the National Institutes of Health, the Centers for Disease Control, and the Indian Health Service.

Immigration increased dramatically in the late nineteenth century and the federal government took over the processing of immigrants. In 1891, the Marine Hospital Service was assigned responsibility for the medical inspection of arriving immigrants to prevent infectious disease from entering the country. In 1902, because of increasing responsibilities of the Hospital Service, the name was changed to the Public Health and Marine Hospital Service.

In 1912 the federal government turned the Marine Hospital Service into the US Public Health Service (PHS) authorized to investigate the causes and spread of diseases, problems of sewage, sanitation and water pollution, and publish health information for the general public. In addition to controlling the spread of contagious diseases, PHS commissioned officers conducted important biomedical research, regulated the food and drug supply, provided health care to under-served groups and supplied medical assistance in the aftermath of disasters.

The Marine hospitals were spectacular examples of government-provided health care. The Nixon administration cut funding to the PHS hospitals program and many were closed or released to local public health services. Eight survived until the early 1980s, when the Reagan administration ended their funding. The PHS hospital in San Francisco on the grounds of the Presidio was used for language training of military officers.

Hunger and Health

In the 19th Century city-dwellers were the first to complain about immigration: Immigrants had caused an increase in crime and disease. Much of that was true because hungry and homeless people do pilfer inexpensive items for sustenance and are more likely to be sick and to die of diseases related to hunger, especially the old and children. In 1873, 20,000 New Yorkers lived in cellars. In Boston a fifth of the population lived in crowded tenements. Simple hygiene was a compound, complex problem. Small pox, typhoid, measles swept from block to block. People died of hunger and hunger-related illnesses living the American Dream.

Child Savers believed that all children should have access to good health and health had many aspects, including nutrition and housing. Children distracted by hunger, children who did not have enough clothing to be warm, children with dirty hair and hands, children wracked by coughing and sneezing, and worried by rashes, ringworm, boils, insect bites and scabies tended to be slow to thrive and slow to learn. Public schools required children to wash their hands and sometimes their faces and feet.

> *Personal Note:* I remember going to the doctor only twice as a child. Once was when I stepped on a nail when barefoot. The nail had almost penetrated all the way through my foot and my parents debated whether to drive it all the way through for cleaning. I supported the negative side. They removed the nail, put my foot in a bucket of coal oil, our antibacterial medication, and the doctor gave me a tetanus shot. The other time my mother took me to the doctor because she thought I was "nervous." Today I would probably have been called hyperactive. The doctor advised mother to feed me more meat. We were a farm family that raised our own meat. We had meat three times a day.

Epidemic: Yellow Fever

Movement south and west exposed more cities to the ravages of yellow fever. In cities, care depended on religious organizations, social organizations and citizen organizations such as the Howard Society that operated hospitals and pesthouses, provided medical care and ensured sanitary burial.

In 1839 a yellow fever epidemic killed a fourth of the population of Galveston, the largest city in the Republic of Texas, and a major port for European immigrants. The Republic of Texas offered no health services. After an epidemic in 1844 citizens organized to care for those sickened by the fever. Many members were "Howards" and the group began to refer to itself as the Howards during the 1847 epidemic that killed one-fifth of the population. In 1853, the fever returned and deaths averaged a dozen a day. The New Orleans Howards sent $1,000 to Galveston. In 1854 the Galveston association borrowed the constitution and bylaws of the New Orleans Howard Association.

In addition to local yellow fever victims, the association aided patients in Indianola and Port Lavaca in 1853. In 1873 they sent aid to Calvert and Marshall, and in 1878 to Memphis, Tennessee, and Vicksburg, Mississippi. Associations were also founded in Corpus Christi (1860), Houston (1867), and Marshall (1873). In 1867 the Howard Association in Corpus Christi built a pesthouse to quarantine the infected. Most fever victims were males between the ages of 15 and 40 leaving many orphans.

Yellow fever had plagued the US since its founding. A Cuban physician, Dr. Charles Findlay, believed that the disease was transmitted by mosquitoes but no one listened. During the Spanish-American War the federal government sent a commission led by Major Walter Reed, M.D. to Cuba to study the disease. More American soldiers occupying Cuba were dying of yellow fever than had died in combat. The commission tested and proved Finley's theory making the Panama Canal a possibility and enabling port cities in the US to protect themselves from mosquitoes and to cover standing water.

The last yellow fever epidemic in the US was in New Orleans in 1905. New Orleans continued to operate a quarantine, fumigating ships and sanitizing clothing and bedding on board. A ship carrying bananas evaded the quarantine and yellow fever popped up in immigrant Italian stevedores who unloaded banana boats. The city declared an emergency and asked for federal help.

President Theodore Roosevelt assigned the Surgeon General of the Public Health and Marine Hospital Service to help New Orleans. The Surgeon General ordered the city to use the procedures that had proved successful in Havana. The city was fumigated. New Orleans citizens got their water from wooden cisterns and the cisterns were ordered to be screened. Still, the epidemic was not immediately stopped. With memories of the Civil War and the occupation of New Orleans by Union troops some citizens were resistant to dictation by the federal government. After the archbishop died from yellow fever, mosquito larvae was discovered in the holy water in St. Louis Cathedral. The city fined those who did not comply with public health rules and the last yellow fever epidemic in the US died.

Health Care: Prevention

The earliest prevention against infectious disease was quarantine. As early as 1743 pesthouses were built to shelter and separate those with contagious diseases. Smoke-houses were built in port cities to disinfect travelers and goods by burning sulphur. Virginia organized a board of health in 1794, New York in 1796 and Massachusetts 1797. Paul Revere headed the Boston board of health in 1799. Massachusetts required plumbing inspection in 1877. Notifying public officials of contagious disease was first required in Brooklyn in 1873. Medical inspection of children's vision, hearing, general nutrition, tonsils and mental condition began in the US in 1894. In 1843 Horace Mann advocated teaching knowledge of the body in order to maintain good health, a matter that is still controversial.

Hospital facilities for children were inadequate and the first hospitals dedicated to the care of children were in Philadelphia 1855; New York City 1857; Chicago 1865 and Boston 1869. In tenements children died by the thousands in summer time. After the story of the cruel treatment of Mary Ellen, the Society for the Prevention of Cruelty to Children began in 1875. Providing shelter and preventing cruelty seemed to satisfy the conscience of the public and the health of children was ignored. More attention was given to older children because their work and mischief was done in public.

In 1879, the US Congress created a National Board of Health because a yellow fever epidemic expanding up the Mississippi River crossed state's borders. The states fought back defending states' rights and it was disbanded in 1883. The rights of quarantine reverted to the Marine Hospital Service. The Hospital service extended its public health activities to controlling infectious disease, pollution of lakes and rivers, and set aside a room as a "hygienic laboratory."

No longer the land of fiercely independent farmers and craftsmen, America had become home to cyclic bank panics that gave extreme wealth and privilege to the rich, misery and dire poverty for the masses, and cost farmers and shopkeepers their life savings. Women organized for "municipal housekeeping" the way they kept house at home. Women volunteers cleaned up neighborhoods and demanded improved public sanitation. Joined by public health nurses they started well-baby clinics, school health services, and infant feeding centers to certify the purity of milk. Water was often added to milk for more profit. Usually the water was okay but it lowered the nutritional value of the milk further endangering the health of children in poor families. The rich had pure milk delivered to their doors and carried into their mansions by servants.

In 1901, the Tenement House Act of New York City required all new construction to install sanitary water closets, with a separate closet inside the apartment for each family.

Life had once been simpler. Food was grown, raised, processed, prepared at home or sometimes bartered from neighbors. Increasingly food was produced in factories and shipped over distances. Consumers had no knowledge of where the food came from, how it was processed, shipped or handled. The New York Medical Society reported that food was often adulterated and could be a health hazard. Bread contained sulfate of copper. Canned goods contained tin, copper and chemical preservatives. Some meat was spoiled and infested with parasites. A state law to prevent foreign matter in food and medicine was written in 1878 by a committee representing the New York Academy of Sciences, Medicine, the College of Pharmacy, and the American Chemical Society but the state of New York could not control interstate commerce in foods and drugs.

Mothers and progressives argued that from a purely mercenary view good health of the poor was an economic benefit to the country. Healthy citizens promoted the general welfare. No one disagreed because no one listened despite the enthusiasm of the volunteers. Public health leaders knew that central planning, business efficiency and scientific knowledge would be required.

Health departments were staffed by the patronage system. Progressives argued that increased pay and qualifications would gain trained personnel and that the pay for saving a child's life should at least equal that of a plumber. It doesn't matter where an epidemic starts, gated communities and private servants will not stop it.

In 1906, Upton Sinclair's *The Jungle* about the life of a meatpacking worker horrified readers and Theodore Roosevelt pressured Congress to pass the first food safety laws—the Pure Food and Drug Act and the Federal Meat Inspection Act.

The Pure food and Drug Act prohibited the "manufacture, sale or transportation of adulterated or misbranded or poisonous...foods, drugs, medicines and liquors. Patent medicines required a label stating the contents and manufacturers were prohibited from using harmful materials in their products. Rather than the different laws of 48 states and territories there was now more uniformity. The Meat Inspection Act authorized federal officials to certify that meat shipped in interstate commerce came from healthy animals and was packed in sanitary conditions.

The Department of Agriculture was given power to establish standards for food products. Agents gave home demonstrations on properly maintaining food.

Nutrition didn't become an issue until World War I. Previously, the concern was providing enough food for the poor with no attention to the need for a healthy diet for children. It was the beginning of school lunch programs that provided milk and sometimes crackers for the children. In 1920, in New York City, the schools provided hot school lunches for 3,000 children. Chicago provided food for undernourished children who applied for work papers.

In 1918, The Child Health Organization of America (CHOA) organized to promote health education, advocating a scale in every school, time allowed every day for teaching health, hot school lunches, teachers trained to teach health habits, every child's weight to be recorded and the record sent home each month. The Secretary of the Interior approved the plan and CHOA furnished most of the literature for school children.

There were the usual complaints of "socialism" and "eliminating jobs" and "reducing profits," but the laws, based on the federal government's right to tax, have contributed to public health and promoted the general welfare when enforced.

New York city established the Division of Child Hygiene in 1908. In 1912, the federal government created the Federal Children's Bureau. In 1915, Birth Registration and the publication of birth and mortality statistics were available to the public.

By 1912, 15 states required that all members of their boards of health be physicians and 23 states required that one member be a physician. The other states had no professional requirements. Civil and sanitary engineers had created clean water supplies and more adequate sewerage systems. Health departments left to them sanitation and focused on the identification and control of infectious diseases. Private doctors complained about the unfair competition by the public provision of services that threatened their income.

Entry into World War I startled citizens by the proportion of young men physically or mentally unfit for military duty. Sensational reports that 47% of young men were unfit for the military boosted support for public health expenditures.

Epidemic: Smallpox

For many centuries, smallpox devastated mankind. The mummy of Egyptian pharaoh Ramses V, who died 1156 BC, shows marks of smallpox. Smallpox in China was described in 1122 BC. In 165 AD, a smallpox plague in the reign of Marcus Aurelius was spread by war in Mesopotamia and northeast Italy. The extent of the plague is subject of debate but seven million people are believed to have died, affecting soldiers, farmers and the economy. The Roman army had to recruit barbarian troops and fear of the plague encouraged spirituality and the spread of Christianity.

In 18th Century Europe 400,000 people died of smallpox every year. One third of the survivors went blind and most survivors suffered disfiguring scars. It was known that survivors could not be re-infected and they were used as nurses as early as 402 BC. The first written account of inoculation recorded a Buddhist nun grinding up scabs from a smallpox victim and blowing the powder into the nostrils of another person in the middle of the 11th century. By the 18th Century that form of inoculation was common in India, China and Turkey.

Smallpox was brought to the Americas by the Spanish and Portuguese, destroying the Aztec and Inca empires. The practice of inoculation in the United States began in 1721 when a ship from the West Indies arrived in Boston with people infected with smallpox. An epidemic broke out in Boston and spread to other parts of Massachusetts. Rev. Cotton Mather wrote a letter to doctors recommending inoculation of those not infected. Only Dr. Boylston responded and with Mather's support, Boylston began inoculating volunteers. As the disease spread so did fear-driven anger regarding a pagan practice. Some Christians believed that God sent plagues to punish sinners. Some repented and prayed but someone else threw a bomb into Mather's house. Mather and Boylston compared those who died from smallpox without inoculation and those who died after receiving the inoculation. The fatality rate for those who were not inoculated was 14%, but only 2% for those inoculated. Inoculation spread in New England.

During the French and Indian War (1754–1767) the commander of the British forces gave blankets and handkerchiefs of smallpox victims to the Indians. Many slaves brought to America were from areas of Africa where smallpox was widespread. In 1775, General Washington was unable to capture Quebec because so many of his troops were sick with yellow fever. The British soldiers had been inoculated. By 1777, all of Washington's troops were inoculated.

Edward Jenner had heard the common belief that dairymaids were some way protected from smallpox. He believed that infecting people with cow pox, a common and less dangerous disease, could prevent the spread of smallpox. In 1796 Jenner used matter from the lesions of a milkmaid to inoculate a young boy. After inoculation with smallpox the child showed no symptoms. That discovery made the eradication of smallpox possible. Like Jonas Salk, the inventor of the polio vaccine, Jenner made no attempt to profit from his important work.

Thomas Jefferson vaccinated members of his family and friends in 1801 and as president directed vaccination of Southern states. Louisiana opposed compulsory inoculation until smallpox broke out in New Orleans. In 1805 Napoleon ordered inoculation of troops who had not had smallpox. Compulsory inoculation began in Bavaria in 1807, Denmark in 1810, Russia in 1812, and Sweden in 1816.

In America inoculation was for the educated upper classes who could afford it. Those who were poor and less educated either could not or did not want to pay for it, or could not imagine allowing foreign matter from a sick person being injected into their skin. Some regarded the growing gap between the rich and the poor as God's will. Diseases were God's way of maintaining a balance between the sheep and the goats.

In 1813 Congress passed the Vaccine Act making certain that smallpox vaccine was available to the American public. In 1827, Boston became the first American city to require children to be inoculated before entering the public schools. In 1832, the federal government established a smallpox vaccination program for Native Americans. Massachusetts passed a school inoculation law in 1855, New York in 1862, Connecticut in 1872, and Pennsylvania in 1895. Enforcement of the law was difficult because of resistance and apathy. In 1894 politicians, clergy, and doctors resisted the city health officer of Milwaukee in his attempt to quarantine smallpox victims. In Chicago,1894, less than 10% of school children had been vaccinated despite a 12-year-old law that required it.

When the last state legislature agreed to a compulsory education bill in 1918 a mechanism was created for elimination of smallpox. School boards required certain immunizations before a child could be admitted to class. Religious and other objections to forced immunization persisted but the last outbreak of smallpox in the United States occurred in Texas in 1949 with 8 cases and 1 death. The US stopped vaccinating the general population in 1972, but continued to vaccinate military personnel because of exposure to smallpox in other countries. Vaccination of military recruits ended in 1990.

Worldwide eradication of smallpox began when the World Health Assembly received a report in 1958 of the catastrophic consequences of smallpox in 63 countries and succeeded in eradicating smallpox in 1977. In 1980, the World Health Assembly recommended that all countries cease vaccination. Unless developed and used by bioterrorists smallpox is a short but important lesson in the history of world health.

Mental Health

In the 17th & 18 centuries the mentally ill were believed to be possessed by demons and were badly mistreated, erroneously blamed for crimes, and sometimes burned as witches. The first institution for the mentally ill in America was in Williamsburg, Virginia in 1773. By 1840 there were eight "asylums" in America. The first attempt to measure mental illness was the 1840 census that included a category for "insane and idiotic." Immigrants were screened for retardation or mental illness.

Straight-jackets, padded cells or confinement to the basement or attic of those who were "not right" were commonplace in both public and private care of the brain damaged or mentally ill. Little was done to distinguish between them.

Personal Note: In a town not far from my father's farm there were rumors surrounding a house where a baby had been injured in birth or had been misbegotten. No one had ever seen the child, that had to have been middle-aged when the house was pointed out to me, except for family members who cared for him or her. If there were any scandal it regarded how the child came to be, not how the person was treated. For all anyone knew he or she received loving care.

In 1908, Clifford Beers changed the treatment of the mentally challenged and mentally ill with his autobiography, *A Mind That Found Itself.* A Yale graduate and successful businessman, Beers was depressed by the death of his brother and attempted suicide. His family placed him in a private mental institution where he received brutal and degrading treatment. His family moved him to other institutions with hope that he would find better care but oftentimes it was worse. The story of his illness and recovery and the incompetent and humiliating treatment he received shocked the nation. Beers founded the Connecticut Society for Mental Hygiene that became the National Society for Mental Hygiene.

In 1915 the Texas legislature established the state's first facility for the retarded, some of whom had been housed at the Austin State Lunatic Asylum until then. Two years later the State Colony for the Feebleminded opened on Austin's outskirts with an initial admission of sixty-five females, ages six to forty-nine.

In 1930, the First International Congress for Mental Hygiene met with more than 3,000 participants from more than 40 countries. The Public Health Service opened a Narcotics Division that later became the Division for Mental Hygiene that studied addiction and the causes, prevalence and means of preventing and treating mental disease. By 1950, three separate groups in America joined to form the National Association of Mental Health, (NAMH).

World War II brought a new emphasis to mental illness. Experts studied how long men could endure constant combat without suffering "shell shock" that was beginning to be changed to "combat fatigue." Studies had not yet begun on the effects of brains bouncing against skulls because of explosives. In 1946, Congress enacted the National Mental Health Act that gave federal funding for psychiatric research leading to the creation of the National Institute of Mental Health (NIMH) in 1949.

In 1947, states began community-based mental health services and improved state mental health institutions. In 1955, Congress authorized the Mental Health Study Act. 1956, Congress established the Psychopharmacology Service Center. Enrollment of patients in mental health institutions declined due to the discovery of drugs such as Lithium and Thorazine. Congress also authorized federal support for community services such as halfway houses, daycare and aftercare. In 1963 Congress authorized community mental health centers as a substitute for custodial care. The act transferred involuntarily hospitalized patients from state mental hospitals into community facilities funded by the federal government. This placed the mentally ill closer to a normal environment with family and friends nearby and resulted in better trained staff and better qualified professionals. 1975, Congress mandated accessibility of all persons to mental health care regardless of ability to pay.

In 1982, the federal share of funding decreased to 11% of the total. State and local tax rates increased but service to the mentally ill decreased. The population of the homeless increased, many of them veterans. By 1985, state taxes accounted for 42%, and local taxes 13% of mental health care. Medicaid decreased and Medicare remained at 2%. Patient fees accounted for 8%, double the amount from 1975.

1987, Medicare added outpatient mental health benefit but with large copayment. 1987, Minnesota's Comprehensive Mental Health Act for adults added an array of mandated services. 1988: Massachusetts was the first state to privatize mental healthcare for efficiency and economy. However, it was hard to find economic benefit, technological promises weren't fulfilled, there were differences in care between the rural and urban areas, and access and quality declined.

1990, Minnesota's Children's Health Plan included mental health benefits. NMHA led to the development of the Americans with Disabilities Act that protected mentally and physically disabled Americans from discrimination in employment, public accommodations, transportation, telecommunications, and state and local government services. 1991, Community Mental Health Centers were authorized to provide limited hospital services under Medicare. 1993, The National Council for Community Mental Healthcare Centers changed its name to the National Community Mental Healthcare Council. The word "centers" was erased and emphasis was put on "community." 1995, Minnesota was one of the first states to pass a mental health bill regulating private health plans. 1996, The Health Insurance Portability and Accountability Act protected health insurance coverage for workers and their families when they changed jobs or lost them. The Temporary Assistance for Needy Families Act required work of recipients, including mothers, child support, increased funding for child care and guaranteed medical coverage.

Epidemic: Influenza

Some believe that the influenza, or Spanish Fever, that killed 600,000 Americans began in this country in Fort Riley, Kansas, March 9, 1918. Before breakfast, a company cook turned up at the base infirmary complaining of a bad cold. By noon 100 more soldiers had reported to the infirmary with the same symptoms. The illness quickly spread to other military bases and to prisons, places where men were confined in close quarters. However, the nation had more important concerns: war was raging in Europe and American soldiers were going there. No one knew they were carrying a virus that would sweep across the world.

By summer influenza was reported in Russia, North Africa, India, China, Japan, the Philippines and New Zealand. Americans had developed great faith in its doctors, medicines and hospitals and the shocking infection, sudden death of friends and relatives with no one able to stop it led to invented causes. German submarines had left German agents with poisons along the east coast, the Gulf, maybe even to the west coast to explain an outbreak at the San Quentin penitentiary. Others blamed German-Americans for spreading the disease. General John Pershing, future president Franklin Roosevelt, and the man in the White House, Woodrow Wilson, survived the illness but their national importance lent credence to the stories of anti-American causes.

One doctor at a military camp reported that there were no military activities because assemblages were forbidden. He also reported 100 deaths a day from the most viscous pneumonia he had ever seen and that his entire activity was restricted to "hunting for rales," a rattling in the lungs that meant certain death. It was just a matter of waiting for them to suffocate. The camp that had normally 25 doctors had more than 250. One barrack had been vacated for the use as the morgue and special trains were required to carry away the dead.

September 5, 1918 the Massachusetts Department of Health alerted area newspapers that an epidemic was underway. Dr. John

S. Hitchcock of the state health department warned that "unless precautions are taken, the disease in all probability will spread to the civilian population of the city." September 13, the Surgeon General of the PHS advised the press on how to recognize the influenza symptoms. He prescribed bed rest, good food, salts of quinine, and aspirin for the sick. On the same date, the Health Commissioner of New York City, declared, "The city is in no danger of an epidemic. No need for our people to worry."

Officials in Philadelphia had seen reports from Boston of a deadly influenza and knew what was coming their way but not what to do about it. More than a quarter of the city's doctors, and a larger portion of its nurses, were serving in the nation's war efforts. At Philadelphia Hospital, 75% of medical and support staff were overseas. Such shortages were a problem before influenza arrived. The Bureau of Health warned of public coughing, sneezing, and spitting, but the Department of Health and Charities assured the public that the illness would not spread beyond the military.

In September, 200,000 people gathered for a fourth Liberty Loan Drive to support the troops and demonstrate patriotism. Within days there were 635 new cases of influenza. Churches, schools, and theaters were ordered closed, along with all other places of "public amusement." Some newspapers condemned the closings as a violation of personal freedom, the very thing the doughboys were fighting for. Church parish houses and state armories doubled as shelters for the sick. Dr. C.Y. White announced that he had developed a vaccine to prevent influenza and the Philadelphia Board of Health vaccinated more than 10,000 citizens. Whether the vaccine was effective became a raging debate.

Bell Telephone Company had so many sick employes they permitted only calls concerning medical matters. Rumors spread of a few whose pockets bulged with money created by sickness, death, misery and grief. Some undertakers raised their prices by more than 500%. Grave diggers quarreled with grieving families over the costs of a grave. Garbage lined the streets as garbage collectors fell ill. Unable to remove all the trash, workers covered the mounds of garbage with dirt. Philadelphia begged the federal government to send embalmers. Medical students tended the sick.

Congress approved a special $1 million fund to enable the Surgeon General to hire additional doctors and nurses for the Public

Health Service; however, many doctors and nurses had been recruited by the military. The PHS had to look for doctors and nurses serving in old-age homes and rehabilitation centers.

In October the crime rate in Chicago had dropped by 43%. Police authorities attributed the drop to influenza among the city's lawbreakers. October became the deadliest month in America's history: 195,000 Americans died of influenza.

November 11, 30,000 San Franciscans celebrated the end of the war, many of them wearing face masks. November 20, in five days, influenza killed 72 of the 80 native American Inupiats in Brevig Mission, Alaska. They were buried in a mass grave. November 21, sirens announced to San Franciscans that it was okay to remove their face masks. 2,122 had died.

December Public Health Service estimated that 300,000 to 350,000 civilian deaths were the results of influenza. War Department records revealed that 20,000 soldiers had died of the illness. More than 2,000 Navajos in Apache County, New Mexico had died. The epidemic continued into 1919, killing approximately 600,000 people, almost as many Americans as those who died in the Civil War. It was the worst epidemic in American history.

> *Personal Note:* My father served in World War I, 360th Infantry Regiment of the 90th Division. He had kept a diary during his days in the trenches. Some years later looking over the record he saw days with no words. Years later, when he encountered a buddy from his unit Dad asked about the missing days. He was told that he had double pneumonia and was out of his head with fever. There was no way to get him to a hospital so his unit led him wherever they went. I often wondered if he wasn't injured in a gas-attack but it was more likely that he had a light case of the "Spanish" flu.

Some of the things Dad brought home from the war were postcards that he had picked up on the battlefield. The postcards were to German soldiers from folks back home. Long after Dad's death I had the messages translated by a professor of German. On one of the cards was a melancholy note to the soldier that his family back home were sick with the "Spanish fever."

Environment: Clean Air

In 1881, Chicago and Cincinnati enacted ordinances to control smoke. In 1904, Philadelphia passed an ordinance limiting smoke in flues, chimneys, and open spaces and establishing a penalty for failure to pass smoke inspections. In the 1930s and 1940s studies were made of the economic and environmental consequences of fuel emissions by the federal government. In 1947 California created Air Pollution Control Districts in every county of the state.

In 1949, a National Air Pollution Symposium was held to alert the public to the growing health concern. In 1955, the federal Clean Air Act declared that air pollution was a danger to public health and welfare but left the states in charge of prevention and control. The Act authorized the Surgeon General of the Public Health Service to study air pollution and provide information regarding the prevention and control of air pollution, but with no authority to punish polluters.

In 1963, the Act was expanded to give the Secretary of Health, Education and Labor power to define air quality and to provide grants to local and state agencies to define their air quality. In 1965, the Motor Vehicle Air Pollution Control Act focused on automotive emission standards. In 1967, the Air Quality Act of 1967 was passed. This amendment allowed states to enact federal automobile emissions standards.

A great leap forward was made with the 1970 establishment of the Environmental Protection Agency (EPA). The EPA set the National Ambient Air Quality Standards to protect public health and welfare. The EPA allowed citizens to sue polluters or government agencies for failure to abide by the act, and required that by 1975 the entire nation meet clean air standards.

"To environmental justice activists, the synergy between pollution and social hardship intersects with barriers surrounding urban communities." A Columbia study, focused on New York City women of black and Dominican descent, noted that disadvantaged communities already dealing with poverty, healthcare and education gaps and racial segregation, face disproportionate exposure to air pollution. Much environmental research focuses on everyday exposures, but in unhealthy workplaces, there's a convergence of economic, gender and environmental injustice that "may pose crippling costs for the whole family." (inthesetimes 6/8/12)

In 1977 there were amendments to the Clear Air Act prohibiting engines needing leaded gas, and requiring improved fuel efficiency and cleaner fuel. Because aircraft emissions released toxins causing birth defects and cancer, restrictions were placed on such emissions with inspection the duty of the Secretary of Transportation.

There were no new acts or standards regarding clean air during the 1980s.

"The annual federal report on air pollution trends has no section on global warming and according to an EPA official, "Some people at pretty high levels in my organization were saying, 'Take it out.'" (*New York Times* 9-15-02)

Tennessee Republican House member Marsha Blackburn has written a bill, with 125 cosponsors, to amend the Clean Air Act to "(1) exclude from the definition of the term 'air pollutant' carbon dioxide, water vapor, methane, nitrous oxide, hydroflurocarbons, or sulfur hexafluoride; and (2) declare that nothing in the act shall be treated as authorizing or requiring the regulation of climate change or global warming.

Epidemic: Diphtheria

The diphtheria bacterium was identified in the 1880s. In the 1890s, the antitoxin against diphtheria was developed. In 1902 Congress passed a law to regulate the sale of viruses, serums, toxins, etc. The legislation also established the Hygienic Laboratory of the Public Health Service that eventually became the National Institutes of Health. In 1905 The Hygienic Laboratory of Public Health and Marine Hospital Service established the strength of diphtheria antitoxin and published the methods of production for use by others.

Diphtheria, called the "strangling angel of children," struck Europe several times and the American colonies in the 18th Century. The United States, still recovering from the flu epidemic in the 1920s, suffered an estimated 100,000 to 200,000 cases of diphtheria per year, resulting in 13,000 to 15,000 deaths per year. Children represented most of the cases and most of the deaths. The most dramatic and dramatized diphtheria outbreak was in Nome, Alaska in 1924.

Nome had only one doctor, four nurses and a 24-bed hospital for Nome and the surrounding Indian communities. The hospital's diphtheria vaccine had expired and the new order had not arrived when winter ice closed the harbor in Seward. During the winter Nome's link to the outside world was the 938 mile dogsled trail to Seward. When a child became ill in an Indian community, the doctor diagnosed it as tonsillitis. The child died and an unusual number of other children showed symptoms suggesting tonsillitis. When another child died the doctor wanted to do an autopsy but the mother refused.

More children died and in desperation the doctor used the expired vaccine with no effect. The doctor called an emergency meeting of the town council and warned that he needed diphtheria vaccine to stop an epidemic. The council immediately quarantined the villages where diphtheria had appeared. The doctor warned major towns in Alaska, the Alaskan governor and the PHS of a public health risk. Native Americans had little immunity to diphtheria. The flu epidemic had killed half the Indian population of Nome and 8% of the Indian population of Alaska.

Public Health Service located enough serum in West Coast hospitals that could be shipped to Seattle and then shipped to Alaska. It was slow but the best that could be done. Then 300,000 units were discovered in the Anchorage Railroad Hospital. It wasn't enough to stop the epidemic but it could delay it until the larger West Coast shipment arrived. The governor ordered it transported by train to Nenana.

The fastest way from Nenana to Nome was by airplane but the planes had been dismantled for the winter, had water-cooled engines and an open cockpit. Winter flying was rare in Alaska because so much winter clothing was required that it was difficult to control the airplane. The board of health unanimously voted for a dogsled relay. The governor ordered the US Post Office inspector to arrange a relay of the best drivers and dogs. The dogs had been used to transport the mail and the inspector telephoned and telegraphed the drivers to set up the relay.

The first driver started out at night with the temperature 50 below zero and falling. The driver ran beside the sled to keep warm but developed hypothermia and parts of his face were frostbitten when he reached Minto. There he warmed the serum and rested for four hours after leaving three dogs that soon died. He made the rest of the run with only six dogs.

Twenty drivers and 150 sled dogs moved the vaccine 674 miles in 127 and a half hours into the teeth of gale force winds reaching 80 miles per hour, despite swirling snow, whiteouts, climbing over a 5000 foot mountain, the deaths of more dogs, frostbite and colliding with a reindeer that tangled dogs and harness. The governor ordered the mushers to wait out the storm but as the storm got worse and snowdrifts threatened to close the trail, they persisted. High winds flipped one sled and the vaccine was buried in the snow. The driver had to feel for the container with bare hands to find it and both his hands were badly frostbitten. The wind chill factor reached 85 below zero.

The vaccine reached Nome February 2 and when thawed proved to be okay, saving Nome and the surrounding Indian villages from an epidemic. Balto, the lead dog on the last relay rivaled Rin Tin Tin in popularity and a statue of him was placed in Central Park in New York City to honor all the dogs. The Iditarod dogsled race each year commemoratives the drivers and the dogs that delivered the vaccine to a part of the nation that few Americans knew of.

Balto and the other dogs became part of a sideshow until children raised funds to move him to Cleveland where Balto spent the rest of his life in the Cleveland Zoo. When Balto was 14, he was euthanized, mounted and displayed in the Cleveland Museum of National History. Togo and his driver, Leonhard Seppala, were believed by many to be the real heroes of the relay because they traveled a greater distance than any other team, 261 miles. Togo and Seppala were given gold medals by Roald Amundsen, the first man to reach the South Pole. Seppala moved to New England and sold Togo and the team to a kennel in Maine. Most huskies in the United States are descendants of those dogs. Togo was also euthanized, and placed on display at the Iditarod museum in Wasilla, Alaska. A future Alaskan vice presidential candidate was given much the same treatment.

The vaccine from Seattle was placed on a tugboat and reached Seward on February 7. The governor ordered half the vaccine to be flown to Nome and the other half shipped by dogsled. The US Navy moved a minesweeper north from Seattle, and the Signal Corps lighted fires to guide the planes. On Feb. 8, half of the second shipment left Seward by dogsled. The airplane failed to start because of overheating due to a broken radiator shutter. The airplane failed the second day as well and the flight was scrubbed. The second relay included many of the same drivers, and faced similar harsh conditions. The vaccine arrived February 15. A reenactment of the race against an epidemic was held in 1975 and took almost twice as long, in better conditions but without the desperation.

The race to save the children was reported daily by newspapers and by radios that were becoming a "necessity." The attention to diphtheria's deadly threat and the means by which it could be easily prevented encouraged parents to have their children vaccinated.

In the 1940s, diphtheria vaccine was combined with tetanus and pertussis (DTP) and used to immunize children before entry in public schools. There have been no more diphtheria epidemics in the US but travelers to some countries do have to be immunized. The latest death reported in the United States was in 2003 to a man who had traveled to Haiti without being vaccinated. In the 1990s there were outbreaks of diphtheria in the states that had formed the Soviet Union but in the US there are rarely more than five cases a year and those are among adults who were not immunized.

Personal Note: I liked school but dreaded the start of school because I hated the vaccinations. A nurse came from Vernon, the county seat, with a small bottle of alcohol in which were embedded the needles for vaccinations. The smart children lined up first knowing that the needles were sharper then. After a shot the nurse dropped the needle in the bottle of alcohol and picked up another needle. The worst shots were typhoid shots that made your arm sore for two or three days. I lingered at the back of the line dreaming of some salvation, some rescue. My mother would rush to the school, pick me up and carry me home to shelter me. Or, perhaps it would be my father who would take my hand and lead me to the car and drive me to the Wilbarger County sales barn, that Dad always called the mule barn, to help him buy a cow or even better a horse.

Instead, the older boys, having gotten their shots waited for the rest of us to get ours so they could punch us on the shoulder that had received the shot. When I have been asked if I was ever bullied in school I have always answered no, because I don't believe I was. A punch on a vaccinated arm caused more imagined pain than real pain. Most of us aggressively guarded our wounded arm so that it moved little if at all. It's better to do calisthenics after vaccinations to keep your arm from getting sore. At least the Marines said so because that's what we did after vaccinations—a lot of arm and shoulder exercises, usually involving an 8-pound rifle.

The school had a hand pump that spouted water from the well into the air through three, maybe four spigots. Boys ran to be the first to pump water; I'm not sure why but I did too. The bigger, older boys could pump fast enough that they could let go to the pump handle and grab a bit of water from a spigot themselves. That was a skill that eluded me.

We were all from families that kept some livestock and we all had outhouses, some attended churches that had outhouses. Typhoid and cholera worried our teachers and government officials, but to us they just meant painful shots.

By 1980, all 50 states had school immunization laws. The constitutionality of school immunization laws was upheld by the US Supreme Court. One result was an increase of private schools and home-schooling to avoid required immunization.

Lyndon Johnson's War on Poverty included access to medical care for the poor and elderly, Medicare and Medicaid. He did not expect organized resistance by hospitals and the medical profession that were rapidly becoming Big Business. Allied with other businesses, they demanded that anything done to help the public must put money into private pockets.

The new diseases were cancer, hypertension, diabetes that could be treated but rarely cured. The present cost for diabetes, now hitting teens who aren't overweight, simply junk food junkies, stagger budgets: one Medicare dollar in three deals with diabetes, with predictions of "$3.4 trillion over the next 10 years to treat pre-diabetes and Type 2 diabetes." (disabetesadvocacyalliance.org) That's comparable to what we spent on WWII, or will on Iraq and Afghanistan.

In the US dialysis treatment for end stage renal failure is generally paid for by the government (taxpayers) and not by the insurance industry. Persons with privatized Medicare (Medicare Advantage) are the exception and must get their dialysis paid through their insurance company, but persons with end stage renal failure generally cannot buy Medicare Advantage plans.

Personal Note: I have an Advantage plan and every time I see a new physician and fill out a form I must declare that I have never had kidney disease or renal failure.

Research had discovered how fluoride prevented dental cavities, how tobacco increased the risk of cancer, the danger of cholesterol, the value of physical exercise and preventive care but citizens did not want the government to tell them what to eat, whether to smoke, and exercise ruined their lifestyle. Those were intrusions of the government into private lives and health insurance companies knew best how to treat the sick and dying and how to discard those whose illness or death was not profitable. By the 1970s public health became providers of the last resort for the uninsured and those on Medicaid rejected by doctors and hospitals.

Prevention: Clean Water

At the beginning of the 20th century hundreds of towns and cities had sewers that were discharging untreated sewage into rivers and lakes contaminating the water downstream. Sand, mechanical, and chemical treatment reduced coliform bacteria in water and reduced sickness and death. In 1912 the Public Health Service Act expanded the mission of the PHS to study problems of sanitation, sewage and pollution. In 1914, bacterial analysis was used by the Public Health Service to set standards for water used in interstate commerce. The standards were adopted by several states for use by their towns and cities.

In 1902 the American Public Health Association (APHA) appointed a committee to study industrial waste. The committee reported that hundreds of different industries produced objectionable waste requiring separate consideration of each, but there was no process for it. In 1908, the US Corps of Engineers studied the oxidation process of New York Harbor, believing that industrial wastes deserved the same attention as human wastes because they were a menace to public health. Industrial waste prevented the disposal of infectious matter by dissolving the oxygen in running water. Oxygen was the natural purifying power of water. Re-aeration of water was the method for reducing or eliminating industrial wastes in water.

In the period of 1909 to 1913, the percentage of deaths from tuberculosis in stonecutters fell from 26.3 to 19.7. metal grinders from 39.2 to 29.1, molders, founders, and casters from 19.7 to 17.4; in other iron and steel workers from 24 to 17.2, in plumbers from 32.5 to 22.6. The sickness rate was 2 and one-quarter percent of wage owners constantly ill and incapacitated.

State health departments usually responded to industrial waste only when the waste reduced the potability of water. Scientists called for cleaner streams by stopping industrial waste at its source. They attracted little attention until they were joined by sportsmen, corporations that sold sporting goods and equipment such as boats, tackle, guns and camping gear, and corporations that required high quality water. Many states had Fish Commissions but they had little power against industries. In 1917, the Pennsylvania Legislature passed a law prohibiting the release into streams of any matter harmful to fish. Six years later the legislature gave the authority over streams to the Sanitary Water Board. The Board rated some streams as non-recreational and incapable of supporting fish, thereby opening them to further pollution.

Even states with tough water regulations exempted some rivers and industries from enforcement. It was the "Roaring 20s" and health departments were slow to restrict industrial polluters because tycoons had powerful friends in government and the press to whom they complained about the loss of jobs and profits and the freedom to run their corporations their way. Tycoons also had lobbyists to be sure that their demand and their money were shown in the office of everyone who could help or hinder them.

Because of its connection to contagious diseases, water pollution was the concern of state departments of health in most states. Health departments were headed by doctors who showed little concern for industrial pollution, and that from automobiles that were become more common. Fish die-offs, the death of other aquatic life and vegetation did not trouble state departments of health because that was not within their jurisdiction.

State conservation commissions were begun in some states in the 20s to cooperate with state departments of health in maintaining the health of land and water, and to give technical advice to industrialists. However, most had little or no power of enforcement.

Industrial wastes did not normally carry disease, except for tannery and wool scouring wastes that might contain anthrax. The United States Geological Survey's interests in lakes, rivers and streams were broader than merely the relationship of clean water to public health. In 1903 the USGS had formed a Division of Hydro-economics to study the economic value of water supplies and the economic injury of heavy pollution.

In 1924, Congress prohibited the intentional discharge of fuel oil into tidal waters and authorized the Army Corps of Engineers to arrest violators. In 1972, the Clean Water Act reduced the Corps' role to the intentional discharge of dredged or fill material.

The Roaring 20s were followed by the Great Depression. Men who couldn't find work left their families looking for work somewhere and hoping that neighbors would be kinder to a mother and children with no man in the house. Those men who did find jobs were scarcely able to feed their families and keep a roof. Paying for medicine or a doctor to help a sick child was a distant dream. Doctors complained of low income and some left private practice to work in the Public Health Service.

The war years brought full employment with millions of men in the military, but also war factories with lessened concern for workers or the environment, new medicines and chemicals, and more industrial waste dumped into streams.

The Federal Water Pollution Control Act of 1948 created water quality programs. The Public Health Service provided financial and technical assistance. In 1965 The Water Quality Act required states to issue water quality standards, and created and authorized the Federal Water Pollution Control Administration to set standards where states did not. In 1969 The National Environmental Policy Act set a national policy enhancing the environment and creating the President's Council on Environmental Quality.

In 1972 Congress authorized the construction of municipal sewage treatment plants with the federal government providing 75% of the cost. The state was supposed to pay the rest. Congress later reduced the federal's financial responsibility. 1974, The Safe Drinking Water Act required the EPA to create standards for safe drinking water and oversee the water quality of states, localities and water suppliers, other than bottle water that is regulated by the Food and Drug Administration. The Clean Water Act of 1977 set goals for ensuring surface waters were safe for sports and recreation by 1983, and eliminating the release of toxic substances in the water and other water pollution by 1985.

The health hazard faced by coal miners had been known for a long time. In the 1880s establishment of state hospitals in the coal fields was a taxpayers' gift to mining companies. It wasn't until 1977 that mining's impact on the environment became a concern. The Surface Mining Control and Reclamation Act established the Office of Surface Mining within the Department of the Interior, and contains two programs, one to regulate the effect of coal mining on the environmental and one to reclaim abandoned mines.

Surface, or strip mining, did not become common until the 1930s. West Virginia wrote laws regulating strip mining in 1939, Indiana in 1941, illinois in 1943, and Pennsylvania in 1945. However, the demand for coal created by World War II encouraged mine operators and regulators to disregard environmental damage. After the war, states expanded regulation requiring that the land could be reclaimed when the mine was closed. But laws varied and mine companies moved to states where regulators were friendlier. By 1973 strip mines produced 60% of the coal.

In 1974 and 1975 Congress sent bills regulating mining and the pollution of air and water to President Ford who vetoed them. They would cost jobs and reduce profits. In 1977 President Carter signed the Surface Mining Control and Reclamation Act.

In 1965, Congress created the Resource and Conservation Recovery Act to confront the volume of municipal and industrial waste. The RCRA was to protect human health and the environment from the dangers of waste disposal, reduce the amount of waste through source reduction and recycling, and manage waste in an environmentally sound way. In 1976, Congress gave EPA authority to control hazardous waste from "cradle to grave"—generation, transportation, treatment, storage, and disposal of hazardous waste.

US News (12/22/03) reported that water assessments required by the Clean Water Act are still being done, but the 1996 amendments intending the assessments to "arm the public with the information necessary to push for improvements" had been so restricted that there is too little information to act upon. "As a result, the program has been fundamentally reshaped from one that has made information widely available to one that now forces citizens to essentially operate on a need-to-know basis," said Stephen Gasteyer, a Washington specialist on water-quality issues.

From 2001 to 2004, Washington, D.C., suffered severe lead contamination of city water. Some tap water contained enough lead to be classified as hazardous waste. A CDC report stated that water contamination "might have contributed a small increase in blood lead levels." New York, Seattle and other cities used the report to justify high levels of lead in their water. In 2007, CDC discovered that many

D.C. children were poisoned by drinking water but did not publicize the finding or alert public health officials and scientists from other agencies, including EPA and HUD. "When it comes to lead in water, you need engineers, chemists and health people to figure it out," one of them said.

A D.C. resident filed a $200 million lawsuit against the D.C. water company, claiming that lead-contaminated tap water poisoned his twin sons as infants, causing them to have ongoing learning and behavioral problems. The House Science and Technology Committee Investigations and Oversight Subcommittee is beginning an investigation into CDC's handling of the D.C. lead crisis. Subcommittee chair Brad Miller, D-N.C. said, "If the CDC tells parents that they shouldn't worry about their children's health, its evidence had better be rock solid. It's hard to win back lost trust." (*Salon* 4/10/09)

EPA has dropped or delayed more than 400 cases of suspected violations of the law such as illegal industrial discharges. (*New York Times* 8/18/08) EPA has overstated the purity of the nation's drinking water for four years leaving millions of people at risk. (*Washington Post* 3/12/04)

At least 46 million Americans are affected by trace amounts of pharmaceuticals in drinking water, up from 41 million people in six months. Estrogen from birth control pills is found in rivers, lakes and drinking water. It has caused reproductive and developmental problems in fish and may relate to the increasing infertility of males in industrial nations. Chicago found a cholesterol medication and a nicotine derivative in its water. Many cities found an anti-convulsant. Colorado Springs found five pharmaceuticals, including a tranquilizer and a hormone. Even in extremely diluted concentrations pharmaceutical residues harm fish, frogs and other aquatic species in the wild and impair the workings of human cells in the laboratory. The overwhelming majority of US communities have yet to test drinking water. (AP 9/12/08)

The EPA reminded the staff of the Army Corps of Engineers of their duty under the Clean Water Act to protect all bodies of water, large and small, from harmful development. The 1972 law was designed to protect "the waters of the United States" from pollution. It requires oil companies, developers, homeowners to seek a permit from the Corps to stop destructive projects and mitigate the damage from others. Two confusing Supreme Court decisions and guidance from the W. Bush administration have created uncertainty about regulation. The Corps has been protecting navigable waterways while ignoring "thousands of miles of smaller streams and millions of acres of wetlands that are critical to the nation's drinking water and aquatic ecosystems." Commercial and farming interests denounced the proposed guide as a "job-killing" regulation from the EPA. The White House has not yet released the guidance or explained to Americans why it is essential for keeping this country's water clean and safe. (*New York Times* 6/21/12)

Epidemic: Poliomyelitis

Although the effects of polio are depicted in Egyptian drawing it was not a cause of major epidemics until the 20th Century when it became a frightening childhood disease. Swimming pools were closed. Movie theaters that featured western B movies appealing to children were closed. Because the outbreaks occurred most often in the summer there were hopeful rumors among my friends at church that school would not start because of polio.

> *Personal Note:* My brother, sister and I heard our parents whispering about the dreadful ravages of polio and although it scared us we children did not talk about it at home or school. Although some parents allowed their children to skip church for fear of contagion, our mother took us to church every Sunday convinced that polio was less likely to strike a believer who risked going to church. I didn't know anyone who had actually contracted the disease but I heard and read stories of victims in breathing chambers, and saw crippled children. We feared polio more than we feared the Soviet Union or the atomic bomb. They seemed remote. Polio hobbled our tomorrow.
>
> In my first professional job teaching Speech and Drama at Gardner-Webb College (now university) there was a student, Martha Mason, who, except for her head, was encased in an iron lung. I talked to her because she wanted to take a speech class but the logistics were too difficult and she abandoned the idea. It was my loss because she went on to Wake Forest University where she graduated at the top of her class. She lived the rest of her life in an iron lung but before she died wrote, *Breathing: Life in the Rhythm of an*

Iron Lung. There are many such stories but the most famous survivor of polio was Franklin D. Roosevelt.

Much later I knew a man, a writer and successful restaurant owner who had overcome most of his childhood disabilities as a result of polio, only to see it recur in his later years, eventually resulting in his death. Post-polio syndrome that occurred 10 to 40 years after initial infection produced symptoms such as muscle weakness, pain, fatigue, difficulty breathing and intolerance of cold temperatures. PPS affected 25% of "non-paralytic" and 50% of paralytic polio victims. Treatment was rest, speech therapy to assist with breathing, use of braces, crutches, wheelchairs, occupational therapy and non-steroidal anti-inflammatory drugs to ease pain when necessary.

Polio was not so severe in earlier times because of a paradox. Improvements in sanitation, water supplies and sewage disposal resulted in children who were not exposed to the polio virus found in fecal matter. Improvements that had saved them from some childhood diseases made them vulnerable to others.

In the United States, 1952 was the worst year with Public Health Service reporting more than 2,600 cases in a single week. By year's end there were almost 58,000 cases, 3,145 dead and more than 21,000 with disabilities. Later PHS reported that 1.63 million Americans had survived polio, 50,000 out of every 8 million citizens. Because most of the victims were children, parents gave money to institutions trying to combat the crippling illness and doctors, medical research institutions, health organizations worked unstintingly for a cure. For Rotary International the eradication of polio was a cause. Some saw a fortune to be made with a cure, some thought of fame, others were intrigued by the challenge.

By 1977 there were 254,000 Americans who had been paralyzed by polio. Physical therapy gained popularity. Family and friends demanded more governmental consideration for the disabled. But through school vaccination programs polio was slowed and eventually stopped in the United States. The battle moved on to other countries working for total eradication of the disease as had been done by smallpox through the World Health Organization.

Dr. Jonas Salk who sought a career in medical research rather than the more profitable medical practice began search for a cure in

1948 and funded by the National Foundation of Infantile Paralysis assembled a skilled research team. Once he had the vaccine he carefully tested it with the help of 20,000 doctors and Public Health officers, 64,000 school personal and 220,000 volunteers. More than 1,800,000 school children took part. A cure for polio became a national responsibility. News of the vaccine's success was published April 12, 1955. We didn't have children but we intended to and our sigh of gratitude and relief was echoed across the nation.

In 2011, India declared for the past 12 months the country had been "polio free." That leaves three countries that are not yet polio-free, Nigeria, Pakistan and Afghanistan. The World Health Organization says that 2.7 million children have never had polio vaccine. The possibility of a polio epidemic in Nigeria is ever-present. Violence in the north and religious rejection have been problems although Muslim clerics have supported vaccinations.

A Taliban leader in the north-west tribal regions of Pakistan has banned polio vaccines until the US stops its drone attacks in the region. The situation has been exacerbated by the CIA's use of a Pakistani doctor going door to door in Abbottabad offering polio vaccine while gathering evidence that Osama bin Laden was residing nearby. That caused doubt concerning all humanitarian efforts in the region, including Afghanistan where there is a security problem and lack of information regarding the presence or possibility of the vaccine. (*The Guardian* UK 3/2/12 and *India Daily News* US 6/24/12)

Why Profiteering by the Pharmaceutical and Medical Industry is Wrong

Personal Note: Jonas Salk was a national hero and a savior of children around the world. In the 60s we had two daughters and we would have indebted ourselves for life to save them from being crippled or worse. Countless others would have willingly become indentured workers. However, when asked who owned the patent, Salk responded, "There is no patent. Could you patent the sun?" Born of Jewish Russian parents who had little formal education but saw to it that their children were educated, Jonas Salk became the foster parent of children around the world with no thought of the money he could make by withholding the vaccine from the children of the poor.

Thalidomide became a popular "wonder drug" from 1957 to 1961 as a tranquilizer, painkiller, that cured coughs, colds, and prevented morning sickness and insomnia. In 1961 it was withdrawn because a side effect was severe, life-threatening birth defects if taken by pregnant women. More than 10,000 children in 46 countries were born with deformities caused by thalidomide. Before then scientists did not believe any drug could pass to the fetus.

In the United States, Dr. Francis Kelsey, a pharmacologist, refused FDA approval despite pressure from a drug company. That reduced the number of babies born with defects in the US, but millions of samples had been given to doctors as samples to demonstrate its effectiveness as a sedative and to prevent morning sickness. In 1962, Congress required testing for safety during pregnancy before approval of drugs for sale.

Thalidomide can still be used to treat multiple myeloma, leprosy and certain complications of HIV. Women of childbearing age must use birth control or have had a hysterectomy to take the medication. The approval of use for cancer came after 7 years of testing. One drug company used those 7 years to sell their form of thalidomide "off-market" making $300 million a year while the drug was approved only for leprosy.

Feb. 10, 2005, Dr.Sidney Wolfe, editor of Public Citizen Health Letter, testified to the House Health Subcommittee that in 1998, Public Citizen Health Research surveyed FDS medical officers who were the primary reviewers for Drug Education and Research and found that of 53 FDA medical officials 27 thought a drug too dangerous to be approved but it was approved anyway. Seventeen declared the current FDA standards of review "lower" or "much lower" than those in 1995. Several medical officers reported they had been instructed by supervisors to censor their reports.

The FDA investigated the high turnover rates among scientists and physicians in the agency. About one-third of medical officers were not comfortable expressing different scientific opinions, and about the same number believed that decisions adverse to a drug were "stigmatized" by the agency. Several reviewers believed decisions should be based more on science and less on corporate profits, and 18% had felt pressured to recommend drugs despite their concerns about the drug's "safety, efficacy or quality."

March 1997, Rezulin was marketed. December 1997 the drug was withdrawn in the UK after 130 cases of liver damage and 6 deaths. July 1998, the Health Research Group petitioned FDA to ban Rezulin after 260 cases of liver damage and 26 deaths. Rezulin was withdrawn in March 2000 after 63 liver deaths and 7 liver transplants. Dr. Wolfe also mentioned Trovan, Baycol, Crestor, Vioxx, Bextra, Meridia and the 85% decrease from 1998 to 2004 in FDA enforcement actions about illegal prescription drug ads.

According to the Associated Press (7/2/12) GlaxoSmithKline LLC will pay $3 billion and plead guilty to promoting two popular drugs for unapproved uses and for failing to disclose important safety information on a third in the largest health care fraud settlement in US history. "The company's improper marketing included providing doctors with expensive resort vacations, European hunting trips, high-paid speaking tours and even tickets to a Madonna concert." The corporation also agreed to be monitored by government officials for five years to ensure the company's compliance. "For far too long, we have heard that the pharmaceutical industry views these settlements merely as the cost of doing business," Acting Assistant Attorney General Stuart Delery said at the news conference. A recent settlement with Abbott Laboratories also included continuing compliance monitoring.

Pfizer Inc., the world's biggest drugmaker. paid $2.3 billion in criminal and civil fines for improperly marketing 13 different drugs, including Viagra and Lipitor. Pfizer also encouraged doctors to prescribe its drugs with free golf, massages, and junkets to posh resorts. It is illegal to promote uses for a drug that have not been approved by the Food and Drug Administration—a practice known as off-label marketing.

GlaxoSmithKline illegally promoted the drug Paxil for treating depression in children from 1998 to 2003, although the FDA did not approve it for anyone under age 18. The corporation also promoted the drug Wellbutrin off-label although it was approved only for treatment of major depressive disorder. From 2001 to 2007 GlaxoSmithKline failed to report to the FDA on safety data from some post-marketing studies and from two studies of the cardiovascular safety of the diabetes drug Avandia. Since 2007, the FDA has added warnings to the Avandia label about increased risk of congestive heart failure and heart attack. The company also resolved accusations that it paid kickbacks to doctors to prescribe certain drugs.

A three-judge panel of the US Court of Appeals for the Third Circuit ended the practice of brand-name drug companies bribing generic competitors to delay bringing generic drugs to market lowering the price of the medication. The court saw it the way common citizens saw it, as "prima facie evidence of an unreasonable restraint of trade." (*New York Times* 7/18/12)

Dr. Wolfe ended his testimony by discussing medical malpractice and product liability where the costs are high for the alleged victim, and the likelihood of winning is very low compared to other types of tort suits, creating an enormous imbalance in favor of the doctor, hospital, drug company defendant. Dr. Wolfe believed that the legal system should be fair, balanced, and accessible to all Americans.

A woman seriously injured by generic drugs sued the manufacturer over its failure to warn of risks. The manufacturer knew the risks were much greater than when the FDA approved the labeling. When the woman took the drug, the label indicated that the risk of a disorder she developed was 1 in 500. In reality, it was about 1 in 5 patients developing the disorder. Despite mounting evidence none of the companies that manufactured the drug proposed that the FDA modify the label. The five mercenary "justices" on the Supreme Court ruled that the manufacturer was not obliged to seek a change to the labeling even though the manufacturer knew the labeling was wrong. Profits are sacred, lives are not. (People for the American Way, Pliva v. Mensing) (*New York Times* 8/6/12)

HCA, the largest for-profit hospital chain in the country, is confronting evidence of unnecessary cardiac treatments at some of its medical centers in Florida after a nurse's complaint prompted an internal investigation. The inquiry found that the complaint was far from the only evidence that unnecessary—even dangerous—procedures were taking place at some HCA hospitals, driving up costs and increasing profits.

HCA, with 163 facilities, had uncovered evidence as far back as 2002 and as recently as late 2010 showing that some cardiologists at several of its hospitals in Florida were unable to justify many of the procedures they were performing. In some cases, the doctors made misleading statements in medical records that made it appear the procedures were necessary, according to internal reports.

Hinckley Institute of Politics, 3/28/12, reported 700,000 bankruptcies each year are attributable to enormous medical bills, a tragedy unknown throughout the rest of the industrialized world.

Personal Note: In 1971, the book *Our Bodies, Ourselves* argued that profit motivated doctors to give needless hysterectomies when women were dying of preventable or curable diseases. In 1968, in Tennessee I met a young doctor at a party. I asked why he wanted to be a doctor. He said it was because he wanted to make a million dollars by the time he was 30 and he had done that. Even considering that he said "made" rather than "saved" I found that hard to believe and asked how that was possible. He said that if a young woman came to him with a "female complaint" he knew what she wanted was a hysterectomy so that's what he did.

That's anecdotal and probably an exaggeration. Maybe it was a joke, but it reveals the thinking that caused the authors of *Our Bodies, Ourselves* to mention it. Later, visiting a cousin in a small town in West Texas I expressed surprise that such a small town had a doctor and a clinic. Don't go to the doctor, my cousin said. "I believe he has removed the gall bladder of every patient he has had."

Personal Note: In January 2010, my wife had a persistent pain in her hip that made it difficult for her to walk. She saw six specialists, each of whom required his own x-rays and MRIs and performed his specialty, including painful deep shots into her joints and muscles, physical therapy that worsened her symptoms, and back surgery. She was then passed to the next specialist. Over the months she went from a limp, to a cane, to a walker and before Thanksgiving was in a wheelchair.

She went back to the beginning and a doctor examined the numerous x-rays and MRIs and saw a fractured femur that had steadily gotten worse until it was near breaking. I encouraged her to see my physician, took her in her wheelchair to a primary care physician and the doctor had her admitted to emergency. Later, the doctor told us she thought my wife was dying. Her femur was so near breaking that at the hospital they were afraid to move her and brought an x-ray machine to her room and scheduled her for surgery late that evening. Later, the surgeon came and asked if she would mind waiting until morning because he had been in surgery all day and was exhausted. She would rather he be fresh and clear-headed. He would put a metal rod from her hip to her knee the first thing the next morning. He did and after recovery she was able to stand on both feet without pain for the first time since the beginning of the year. Three days later she was in rehab and we celebrated Christmas there. Since then it has been a matter of regaining strength and endurance.

Public safety must partner with profit in the drug and medical industries. Otherwise, there must be stiff regulations with criminal consequences, including jail for those ultimately responsible. Murder for profit is deadlier and more common than murder for hire. Allowing drug companies to charge Medicare higher prices for drugs than some nations pay, and not allowing Medicare to reimport drugs from Canada was another crime by the W. Bush Administration. That corporate "bail out" or hand out has cost lives.

Prevention: Tobacco

Tobacco products cause 438,000 premature deaths every year and are harmful to fetuses. Tobacco corporations profit and taxpayers pick up the tab for those dying a lingering death. Tobacco executives lied to Congress without rebuke and obstructed justice until a whistleblower leaked the information the tobacco companies had kept secret. The Justice Department prosecuted, seeking to reclaim some of the money that taxpayers lavished on the killers courtesy of "their" elected representatives. In 2005, after a nine month trial, appointed "Justice" Department officials overrode the objections of career lawyers running the tobacco racketeering trial. Robert McCullum, who had been partner in a law firm that represented one of the defendants, ordered the lawyers to reduce the penalty for all those years of lies and deaths and handouts by $120 billion. The top lawyers for the trial team warned that it would "create an incentive for defendants to engage in future misconduct by making the misconduct profitable." (*New York Times* 6/16/05) But that was the point.

The leader of the prosecution team stated that W. Bush administration political appointees repeatedly ordered her to take steps that weakened the government's racketeering case, demanded that she and her trial team drop recommendations that tobacco executives be removed from their corporate positions as a possible penalty, instructed her to tell key witnesses to change their testimony, and ordered her to read verbatim a closing argument they had rewritten for her. "I couldn't even look at the judge," she said. US District Judge Gladys Kessler ruled last August that tobacco companies violated civil racketeering laws by conspiring for decades to deceive the public about the dangers of their product.(*Washington Post* 3/22/07)

Millions of deaths for profit but not one day in jail, courtesy of a "pro-life" administration.

Hospital Dumping

The 20th Century showed little change from 19th Century racial discrimination in health care. Civil Rights activists understandably distrusted giving states control over the health of people of color. Some states maintained separate hospitals with no access to black people who lived far from concentrated black populations. Blacks also distrusted insurance companies that had a history of "redlining" black people, knowing that few had the money or the time to fight discrimination in white courts that were also discriminatory.

In 1946, Congress passed the Hill-Burton Act that provided federal grants and federal loans to improve America's hospitals. Hospitals that received funding were not permitted to discriminate on the basis of race, color, national origin, or creed but did allow "separate but equal facilities" in the same area. That segregation was struck down by the Supreme Court in 1963. The hospitals were required to provide a "reasonable volume" of free care to residents who needed care but could not pay for it. The bill also required proof of the economic viability of the locale meaning that most hospitals receiving the grants were in middle-class areas. When Medicare and Medicaid became available the hospitals were required to participate in them.

There was no definition of "reasonable volume" of free care and some hospitals did not provide any. In 1973, the bill was supposed to expire but was extended for an additional year because of complaints and lawsuits by the poor. In 1975, the Act became Title XVI of the Public Health Service Act changing the 20-year commitment to perpetuity and defined reasonable volume.

Despite Title XVI and Medicare and Medicaid, in 1971, "hospital dumping" in Chicago gained public notice. Hospitals, usually private ones, transfered patients who were uninsured or could not pay to another hospital, usually a public one. Stories about hospital dumping became common as did such transfers of the sick and dying to another hospital that sent them to yet another hospital until they went home unaided or died of iteration.

The Reagan administration rolled back federal funding for public health and other social programs. Federal block grants to the states went to state health agencies leaving them to manage Medicaid programs and health care for the uninsured and the indigent. Cuts to other social programs led to increased poverty, teen pregnancy, family violence, and homeless people, including veterans.

In 1985, Congress passed COBRA that required most hospital to provide an examination and needed stabilizing treatment, without consideration of insurance coverage or ability to pay, when a patient came to an emergency room for attention to an emergency medical condition or to a woman in labor.

In 1986, Congress enacted the Emergency Medical Treatment and Active Labor Act (EMTALA) to sharpen COBRA's fangs. The new law applied to all people not only the poor, and to all hospitals that participated in Medicare. It was passed, in part, because most state tort law did not cover failure to treat. However, for personal injury EMTALA permitted only those damages available under the law of the state in which the hospital was located. In many states "tort reform" bills were being planned to take away the right of a citizen to sue doctors and/or hospitals by making the award, if successful, so small no lawyer could profitably pursue the case.

By 1988, almost three-quarters of all state and local health department funding went to personal health services. 1989, In a letter to the editor of the American Journal of Public Health, Drs. Kellerman and Hackman wrote that the "growing competition in the health care marketplace, federal and state efforts at cost containment, and rising numbers of uninsured patients are threatening the solvency of public and private hospitals alike."

1991, the Journal of the National Medical Association discussed the uninsured population and "patient dumping," the transfer of a patient from a private hospital to a public hospital because of the patient's lack of insurance or inability to pay. The article highlighted the need for reform of the American health care system and suggested the Canadian health system as an alternative model.

Hospital dumping included homeless dumping. Hospital personnel left homeless patients, some mentally ill, on the street rather than placing them with a relative or in a shelter. Some of those dumped returned to life on the street, others didn't know how to live on their own. Some of the mentally ill could not find an institution that had a place for them.

As late as 2006, AP reported that authorities in Los Angeles were investigating suspected dumping of the homeless on Skid Row after ambulances left five people there. In 2007, AP reported that a hospital van left a homeless paraplegic in a soiled hospital gown with a broken colostomy bag.

> *Personal Note:* Jean and I know a young woman who has a persistent health problem but is not financially able to buy insurance. For treatment she has to go to emergency four or five times a year. On one occasion in 2011, she was discharged although she was not well enough to go home alone. She fainted at a bus stop while waiting for a bus to her neighborhood, was picked up by an ambulance, taken back to the same hospital and taxpayers paid several thousand dollars more. With Obamacare, if a citizen goes to emergency for temporary treatment and has to return within 30 days for addition treatment of the same problem the hospital will have to pay a fine. If the fine is stiff enough and is enforced hospital dumping may end, along with procedures to end repeated treatment of a recurrent medical problem.

Prevention: Chemical

In 1910, Congress enacted the first pesticide legislation to protect farmers and consumers from adulterated products. Chemical research and development during World War II discovered new pesticides. After the war the use of pesticides exploded. Federal laws did not cover environmental damage or human health risks. In 1947, Congress passed a new insecticide act to address those problems, giving the

Department of Agriculture responsibility for regulation. Later, authority to control pesticides was given to the EPA. The law has been amended many times to deal with the increasing number of pesticides, the increasing volume of pesticides, and increasing knowledge of the effects of pesticides.

In 1976 Congress passed the Toxic Substances Control Act (TSCA) regulating new and existing chemicals, specifically PCB. Manufacturers must notify the EPA before making or importing chemicals not on the TSCA inventory if they are to be used for commercial purposes. EPA shares this control with the Federal Food, Drug and Cosmetic Act.

Superfund is the common name for the Comprehensive Environmental Response, Compensation, and Liability Act of 1980 (CERCLA), a federal law designed to clean up sites contaminated with hazardous substances such as Love Canal in New York and Valley of the Drums in Kentucky. The law authorized EPA to identify parties responsible for contamination of sites and compel the parties to clean up the sites. Where responsible parties cannot be found, the Agency is authorized to clean up sites itself, using a special trust fund. The EPA published the first Hazard Ranking System in 1981, and the first National Priorities List in 1982. Superfund was ineffective during the Reagan administration. During his two terms, only 16 of the 799 Superfund sites were cleaned up, and $40 million of $700 million in recoverable funds from responsible parties were collected.

The day after the World Trade Center collapse, a top federal scientist warned in a strongly worded memo against the quick reoccupation of buildings in lower Manhattan because of possible dangers from asbestos and other toxic materials in response to a White House request for a health advisory. "We are concerned about even being asked to write a document for the public about reentry at this point. Does this mean that unrestricted access to the WTC vicinity is imminent?"

The EPA's inspector general revealed in 2003 that the W. Bush White House rewrote early agency press releases to downplay environmental hazards and put Wall Street back in business selling toxic assets that wrecked the economy. Six days after 9/11 federal and city officials allowed thousands of people to return to their homes and workplaces in lower Manhattan, while rescue and firefighting operations continued in a sharply restricted zone around Ground Zero.

The EPA had analyzed dust samples in lower Manhattan and one-third showed asbestos levels higher than the agency's 1% danger threshold. Doctors reported that one-third of nearly 7,000 Ground Zero workers at Mount Sinai were still experiencing health problems related to their work at the site. (*New York Daily News* 10/28/03)

On May 8, 2012, *The New York Times* reported that a senior EPA chemist who argued that she was removed from her job in retaliation for accusing the agency of underestimating the toxicity of dust at ground zero has been reinstated with back pay by an administrative board. The chemist sued under the federal Whistle-Blower Protection Act, saying she was being punished for charging that the agency had relied on data that it knew mismeasured the pH levels of the dust released by the World Trade Center collapse in 2001.

Exposure to lead paint threatens the health of 1.4 million American kids every year. Safety regulations were supposed to be in place in 2005 but the EPA secretly delayed the requirement. EPA spokeswoman Eryn Witcher said the agency had not abandoned the possibility of issuing mandatory regulations but was exploring voluntary alternatives that might be more effective, as well as less costly. Complying with the regulations would cost industries between $1.7 billion and $3.1 billion a year. However, an agency estimate shows implementing lead-paint regulations would provide health benefits from $2.7 billion to $4.2 billion annually. (*Los Angeles Times* 5-10-05) That wasn't enough public health benefit for the loss of profits to private pockets.

After Katrina, toxic chemicals in the New Orleans flood waters will make the city unsafe for full human habitation for a decade, a US government official said (*The Independent* UK 9/11/05). New Orlean's "Cancer Alley" of 66 chemical plants, refineries and petroleum storage depots pump out 600 million pounds of toxic waste each year. Other dangerous substances are in storage tanks or at the port of New Orleans. "No one knows how much pollution has escaped through damaged plants and leaking pipes into the toxic gumbo now drowning the city and no one is trying to find out." The water being pumped out of the city was not being tested for pollution and would damage Lake Pontchartrain and the Mississippi river, and endanger people using it downstream. EPA's budget had been cut and "inept political hacks" had been put in key positions.

Those who escaped death in Katrina faced new hazards posed by their government: high levels of formaldehide in trailers provided by FEMA. A study by the Lawrence Berkeley National Laboratory appear to confirm the role that "manufacturers' practices and weak federal regulation played in the public health disaster." (*Washington Post* 7/3/08)

While the power-plant industry is raking in the benefits of the White House mercury policy, children are not so lucky. Mercury, a toxic metal, can cause neurological damage in children, especially newborns. [In 2004], a scientific study found nearly one out of every six pregnant women had mercy levels higher than danger level. (*Washington Post* 4/24/05)

Contaminants and waste products that once spewed through the coal plants' smokestacks are now captured as solid waste, kept in huge piles near cities like Pittsburgh, St. Louis, Tampa and on the shores of Lake Erie, Lake Michigan and the Mississippi River. Studies have shown that the ash can leach toxic substances that can cause cancer, birth defects and other health problems in humans, and can decimate fish, bird and frog populations in and around ash dumps. (*New York Times* 1/6/09)

The coal ash pond that ruptured and sent a billion gallons of toxic sludge across 300 acres of East Tennessee was only one of more than 1,300 similar dumps across the United States. Most of them are unregulated and unmonitored and contain billions of gallons of fly ash and other byproducts of burning coal. These dumps, which reach up to 1,500 acres, contain arsenic, lead, mercury and selenium, that the EPA considers a threat to water supplies and human health. Yet they are not subject to federal regulation and there is little monitoring of their effects on the environment. In 2007, according to a coal industry estimate, 50 tons of fly ash went to agricultural uses, like improving soil's ability to hold water, despite warnings about high levels of arsenic.

A 2005 study by the Center for Health, Environment & Justice looking at just four states—Massachusetts, New York, New Jersey and Michigan—found 500,000 children attending schools within half a mile of known toxic dumps. The 99th Street Elementary was built on top of 20,000 tons of industrial waste. Elementary school children played with ooze such as Lindane and phosphorous rocks bubbling up on the playground. "When you threw (the phosphorous rocks) at a hard surface, they would explode like a firecracker." Some of the children were badly burned. Only seven states have laws preventing building schools on or near toxic waste where land is cheaper. (CNN 8-22-08)

The Independent (UK) reported that industrial chemicals are damaging the intellectual potential of the next generation and may increase the incidence of conditions such as Parkinson's disease. Scientists from the Harvard School of Public Health say at least 202 chemicals are known to damage the brain and their effects at low levels of exposure are unknown. Fetuses and children are exposed when the chemicals seep into ground water, are carried in air or contaminate food.

April 2, 2007, the Supreme Court ruled that the EPA had to decide immediately if it was going to regulate carbon dioxide emissions. One year later, EPA still delayed implementation. Seventeen states filed suit against the EPA for flouting the Supreme Court's ruling. The lawsuit seeks to compel the EPA to act within 60 days. Other states intend to sue the EPA "if it does not act soon to reduce pollution from ships, aircraft and off-road vehicles." (Think Progress 4-02-08)

March 2006 a British Petroleum pipeline ruptured in Alaska's North Slope spilling 267,000 gallons of crude oil across frozen tundra, the second largest spill in Alaska's history. The spill went undetected for nearly a week because the leak detection equipment, that employees had warned BP managers about, malfunctioned. Scott West, special agent-in-charge at the EPA Criminal Investigation Division, who had been probing alleged crimes committed by BP and the company's senior officials, was confident that the thousands of hours he invested in the criminal investigation would result in felony charges.

BP and senior executives received advanced warnings from dozens of employees who worked at its Prudhoe Bay facility that unless immediate steps were taken to repair the severely corroded pipeline, a disaster on par with that of the 1989 Exxon Valdez spill was only a matter of time. West was also told the pipeline was going to rupture six months before it happened. The Justice Department shut down his investigation into BP in August 2007 and gave the company a "slap on the wrist" for environmental crimes that should have sent some BP executives to jail. BP, which reported net profits of about $17.2 billion in 2007, paid a fine of $20 million that was more encouragement to ignore regulations than a deterrent.

Chuck Hamel, an oil industry watchdog, operates Anwrnews. com, "established by and for the many concerned Prudhoe Bay

BP operators who fear for their lives and the environment due to violations of government regulations and requirements by BP." One letter expressed concern about safety and maintenance issues because of "inadequate staffing." The employee wrote, "We had suffered a major fire, which burned a well pad module to the ground and nearly cost one of our operators his life. We had suffered two job fatalities and a third serious injury to personnel in the months before the letter was sent." BP failed to do internal inspection by sending electronic monitors through the pipeline to detect defects. BP had not conducted such an inspection for eight years and ignored and or retaliated against employees who suggested the company do so. West's last statement was that BP did what corporations do. "It was the government that let us down." (Jason Leopold, truthout 5/19/10)

Econowatch.org revealed that in September 2008, nearly two years before the Deepwater Horizon blowout in the Gulf of Mexico, a BP rig had blown out in the Caspian Sea. BP concealed the information from US regulators and Congress, but Chevron, Exxon and the W. Bush State Department knew. Had they not concealed the facts the Deepwater Horizon blowout might not have occurred. One of the classified government documents revealed by wikileaks.org was a cable from Bill Schrader, President of BP, to the US Embassy. The cable stated that the September 17 shutdown was the largest emergency evacuation in BP history. "Given the explosive potential, BP was quite fortunate to have been able to evacuate everyone safely and to prevent any gas ignition...Due to the blowout of a gas-injection well there was 'a lot of mud' on the platform." The cement that failed had been mixed with nitrogen to speed drying, a risk process that was repeated on Deepwater Horizon.

Robert F. Kennedy Jr., senior attorney for Natural Resources Defense Council, calls the concealment of this information, "criminal. We have laws that make it illegal to hide this." Cables reveal that BP's oil-company partners, Chevron and Exxon, also concealed the information from Congress, regulators and the Securities Exchange Commission. The State Department was involved because BP's US partners and the Azerbaijani government were losing $50 million a day because the platform was shut down. The Embassy cabled Washington that BP's partners were upset because BP was limiting information to them.

Kennedy was concerned by the connivance of the State Department, headed by Secretary of State Condoleezza Rice. "BP felt comfortable—and Chevron and Exxon—in informing the Bush State Department, which was run by Condoleezza Rice, and they felt comfortable that that wasn't going to come out." The US Securities Exchange Commission requires companies to report "material" events. BP filed a statement that contradicted the statements of three eyewitnesses and the secret statement of BP's Azerbaijan President in the WikiLeaks cable. "The three big actors, Chevron, Exxon and BP all concealed this from the American public," concluded Kennedy. "This is a criminal activity."

Why would the Azerbaijan government cover up a disaster? According to an insider, Les Abrahams, it has to do with at least $75 million in bribes that he paid to Azeri officials in Baku. Abrahams was a BP executive in Baku in the 1990s working simultaneously, at BP's insistence, with MI6, British intelligence. Greg Palast met with Abrahams in London who said he was joined in his payoff runs by BP's CEO and Chairman Lord Browne who insisted on handing over a "sweetener" himself. At the time, unlike US law, Britain had not made bribery of foreign officials a crime. gregpalast.com/Guardian.co.UK

> *Personal Note:* Jason Leopold and Greg Palast are in my opinion the best investigative reporters in America. They are so good that they don't work for major American media because they investigate stories that the military/industrial/ media complex does not want reported. Greg Palast, who has written two best-seller exposes, *Armed Madhouse* and *The Best Democracy Money Can Buy*, received the George Orwell Courage in Journalism Award for his BBC documentary "Bush Family Fortunes." The controversial Jason Leopold is lead investigative reporter for Truthout.

The Senate approved trade sanctions against Burma but dropped efforts to eliminate a big tax break to Chevron because of its ties to the repressive military junta. Ecuador has sued Chevron for dumping toxic waste in Ecuador's rain forest. "Activists have described the disaster as an Amazon Chernobyl." A court-appointed expert recommended that Chevron pay $16 billion to clean up the mess. Chevron has asked Bush to punish Ecuador if they do not drop the lawsuit. (Newsweek 8-3-08)

For more than seven months, the Center for Disease Control and Prevention blocked the publication of an exhaustive federal study of environmental hazards in the eight Great Lakes states, because it found "low birth weights, elevated rates of infant mortality and premature births, and elevated death rates from breast cancer, colon cancer, and lung cancer." (Center for Public Integrity 2-7-08)

According to new research from the the National Birth Defects Prevention Study, working pregnant women who are exposed on the job to toxins known as polycyclic aromatic hydrocarbons (PAHs) are more likely to have children with gastroschisis, a rare birth defect in which the intestines stick out from the baby's body, generally requiring surgical repair. The researchers noted, "assessing workplace exposure to PAHs is important because 'more than 95% of employed women in the US remain employed during pregnancy' and 'an increasing number of women are being exposed in their jobs to chemicals that can harm the fetus.'" The researchers especially noted exposures among women working as "cashiers in fast food restaurants." PAH causes health problems that can shape a person's life from developmental disabilities to childhood obesity to behavioral issues such as anxiety or attention problems that could impact cognitive development and ability to learn. "The ramifications of toxic childhood environments are a global issue."

The New York Times (5/20/12). The area around Treece and the neighboring town, Picher, was the No. 1 producer of zinc and lead in the country in the 1920s, supplying metal for most of the ammunition in World Wars I and II. Thousands of people from the Ozarks flocked to the two towns to work the mines. By 1981, when the Environmental Protection Agency ranked the area as the most contaminated in the country, only a few hundred people remained. By 2010, Picher had been abandoned almost entirely, and only 170 residents still lived in Treece.

The Treece area is dotted with toxic towers of contaminated stone, that reach heights of 200 feet. The dust contains enough metal that it gave young children in Treece blood-lead levels three times higher than the national average. Tar Creek in Treece is the color of orange juice, and it smells like vinegar. When the mining companies left, they shut off the pumps that kept abandoned shafts from filling with groundwater. Once water flooded the tunnels, it picked up all the trace minerals underground—iron, lead and zinc—and flushed them into rivers and streams. Another problem in Treece is that the ground keeps caving in. In 1966, a 300-foot-wide, 200-foot-deep abyss swallowed up the road out on the edge of town. Somehow no one died. "I don't want to scare you," Treece's mayor at the time, Bill Blunk, told Enzinna in 2010, "but we're literally standing over our graves right now."

The Environmental Protection Agency put Treece on its inventory of the most environmentally devastated places in the country and, along with the Kansas Department of Health and Environment, approved a plan to use $3.5 million to get every resident to abandon the town. The KDHE hired wrecking crews to demolish the last few buildings in town. Among other concerns, they feared meth dealers would set up labs in empty homes, which is what happened years earlier when Picher was abandoned. In April 2012, officials gave up on their plan to turn Treece into a wildlife preserve because the Kansas Department of Wildlife wasn't interested in taking over the land. One employee said, "That land is inadequate for supporting wildlife, or, from what I hear, any other kind of life."

Dec. 19, 2011, the medical journal "Gut" released a study showing that after controlling for age, sex, smoking, diabetes and other factors, scientists found that the subjects with the highest levels of arsenic were at twice the risk for pancreatic cancer, compared with those with the lowest concentrations. Those with high levels of cadmium were at three times the risk for pancreatic cancer, while those with the highest levels of lead were at six times the risk.

The New York Times (5/8/12). The Ecology Center, a nonprofit environmental organization that reviews consumer products, released a study at the website HealthyStuff.org on potentially hazardous chemicals in gardening tools. The group tested nearly 200 gardening products, including hoses, gloves, kneeling pads and tools, for lead, cadmium, bromine, chlorine, phthalates and bisphenol A. Over all, they found that two-thirds of the products tested contained levels of one or more chemicals in excess of standards set for other consumer products. For example, 30% of all products tested, because kids are going to be playing with them, contained lead exceeding the standard for children's products.

The research team left a section of garden hose filled with water out in the sun over multiple days. When the water was tested it was found to exceed federal standards for safe drinking water for several chemicals—including four times the standard considered safe for phthalates, 18 times that for lead and 20 times that for BPA. Unlike residential plumbing fixtures, which must comply with the Safe Drinking Water Act, the brass fittings on hoses are not regulated, even though 30 percent of those tested in the study were found to exceed safety limits for lead.

By 1991, it had been apparent for more than twenty years that insecticides and herbicides were contaminating the land and the water supply. The government could have shifted big agriculture companies from these dangerous and unnatural chemicals. Instead Big Ag genetically modified seed to make it resistant to an herbicide, Roundup, that would destroy every living plant around it except the seed plants owned by the corporation that formulated Roundup. Monsanto aggressively pursued royalty payments from anyone who had those genetically modified plants in their fields, no matter how they got there, and even if the farmer didn't want them there. Jane Smiley

The *Washington Post* (7/2/12) reported that according to the Centers for Disease Control, about two million people acquire bacterial infections in US hospitals each year. Approximately 70% of those are resistant to at least one antibiotic and antibiotic resistance is increasing. The FDA, the CDC, the American Academy of Pediatrics, and the American Medical Association have noted the link between non-therapeutic uses of antibiotics in food animals and the crisis of antibiotic resistance in humans. Yet the FDA, the federal agency in charge of safeguarding the public health, has done little to protect us although the CDC has stated that antibiotic use in animals has directly led to the emergence of resistant bacteria. The CDC also states that antibiotic resistance in the United States costs an estimated $20 billion a year in excess health care costs, $35 million in other societal costs and more than 8 million additional days that people spend in the hospital. Yet, beef and drug producers oppose regulation.

"A federal judge said the FDA had done "shockingly little" to address the human health risks of antibiotic use in animal feed." (Reuters 6/5/12)

2012, A federal appeals court overturned the Environmental Protection Agency's effort to reduce emissions of dangerous chemicals from coal-burning power plants. The US Court of Appeals for the D.C. Circuit struck down the EPA's Cross-State Air Pollution Rule, which would have sharply limited emissions of sulfur dioxide and nitrogen oxide at plants in 28 states. The EPA estimated the rules could save up to 34,000 lives per year and result in tens of billions of dollars in health benefits. After a major campaign by utilities and corporate groups, the appeals court ruled 2 to 1 that the regulations exceed the EPA's authority.

Is such neglect of public welfare benign or malignant?

Unborn US babies are soaking in a stew of chemicals, including mercury, according to a report by the Environmental Working Group based on tests of umbilical cord blood that reflects what the mother passes to the baby through the placenta. "Of the 287 chemicals we detected in umbilical cord blood, we know that 180 cause cancer in humans or animals, 217 are toxic to the brain and nervous system, and 208 cause birth defects or abnormal development in animal tests," the report said. A Government Accountability Office report said the Environmental Protection Agency does not have the powers it needs to fully regulate toxic chemicals. (Reuters 7/14/05)

In 2012, Republican candidates running for the Republican presidential nomination vowed to reduce the power or eliminate EPA. They also vowed they were "pro-life." Fact-check please.

Epidemic: HIV/AIDS

AIDS in America may have begun as early as 1969. By the late 70s and early 80s, doctors were aware of men dying of diseases that should not have been deadly. Doctors began to associate the illness to gay men. By 1982, doctors knew that the disease was not restricted to gay men. It also appeared in women, drug users, those who had received blood transfusions, and babies. Despite recommendations from the Centers for Disease Control, to avoid blood shortages the Red Cross and other blood banks did not ban bisexual and gay men from donating blood.

The early association with homosexuality caused a stigma that the disease still carries. Some declared that it was a God-given pox on abominable homosexuals and they were not to be helped or pitied. They were to be condemned by the righteous and God would rid the world of the homosexual lifestyle forever.

> *Personal Note:* God had never done that before, but now the Almighty was going to do it for the pleasure of the "Religious" Right.

Although doctors, scientists and other health-workers recommended condoms to lessen risk, some religious groups wanted to deny gays condoms and sterile needles. "Let them die," they chanted.

It was God's will. Charles Stanley, pastor of the First Baptist Church of Atlanta and associated with the Moral Majority, preached that HIV/AIDS was God's punishment for homosexuality. Such statements influenced right wing attitudes toward HIV/AIDS. That opposition still exists and in some ways is stronger than ever.

In 1982, a man was arrested in his Atlanta bedroom for engaging in oral sex with another man. The same year the Centers for Disease Control (CDC) in Atlanta announced that AIDS was an epidemic. A reporter asked a White House spokesperson about Reagan's reaction to the announcement. The spokesperson replied, "What's AIDS?" When asked if anyone in the White House knew that the CDC had declared an epidemic in America, the answer was, "I don't think so." The silence of the government spurred gay activists into action.

The government failed to respond to the epidemic but non-governmental organizations (NGOs) had. In 1982, the NGO Gay Men's Health Crisis published 50,000 copies of a newsletter about AIDS and sent them to doctors, hospitals and the Library of Congress. The CDC found that AIDS was not restricted to gays. By the end of 1983, 1,292 people had died.

Despite bigotry on the part of many and Georgia's law against sodomy, in 1985 Evangelical Outreach Ministries, a synagogue and other religious organizations served the gay community in Atlanta. The AIDS National Interfaith Network declared itself to be "the AIDS people to the religious community and the religious people to the AIDS community." By 1985, the largest NGO serving gays was the religious community.

In 1985 the first blood test to identify antibodies to HIV became commercially available for use in blood transfusion centers. Later, Reagan publicly mentioned AIDS for the first time to announce that AIDS had been one of the top priorities. However, he refused to talk about safe sex or the use of condoms. His plan was to stop immigrants with AIDS from entering the country. He also advocated sexual abstinence. Both gays and non-gays joked that was easier at his age. Movie star Rock Hudson died from AIDS.

In 1986, the Surgeon General issued the government's first statement regarding prevention of AIDS. He recommended parents talk to their children. Heat treatment was used to kill HIV in blood used in transfusions. Half of all hemophiliacs in American were infected with AIDS. The Supreme Court upheld Georgia's law against sodomy, reinforcing the belief of many that the government was going to do nothing about a spreading epidemic.

1987, Reagan gave his first "major speech" on AIDS, calling it "public enemy number one." He was criticized for doing nothing except opposing AIDS. V.P. George H. Bush was ridiculed when he called for mandatory HIV testing.

Clinical trials of AZT demonstrated that the drug could slow the attack of HIV. In 1987, the FDA approved AZT as treatment for AIDS but anger was growing over the length of time it took to get access to AIDS drugs. J. B. Stoner, a white supremacist, led a mob passing out "Praise God for AIDS" tracts. Act-UP, a gay rights advocacy group picketed Wall Street demanding a national policy to end the epidemic. 1988, ACT-UP returned to Wall Street. In 1989, the Secretary of Health announced a turning point to change AIDS "from a fatal disease to a treatable one." The results from clinical trials of ACTGO showed the drug could slow the process from AIDS to HIV.

The celebration was short-lived. The drug cost $7,000 a year. Many suffering from AIDS had already been dropped from health insurance rolls, and most others did not have insurance that would cover the price. The joy quickly turned to anger in the belief that the drug company was profiteering from suffering and death. ACT-UP members chained themselves to the VIP balcony at the New York Stock Exchange protesting the price. The drug company cut the price by 20%.

In 1989, Act-Up disrupted a mass at St.Patrick's Cathedral in New York, and threw condoms to the worshipers to protest the Catholic church's stand against AIDS education and condom distribution. The Vatican did not change its opinion. Use of condoms to stop a deadly epidemic and save lives might prevent the birth of an unwanted child.

"Stop the Church," a documentary about the protest, scheduled to air nationally on PBS, was canceled.

By 1993, AIDS was the fourth leading cause of death among women between 25-44 years old. One to two thousand children were infected with HIV each year through their mother. In 1994, the CDC promoted condom use to prevent spread of the epidemic. Such information angered many who did not want their children knowing about such things. It was an epidemic from which they believed they were immune and they didn't want to pay for prevention or treatment. Some of them believed that it was God's punishment of the wicked and it was sinful to try to prevent it or treat it. Others believed use of condoms to save your or someone else's life was wicked.

> *Personal Note:* My congressional "representative" said that the information about prevention was "an insult to the taxpayers who will be forced to pay for something they find personally and morally offensive." That may have been the beginning of the mantra, "let them die," that became popular when Congress tried to make health care available for everyone. National collaboration on anything, a feeling of national togetherness, became a relic of the past lost in the me-ism of the 80s.

In 1995, the CDC declared that AIDS was the leading cause of deaths of all Americans between the ages of 25-44, with more than half a million cases reported to the CDC, more than half of whom had died.

In 1996, California and Arizona voters passed referendums allowing for the medical use of marijuana; 34,947 Americans died of AIDS that year. The epidemic was noticeably high in racial and ethnic minorities because few had health insurance or could afford treatment.

In 2001, nearly 775,000 cases of AIDS had been reported to the CDC, resulting in 448,060 deaths. The rate of infection did not decline despite new drugs. The rate of deaths did decline leaving more people to require treatment and spread the illness. More prevention became imperative. One church's fear of condoms denied freedom of religion to others and promoted sickness and death for victims of AIDS.

In 2006, the Ryan White HIV/AIDS Program was reauthorized providing federal funding for Americans unable to pay for their treatment. Ryan White was expelled from school because he had been infected with AIDS by blood transfusion and parents did not want their children around anyone who might have the disease. The reauthorization also was controversial because 5 new cities were added as recipients of funding without an increase in financing, and funds were shifted to rural areas and the South cutting funding where the epidemic had started, San Francisco and New York.

On July 13, 2010 the White House released the National HIV/AIDS Strategy (NHAS). This ambitious plan is the nation's first-ever comprehensive coordinated HIV/AIDS roadmap with clear and measurable targets to be achieved by 2015. The United States will become a place where new HIV infections are rare and when they do occur, every person regardless of age, gender, race/ethnicity, sexual orientation, gender identity or socio-economic circumstance, will have unfettered access to high quality, life-extending care, free from stigma and discrimination.

Prevention: Radioactive Uranium

For 40 years nothing was done to control nuclear waste that was placed in different kinds of temporary storage despite its radioactivity that had a half-life of danger of more than a million years. Nothing else that humans have made has lasted half that half-life but nuclear plants were running out of storage.

In 1982, the Nuclear Waste Policy Act wrote a timetable and procedure for permanent storage of radioactive waste by mid 1990. The act permitted state governments to veto a waste facility in their state unless Congress voted to override the veto in a battle over states rights.

The Department of Energy (DOE) was tasked with constructing, operating and closing the facility. The EPA was tasked with creating public health and safety standards for releases of radioactive material from storage. The Nuclear Regulatory Commission was tasked with publicizing regulations governing the facility. The Office of Civilian Radioactive Waste Management was created in the Department of Energy to execute the plan.

The DOE was required to recommend three sites to the president in 1985, along with a statement of environmental impact on each site. The president was to recommend one site for the first storage facility in 1987 and for a second facility in 1990. The act also required the federal government to take responsibility of the nuclear waste at the reactor, transport it to the storage site and be married to it happily ever after.

December 1987, Congress designated Yucca Mountain, Nevada to be the permanent storage facility for all nuclear waste. The plan was added to the 1988 federal budget. In 2002 the Secretary of DOE recommended the Yucca site and President W. Bush approved. Nevada vetoed the plan but the veto was overridden by Congress. In 2004, the Court of Appeals upheld Nevada's veto because the plan for 10,000 year storage did not meet the recommendation of storage for 1 million years.

2012 After $30 billion the Yucca Mountain project has been removed from the budget. Radioactive waste is still in temporary storage. Nuclear power plants are still being built with no plans for what to do with the waste.

March 11, 2011 and days following there were earthquakes, a tsunami and meltdowns at 3 nuclear reactors in Japan. News reports following the events tended to blend them so that many people believe that the tsunami caused the meltdown and that Japan is the only place where a tsunami could cause a meltdown. The Japanese Nuclear Industrial Safety Agency warned that Tokyo Electrical Power Company (TEPCO) had failed to inspect recirculation pumps and other critical equipment. TEPCO was ordered to inspect and repair them but there is no record that TEPCO had done that.

Missing from the story was evidence that GE's Mark 1 Boiling Water reactors are defective. According to UK's Independent, GE knew they were defective when they were sold to Japan. Workers at the stricken plant, who had been ordered to evacuate after the earthquake, saw pipes "bursting and buckling." One worker believed that they were cold water pipes and that if enough coolant didn't reach the reactor it would melt down. Radiation leaked from the plant. A radiation alarm, a mile from the reactor, went off eight minutes before the tsunami hit the plant.

The meltdown at the reactors resulted in several hydrogen explosions creating an exclusion zone more than 17 times the size of Manhattan Island that will remain uninhabitable for 100,000 years. There are 23 GE Mark I Boiling Water Reactors in the US. Some of them are located on geological fault lines. Before Kukushima two of them had reported serious loss of coolant.

Knowing that Japan desperately needed Bechtel pumps to cool down the reactors and spent fuel, and maybe save lives, Bechtel raised the price of the pumps from $700,000 to $10 million. If you can't profit from a disaster or a war you're not an American capitalist. (This and much other information in this section is from *Devil's Tango: How I Learned the Fukushima Step by Step* by Cecile Pineda, Wings Press, 2012)

Soon doctors began seeing symptoms in children, nosebleeds, diarrhea, and flu-like illness. By late March 45% of children living near the facility were suffering low-level radiation. Children are more susceptible than adults and the radiation gets into their genitals causing genetic diseases like diabetes, cystic fibrosis and mental retardation passed from parents to children forever.

According to the *Christian Science Monitor*, in 1972 an official with the Atomic Energy Commission, wrote a memo that said the Mark 1's smaller containment design was more susceptible to explosion. In 1976 three design engineers at GE resigned because they believed the Mark 1 design was so flawed it could lead to a "devastating accident." (*New York Times*) In 1980, the NRC stated that the containment design was safe. In 1986, the director of NRC's Office of Nuclear Reactor Regulation said he had lost confidence in the Mark 1 design.

In 2011, about three months after the Fukushima disaster the Associated Press concluded a year-long investigation of US nuclear plants that were designed to be shut down after 40 years. AP reported that the NRC and the nuclear industry Regulators and the nuclear industry had rewritten the standards so the plants could continue to operate.

Japanese officials assessed the accident as Level 4 on the International Nuclear Event Scale. Since then the level has been raised to 7, the maximum level. The Chief Cabinet Secretary announced that the plant will be decommissioned.

Radiation blew out to sea which was lucky for Tokyo and Japan but unlucky for the United States and Canada. By June, 2011, The Center for Disease Control reported that infant mortality had risen 35% in 8 northwestern cities. May, 2012 Fukushima radiation was found in seafood off the US west coast. July, 2012 small "buckyballs" were found on California beaches. According to the University of California, Davis, the uranium filled nanospheres were "created from the millions of tons of fresh and salt water used to try to cool down the three molten cores of the stricken reactors." The balls were reported by EnviroReporter.com as being able to move quickly through water without disintegration.

> *Personal Note:* If you're old enough you may remember how far Japan seemed from the US when the Army, Navy, Air Force and Marines were fighting for footholds from which to launch attacks on other footholds until the US military could stage for an invasion of Japan. The distance is not nearly so far for radiation.
>
> My wife and I visited the Chernobyl Museum in Kiev, Ukraine. Chernobyl itself is deadly and will remain so for millenniums. There were pictures of the families who lived near the plant and pictures after they left hurriedly leaving tricycles, stuffed animals, clothing, furniture behind. The

Soviet government had lied about the incident until the news appeared in *The New York Times*. There was a copy of *The New York Times* headlining the news in the Museum.

There were also stories of the deaths of the helicopter crews that dumped cement on the facility to contain it, and of the raw military recruits who were brought in to bury the facility without knowing the risks.

Most interesting were two survivors—one an engineer, one a fireman. Both knew the danger. The engineer said that when he heard the alarm he thought, "This is the end of the world. I must do something to stop it." The fireman also rushed to the scene knowing he must do whatever he could. Both went through years of radiation treatment but managed to survive although thousands farther from the accident didn't. Scientists are studying them and their children hoping to find something that might enable others to survive future accidents.

That appears to be the best hope for all of us. A few survivors, a tiny remnant, will remain. No doubt there will be mutations. No one seems to be sure what they will be. A superhuman race? Mute beasts who can no longer stand erect?

Bombs, missiles, artillery shells, tank shells contain high amounts of radioactive uranium, usually depleted uranium (DU). The three-week Persian Gulf War caused 467 wounded American soldiers out of 580,400 who served. Nine years later, 11,000 were dead and 325,000 were on permanent disability. The second war on Iraq was much longer with more use of DU weapons that leave uranium dust when fired and when exploded. When inhaled, it goes into the body and stays there. It has a half-life of 4.5 billion years. That dust has now been blowing around Iraq for more than 20 years, a danger to soldiers who are deployed there for a year or more, and Iraqi citizens, especially children, who will breathe it for the rest of their lives.

Depleted Uranium targets DNA

In 2004 American Free Press reported that 8 out of 20 men who served in W. Bush's 2003 war on Iraq now have malignancies, 40% in 16 months. And they bring DU home. It has been found in their urine and semen. Some women who were sexual partners of veterans of Iraq have developed endometriosis and have required hysterectomies.

In a study group of 250 soldiers in Mississippi who had fathered normal babies before the Gulf War, 67% have fathered babies with birth defects after the war. Some babies had missing legs, arms, organs and/or blood diseases. The Department of Veterans Affairs does not keep records of birth defects in the children of veterans.

The number of disabled vets reported up to 2000 has been increasing by 43,000 every year. Brad Flohr of the Department of Veterans Affairs told American Free Press that he believes there are more disabled vets now than after World War II.

In 2003 scientists from the Uranium Medical Research Center (UMRC) studied urine samples of Afghan civilians and found that 100% of the samples taken had levels of non-depleted uranium 400% to 2000% higher than normal levels. The UMRC research team studied six sites, two in Kabul and others in the Jalalabad area. The civilians were tested four months after the attacks in Afghanistan by the United States and its allies. (*New York Daily News* 4/5/04)

The US pressures North Korea and Iran to shut down their nuclear weapons development programs but the US is making little effort to recover enough weapons grade uranium to make about 1,000 nuclear bombs that the US government scattered over 43 countries. The US is charging countries $5000 per kilogram to return it. The White House has also underfunded the Nunn Lugar initiative to dismantle potentially dangerous nuclear activities in the former Soviet Union. (*New York Times* 3/4/07)

Climate Change

The World Health Organization expects 300,000+ deaths linked to climate change by the year 2030. The American Lung Association attributes 24,000 premature deaths, 550,000 asthma attacks, 38,000 heart attacks, and 12,000 hospital admissions annually to coal-fired power plant pollution. John Young of the Waco Tribune pointed out that while there is some disagreement between scientists regarding human-caused global warming, "They do not disagree on how those emissions strain the lung's bronchioles, with asthma deaths, lung cancer and more. You can't dispute that."

You can ignore it. But why would you ignore measures that would not only save lives, they would improve the quality of life and the futures of children? Because it would reduce profits.

Former EPA official Jason Burnett revealed how the W. Bush White House censored and distorted climate change science to protect corporate interests. Office of Management and Budget officials tried to define carbon dioxide (CO_2) from power plants as different from CO_2 from cars and trucks in order to shield industrial power plants from regulations required by the Supreme Court. (*Washington Post* 7/29/08)

EPA has estimated a reduction in ozone to 70 parts per billion "could result annually in 2,300 fewer nonfatal heart attacks; 48,000 fewer respiratory problems, acute bronchitis and asthma attacks; 7,600 fewer respiratory related hospital visits, and 890,000 fewer days when people miss work or school." Big industries are lobbying to block the new limits. "It could trigger layoffs nationwide," said Sen. George V. Voinovich. (AP 3/6/08)

The EPA and "the science of global warning are under relentless Congressional attack." (*New York Times* 6/28/12)

Prevention: Incidental Death

When profit is more sacred than life, secrecy must also become sacred. "Important business and consumer information is increasingly being withheld from the public" reported *US News and World Report*. (12-12-03) The day Bush took his oath of office, Attorney General Ashcroft encouraged "agencies to deny Freedom of Information Act requests if a 'sound legal basis' exists.'" The commitment to secrecy extends to transportation, communications, energy, and "other systems that make modern society run."

According to new Transportation Security Administration rules information can be withheld from the public if it's "impractical" to release it. Homeland Security (HS) encourages companies to submit information about critical infrastructure to aid HS in protecting those facilities. "When a company does this, the information is exempted from public disclosure and cannot be used without the submitting party's permission in any civil proceeding, even a government enforcement action. Critics see this as a get-out-of-jail-free card, allowing companies worried about potential litigation or regulatory actions to place troublesome information in a convenient 'homeland security' vault."

For two years documents related to Ford-Firestone tire accidents that resulted in 88 deaths were suppressed by the court. "When companies are sued for selling unsafe consumer products or creating environmental hazards, the cases too often end with court orders that keep vital health and safety dangers secret. This practice works out well for the wrongdoers, but it is bad for ordinary Americans who need to know about these threats." March, 2008, the Senate Judiciary Committee approved "a modest but potentially life-saving bill that would require federal judges to consider public health and safety before granting a protective order, sealing court records or approving a settlement agreement." The measure was first proposed 15 years ago. (*New York Times* 3-12-08)

Some 60% of new infectious diseases originate in animals and two-thirds of those are in wild animals. The US Agency for International Development has enlisted experts—veterinarians, conservation biologists, medical doctors and epidemiologists—in a project called "Predict" to determine, based on how people alter the landscape, where the next diseases will "spill over" from wildlife into humans, how to spot them before they can spread, and how to prevent them from "leaving the woods." A study by the International Livestock Research Institute discovered that more than two million people a year are killed by diseases that spread to humans from wild and domestic animals. That number is likely to grow due to human encroachment on woods and wildlife. (*New York Times* 7/14/12)

A twelve-year-old boy died of a toothache. An $80 tooth extraction might have saved him if his family had not lost its Medicaid. After two operations and more than six weeks of hospital care at a cost of more than $250,000 the boy died.

Prevention: Reproductive Health

Historically, a man's power is in his ability to impregnate a woman whether she is willing or not and to force her to bear his child whether she wants to or not. That puts men in charge of reproduction and patriarchal societies have always had birth on demand. For that reason, in many countries life expectancy for women is shorter than that for men because of repeated pregnancies. Pregnancy and child-bearing are health issues and should be treated as such. To claim that it is a religious matter is to deny others their religious freedom.

Both contraception and abortion are legal in the US, and have been so for some time. Reproductive freedom made it possible for women to succeed in trades and professions where they had previously been shutout because of pregnancy and childcare. There has never been equality but over time law, science and religion have stripped away men's supremacy over women and men want it back. Religion and government are the tools they wish to use.

Although America is still a democracy with a Constitution, we aren't a lawful nation under a Constitution. Reagan and H.W. Bush violated the Constitution with impunity to fight secret and illegal wars of terror against the indigenous people of Central America.

W. Bush and Cheney violated the Constitution to start two undeclared wars and authorized torture. The Constitution and treaties signed by the US, that are the law of the land, require that Bush, Cheney and others in that administration who authorized, permitted, or participated in torture be prosecuted or turned over to a lawful nation that will prosecute them. Until then we will not be a lawful nation or one under a Constitution.

Elected officials, and others who have taken an oath to "uphold the Constitution," are happy to divert attention from that fact by keeping the "unborn," and women and their rights to private property at the top of the page and top of the hour. The "Religious" Right claims that life begins at conception. That is not a scientific fact and it is not the law. It's not even the belief of many religious people, maybe including the majority of Christian Americans. It is an attack on the religious freedom of all, with some government support, including that of some courts.

Although some 98% of American women have used birth control, including those in the "Religious" Right, there is a well-financed attack on contraceptives and abortion, meaning birth on demand. Who has the right to treat women as though they were brood animals? Men and male-dominated organizations like churches and governments is the only possible answer.

That's not pro-life, of course, except in some extreme Orwellian sense of wrong is right. Of the 33 countries that the International Monetary Fund describes as "advanced economies," the United States now has the highest infant mortality rate according to the World Bank. Dead last. That is the sign of a nation that does not believe life is sacred. A mother in the US has a ten times greater chance of dying in childbirth than a mother does in Ireland. That is the result of treating a health issue as a means for political power.

No honest person dare call that "pro-life." Yet, some hypocrites, cloaked in religious language, want to strip the EPA of its power to protect fetuses, babies, infants, and children, and strip women of their right to their most private property. Some wear red to hide their blush of shame.

The Catholic Church has not yet been able to force that on all women but desires to do so regardless of their religious freedom and that of their churches. To them and to others it is not a health controversy but a matter of domination. The way to male domination and the humiliation of others is rape. You learn in first grade that bullies are cowards and cowards are bullies. The most cowardly bullies are those who bully women.

Texas and some other states now require that a woman who wants a legal abortion, for whatever reason, must submit to a vicarious, legitimate rape by the Texas governor and Legislature. The bully-cowards require a sonogram that includes the insertion of a foreign object in the vagina of an unwilling woman. That is the legal definition of rape. The governor knows that, the legislators know that, the doctors know that. They also know that a woman will feel that she has been raped and the guilt and shame that she is not able to protect herself from superior powers will humiliate her. How she will feel about her husband, father, brothers, doctors, pastors, rabbis, priests, imams, the law and the Constitution that failed to protect her is unknown. Where were the mothers? Where were the sisters?

In 1964, 28-year-old Kitty Genovese was attacked before she could get from her car into her apartment building. Her screams and cries awakened her neighbors who looked out their widows to see her being attacked. The attacker left. The neighbors went back to bed. Kitty had been stabbed twice but tried to stagger to her apartment at the back of the building. The attacker returned, followed the blood trail to the back of the building and stabbed her some more. Then left. She made it into the building when he returned the third time, raping her while she was dying. That's the metaphor for the government of Texas and other cowardly states' attack on women.

For the bully-cowards of Texas, vicarious rape wasn't quite enough dominance. The bully-cowards also dictated exactly what the doctor has to say to a woman seeking an abortion on pain of losing his license. One Texas legislator proposed that the mandated declaration by the doctor be medically correct. The proposal didn't make it out of committee. Not a single Republican supported it, not even the pediatrician on the committee supported it. Truth wasn't the point. Dominance and humiliation of women was the point. I don't know of a single physician or medical society that has opposed the government dictating medical advice.

Blood tests are now available that can determine paternity as early as the eighth or ninth week of pregnancy and are much cheaper than DNA tests. For every single mother there is a father who should bear financial responsibility for his child until the age of 18, or longer if the child goes to college. Making single mothers solely responsible for children has been detrimental to the health, education and economic mobility of mothers and children, and expensive to taxpayers. If the tests gain legal acceptance the father would lose plausible deniability, become financially liable for support of the child reducing both abortions and unwanted children. It would also quickly end the opposition of male-dominated institutions like the church and state to a woman's right to her own body.

If you really wanted to reduce abortions, you'd have to ask yourself: Why does "godless" France, where abortion is nearly free (it's covered by their universal health insurance), have 20% fewer abortions per capita than we do? The answer is: Because France has religious freedom and reproduction is a health matter and not about the power of men or of one church to force its dogma on all others at the cost of their own religious freedom.

Healthcare: History

Theodore Roosevelt believed that conservatives must have something they wanted to conserve other than their personal wealth, however great or small it might be. He was committed to conserving America's natural resources for future generations with national parks, national forests, and the preservation and maintenance of public lands. He opposed the ravage of the earth by the powerful to rob the nation of its resources and leave nothing but hazardous waste, polluted water and air, denuded forests, leveled mountains and yawning pits reminiscent of a child's view of hell.

TR also believed in conserving the nation's health and as a progressive proposed national healthcare. When workers were sick they lost wages. Because of that loss due to illness, especially disability, families fell into poverty they could rarely escape. The AFL supported TR's plan. Women trade unionists and suffragists favored the proposal because it included maternity benefits for women workers. Other labor groups supported American Association for Labor Legislation because it wanted to protect both workers' health and their wages. The AALL believed research and information would inspire the nation to universal health care and a livable wage. TR lost the election and his chance at national healthcare but he recognized the problem.

Franklin Roosevelt's Social Security Act, 1935, included help for the nation's elderly, sick and disabled, and gave citizens some power to resist unfair and unsafe business practices that ruined the lives of some and left others crippled, ill and a burden on their families. Roosevelt wanted the federal government to take the lead in dealing with public health and poverty. But congressional Democrats from the South, since returning to the government after the Civil War, tried to restrict the federal government's power in the interest of states' rights.

After World War II, Truman made universal health care part of the Democratic Party's Platform. Truman was probably America's stoutest opponent of Communism, yet like FDR he was accused of being soft on Communism, and members of his administration were accused of being "pinkos, fellow travelers or members of the Communist Party." Anything Truman tried to do for citizens was attacked as "Communism" or "Socialism" and it was a time when many Americans feared the Soviet Union and some feared a Communist takeover from within. Truman was able to expand Social Security coverage.

Lyndon Johnson took up the torch for the people and in addition to the Civil Rights Acts was able to establish Medicare and Medicaid. He was denounced as "un-American" and a "socialist" but the American Medical Association that had earlier opposed national health care worked for a compromise. Ronald Reagan made a TV ad warning that universal health care would lead to a Socialist dictatorship and the loss of all social freedoms. Freeing the people from the tyranny of health insurance companies was the loss of personal freedom.

Richard Nixon was the next to propose national health insurance for all Americans, perhaps driven by his own experience with family illness. Democrats believed Nixon's plan that mandated all employers to provide health insurance, was to increase profits for health insurance companies. Senator Edward Kennedy was able to effect a compromise and agreed to help pass the plan through Congress. The Watergate crime brought more opposition to the plan.

Gerald Ford tried to reintroduce national health care but there was unrest in the Middle East and the price of oil surged. The economy fell into recession. Jimmy Carter also believed in national health care but the economy, US failure in Vietnam, and the oil embargo made implementation impossible.

Bill Clinton proposed a national health insurance plan with the usual opposition, a slicky slide to Socialist dictatorship, cost jobs, reduce profits, and a national media campaign that the federal government would dictate your doctor and what care you would get. The AMA was so wedded to the medical/pharmaceutical/insurance complex that doctors gave insurance companies the power to dictate what treatment an insured patient could receive, and what medications a patient could get with co-pay.

Barack Obama was the first president, almost a century later, who was able to pass a national health insurance plan. The US ranks last among industrial nations in avoiding death by preventable disease. (*Democracy Now* 1/9/08) That is now likely to change.

Two health economists, David Cutler of Harvard and Karen Davis, president of the Commonwealth Fund, have calculated that over the first decade of Obamacare total spending will be half a trillion dollars lower than under the status quo. "Ten percent of the population accounts for 60 percent of the health outlays," Davis said. "They are the very sick, and they are not really in a position to make cost-conscious choices."

It could be even better. The Congressional Budget Office said that permitting Medicare to bargain for drugs as the VA does, or reimporting drugs from Canada, would save $1 trillion in 10 years. Beginning with his January 2003 State of the Union address, W. Bush pledged to keep the total cost of the drug benefit to $400 billion over 10 years...shortly after Bush signed the program into law in December 2003, the White House revised its projection to $534 billion...March 2004, Richard S. Foster, Medicare's chief actuary for nearly a decade, said administration officials threatened to fire him if he disclosed his belief in 2003 that the drug package would cost $500 billion to $600 billion. 2005, The White House released budget figures indicating that the new Medicare prescription drug benefit will cost more than $1.2 trillion in the coming decade. (*Washington Post* 2/9/5) If you're ever asked what a lie costs, you can cite that figure.

It could still have been better. Medicare overhead is 3%. Streamlining payment through a single nonprofit payer such as an upgraded Medicare would save more than $400 billion per year, enough to provide comprehensive, high-quality coverage for all Americans. All Americans, including elected or appointed government officials should be allowed to enroll in Medicare. Those who do not can choose their own private insurer but if that insurer ever drops them from care they will have to pay a penalty to enroll in Medicare. Unchecked corporate greed tramples human need, human dignity, and families.

A recent study revealed that the year's earnings of CEOs of Health Insurance corporations were: Cigna CEO $19 million, United Health CEO $13.3 million, WellPoint CEO $13.2 million, Coventry CEO $12.9 million. Aetna CEO $10.5 million, Humana CEO $7.4 million.

The United States has never ratified the social and economic rights sections of Article 25 of the Universal Declaration of Human Rights of 1948, including the right to health. In America, health care is a commodity to be bought and sold like, well, like slaves were before their emancipation. To that extent Barack Obama can be ranked with Abraham Lincoln.

The Great Leap Backward

The Reagan administration kicked off the relentless march back to the Roaring Twenties, for the affluent district a time of self-indulgent *Great Gatsby* wealth. For the effluent community it was grinding Great Depression *Grapes of Wrath* poverty. It was the time of "get it while you can" philosophy for employers and "pie in the sky someday" religion for the employed.

It was the kind of America that Reagan, the Bushes, rich Republicans and the "Religious" Right dreamed of and longed for—profligate wealth and luxury for them, and unseen and unacknowledged poverty and ignorance for wretched children. If the federal and state governments had been parents, they would have been guilty of child neglect, child abuse, child endangerment and depraved indifference.

Even in the Roaring Twenties there were people who weren't drunk on gin and greatness, who saw clearly the doom ahead—the Great Depression and the Great War. Neither in the sense of the best but rather in massive and totally destructive. The "greatest generation" is the title of a book. Every generation will have challenges but the greatest challenges are measuring up to the generation that wrote the Declaration of Independence, the Constitution, and won the Revolutionary War giving us a democratic republic, and preserving their gift.

The Recession is not the only blowback to the Reagan/Bush policies. The blowback to Reagan allowing the contras in Central America and "freedom fighters" in Afghanistan to finance their wars through drug smuggling is children born with addiction, young black men who can't find jobs but find a few dollars as middlemen between drug smugglers and yuppies, an expensive and continuing "War on Drugs" begun by Nixon but steadily expanding and filling for-profit penitentiaries. And, of course, 9/11. Reagan recruited, armed, and trained—some in the US—Islamic extremists to fight the Soviets in Afghanistan. The problem with mercenaries is that they only get paid when they fight. When they're not paid, they fight their paymasters. On 9/11, Richard Clarke, National Security adviser said, "The chickens have come home to roost."

More blowback from Reagan's terror wars in Central America is that every other country knows that we are a terrorist nation and a state sponsor of terrorism. The sympathy for 9/11 waned quickly when the federal government decided to wage a war of terror in "The Global War Against Terror." "Our terror is greater than your terror" is a realistic threat but it is also a challenge to "bring it on."

The Bushes wars on Iraq, the opening of Iraq's oil fields to foreign companies, the present and future horror of depleted uranium may result in greater blowback than 9/11. The Bible says that you reap what you sow. If you sow bombs the bloom is not likely to be from flowers.

The consequences of deregulation have not been only the Savings and Loan debacle that cost taxpayers billions but made a few, including Neil Bush, rich. Or the Enron collapse. When asked the reason for the success of Enron, Kenneth Lay said it was deregulation. That was also the cause of Enron's collapse, that and the oil and gas refinery in Pakistan that never opened because Enron could not secure a pipeline from the Caspian Sea oil fields to Pakistan through Afghanistan. Taliban, that did not attack us, barred the way. Or the collapse of Lehman Brothers, or the near collapse of the banking industry and the global economy.

The Republicans propose that persons who can breathe have to bailout corporate persons that can't breathe or be jailed for crimes, including fraud. According to Paul Krugman (*New York Times*), the answer is "regulation that limits the frequency and size of financial crises, combined with rules that let the government strike a good deal when bailouts become necessary. Remember, from the 1930s until the 1980s, the United States managed to avoid large bailouts of financial institutions. The modern era of bailouts only began in the Reagan years, when politicians started dismantling 1930s-vintage regulation."

Financial institutions evolved, as Novel Laureate economist Krugman points out. "The institutions that were rescued in 2008-9 weren't old-fashioned banks; they were complex financial empires, many of whose activities were effectively unregulated—and it was these unregulated activities that brought the US economy to its knees. Worse yet, officials lacked clear authority to seize these failing empires the way the FDIC. can seize a conventional bank when it goes bust." Yet, Republicans have fought efforts to give consumers protection with higher capital standards and more transparency in complex financial arrangements. Bankers' representatives in Congress have tried to cut off funding for consumer protection and "resolution authority." Less than a week after Republicans on the House Financial Services Committee had a campaign fund-raiser the committee's majority passed bills to cripple the Consumer Financial Protection Bureau. According to a *New York Times* editorial, the purpose of the bills was to "deprive the agency of the power to fulfill its mission...and to attract campaign money."

Deregulation and lax regulation has caused unnecessary deaths to mine and oil industry workers, but far greater are the numbers of deaths and disabilities to fetuses, babies, infants and children that will increase until the Environmental Protection Agency is given the money and the bite to stop the destruction of America and its children.

"Free" enterprise for chemical, mining, oil and gas corporations has encouraged their enablers to war on science and critical thinking that limits the fight against climate change. This is not a Republican problem, or a Democratic problem, or an American problem. This is a world problem and it can be denied, it can be disregarded but it cannot be ignored when rising tides cause some island nations to give up their native lands and perhaps their sovereignty. It will take courage from all of us because we do not have the voice of corporate citizens. We do not have the voice of corporate media. We have little representation in Congress and our legislatures. If the end of the world does come soon, even if it is the Second Coming of Jesus, it will be because Mammon is our god. And we sacrifice our children to appease it.

Robert Flynn has published seventeen books and written a two-part documentary for ABC-TV. His latest two novels, *Jade: Outlaw* and *Jade: the Law*, had reference to the "Southern Strategy" by which the South won the Civil War in the latter part of the 20th Century. Robert Flynn's play, "Journey to Jefferson," a dramatic adaptation of Faulkner's *As I Lay Dying*, received a Special Jury Award in international competition at the Theater of Nations in Paris. His novel, *North to Yesterday*, was named as one of the best books of the year by *The New York Times*. He has received two Wrangler Awards from the National Cowboy Hall of Fame, two Spur Awards from Western Writers of America, a Jesse Jones award from the Texas Institute of Letters. He has also received a Lon Tinkle Lifetime Achievement Award from the Texas Institute of Letters, and is a fellow of the Institute.

Notes

Notes

Notes

Wings Press was founded in 1975 by Joanie Whitebird and Joseph F. Lomax, both deceased. Bryce Milligan has been the publisher, editor and designer since 1995. The mission of Wings Press is to publish the finest in American writing—meaning all of the Americas—without commercial considerations clouding the choice to publish or not to publish. Technically a "for profit" press, Wings receives only occasional underwriting from individuals and institutions who wish to support our vision. For this we are very grateful.

Wings Press attempts to produce multicultural books, chapbooks, Ebooks, CDs, DVDs and broadsides that, we hope, enlighten the human spirit and enliven the mind. Everyone ever associated with Wings has been or is a writer, and we know well that writing is a transformational art form capable of changing the world, primarily by allowing us to glimpse something of each other's souls. Good writing is innovative, insightful, and interesting. But most of all it is honest.

Likewise, Wings Press is committed to treating the planet itself as a partner. Thus the press uses soy and other vegetable-based inks, and as much recycled material as possible, from the paper on which the books are printed to the boxes in which they are shipped.

As Robert Dana wrote in *Against the Grain,* "Small press publishing is personal publishing. In essence, it's a matter of personal vision, personal taste and courage, and personal friendships." Welcome to our world.

Colophon

This first edition of *Lawful Abuse: How the Century of the Child became the Century of the Corporation*, by Robert Flynn, has been released as an ebook. In a first occurance for Wings Press, the printed edition follows the ebook, and will be printed on 55 pound EB "natural" paper containing a percentage of recycled fiber. Titles have been set in Colonna type, the text in Minion type. All Wings Press books are designed and produced by Bryce Milligan.

On-line catalogue and ordering
available at
www.wingspress.com

Wings Press titles are distributed
to the trade by the
Independent Publishers Group
www.ipgbook.com
and in Europe by
www.gazellebookservices.co.uk

Available as an ebook or printed book.